Productive Postmodernism

THE SUNY SERIES IN
POSTMODERN CULTURE

Joseph Natoli, *Editor*

Productive Postmodernism

Consuming Histories and Cultural Studies

Edited by John N. Duvall
with an afterword by Linda Hutcheon

State University of New York Press

For information, address State University of New York Press,
90 State Street, Suite 700, Albany, NY 12207

Production by Dana Foote
Marketing by Patrick Durocher

Library of Congress Cataloging-in-Publication Data

Productive postmodernism : consuming histories and cultural studies / edited by
John N. Duvall ; with an afterword by Linda Hutcheon.
    p. cm. — (The SUNY series in postmodern culture)
  Includes bibliographical references and index.
  ISBN 0–7914–5193–3 (alk. paper) — ISBN 0–7914–5194–1 (pbk. : alk.
paper)
    1. Postmodernism. 2. Arts, Modern—20th century. I. Duvall, John N. (John
Noel), 1956– II. Series.

NX456.5.P66 P763 2002   2001049575

10 9 8 7 6 5 4 3 2 1

Contents

Contents

Postmodernism, Architecture, History

Afterword

Illustrations

Preface

This volume grew out of a conference panel I chaired in 1996. My call
for papers asked that panelists think not only about the relation
between postmodernism and history but also about the possibilities suggested by Fredric Jameson's focus on pastiche and Linda
Hutcheon's emphasis on parody as the defining tropes of postmodernism. But well prior to 1996, my own thinking about postmodernism had been shaped by Jameson and Hutcheon. During the 1983
NEH Summer Seminar, "Marxism and the Interpretation of Culture,"
at the University of Illinois, I heard Jameson lecture from his work on
postmodernism and read in galley form the now famous essay "Postmodernism, or, The Cultural Logic of Late Capitalism," which served
as the starting point for his book of the same title. Later, as a teacher
of postmodern fiction, I found in Hutcheon's two books from the
late 1980s—*The Poetics of Postmodernism* and *The Politics of
Postmodernism*—a useful heuristic to introduce and categorize a
number of contemporary cultural narratives. Until her work on postmodern fiction, when someone referred to the postmodern novel, a
fairly small number of highly aestheticized texts, almost invariably
written by white male authors, came to mind. Hutcheon's concept
"historiographic metafiction" clearly allowed one to include a number of women and minority writers under the rubric "postmodernism" who had previously been excluded from the designation.

Although I give students a number of theoretical perspectives
on postmodernism, including those of Andreas Huyssen and David
Harvey, for me, one of the biggest sticking points has always been
how to approach Jameson's and Hutcheon's radically different perspectives on the cultural work of contemporary narrative. The need
to explore their differences seems all the more urgent given the
shared intellectual assumptions of Hutcheon and Jameson, particularly their reliance on Louis Althusser's sense of ideology as unconscious systems of representation. Brian McHale has argued that
Hutcheon's project "is fueled and animated by the anxiety of master
narratives—that is by her desire not to be thought to have invoked,
endorsed, or relied upon one or other totalizing master narrative in
her account of postmodern poetics" ("Postmodernism" 18). For
McHale, Hutcheon's postmodernism fails for its unsuccessful incor-

poration of the master narrative of feminism, as a secure site of social critique, into her claim to disavow master narratives. The Marxist Jameson, in McHale's view, is more successful because as an "unreconstructed totalizer" (23), he is less anxious about Jean-François Lyotard's critique of master narratives; the proof that Hutcheon is wrong about the consequences of "endorsing a master narrative" is that "Jameson's is incontestably the more catholic of the two postmodernsims" (24).

Despite McHale's thoughtful attempt to articulate the Jameson-Hutcheon difference, the matter calls for further exploration since so much applied criticism on postmodern texts is underwritten by the exclusive authority of either Jameson or Hutcheon. So in part this volume is a response to the students in my graduate courses on postmodern American fiction whose questions have pushed me toward, if not the answers, perhaps a better description of the pertinent issues. My hope is that *Productive Postmodernism* will, if not synthesize, at least provide contexts for understanding the differences between Jameson's and Hutcheon's competing versions of postmodernism.

In the work that follows, three Canadian and seven American critics investigate first-world narratives and cultural texts. If our focus is largely on North American texts it is because postmodernism most often has been identified as a first-world phenomenon, and certainly from the perspective of Jean Baudrillard, America epitomizes such first-world culture. Moreover, the kinds of cultural texts that Jameson deploys in his work suggest the extent to which North American cultural texts can serve as a metonymy for first-world culture. However, by bringing Hutcheon's more multicultural sense of postmodernism to bear on these first-world texts, the chapters in a number of instances are able to frame questions about Jameson's emphasis on America.

Following my opening chapter, which lays out what I see as key differences between Jameson's and Hutcheon's postmodernism, Thomas Carmichael's "Postmodernism and History: Complicitous Critique and the Political Unconscious" serves as an alternative overview. While my sense of the two theorists underscores their differing emphases on production and consumption, Carmichael instead reads their positions in a more complementary fashion, seeing points of intersection between Hutcheon's compromised politics of postmodernism and Jameson's political unconscious. After these two overviews, the remaining seven chapters fall into two clusters— "Postmodernism, Fiction, History" and "Postmodernism, Architecture, History"—a division readily suggested by the importance of narrative and architecture to both theorists.

"Postmodernism, Fiction, History" begins with Stacey Olster's "A Mother (and a Son, and a Brother, and a Wife, et al.) in History: Stories Galore in *Libra* and the Warren Commission *Report.*" This essay reads Don DeLillo's novel against the Warren Commission *Report* and texts by and about Lee Harvey Oswald's friends and relatives. Examining this matrix, Olster maintains that *Libra* provides a point of confluence for various theories of historical production. Next, Michael Zeitlin's "Donald Barthelme and the President of the United States" argues that psychoanalysis' investment in the subject still provides a useful purchase on postmodernity that may allow for an oppositional perspective on the totality. Beginning from a theoretical investigation into the persistence of authoritarianism and the father-imago (and linking this to President Clinton's ongoing oedipal wreckage), Zeitlin turns to Donald Barthelme's 1964 story, "The President," to suggest the ways that this fiction explores and challenges protofascist impulses in American culture precisely by keeping alive the possibility of individual psychology.

Turning to African American literature, Kimberly Chabot Davis examines the hybrid enactment of time and history in Toni Morrison's *Beloved* in order to shed a different light on the Jameson-Hutcheon debate. For Davis, Morrison's novel operates in the space between postmodern skepticism toward master narratives and a modernist politics still invested in a coherent historical memory. In "Postmodern Blackness," Davis argues that the power of Morrison's fiction emerges from the productive tension between the traditions of postmodernism and African American social protest. W. Lawrence Hogue approaches the issue of critical purchase through deconstruction. In "Historiographic Metafiction and the Celebration of Differences: Ishmael Reed's *Mumbo Jumbo,*" Hogue sees parallels between Reed's aesthetic practice and Jacques Derrida's project. For Hogue, Reed's fictional undermining of hierarchized binaries confirms Hutcheon's sense of historiographic metafiction while questioning Jameson's version of postmodernism.

The first section concludes with Paul Budra's "Troping the Renaissance: Postmodern Historiography and Early Modern History." He believes that New Historicism's and cultural materialism's focus on the Renaissance, the period in which the nascent narratives of modernity were formed, has trickled down to popular representations of the early modern period. Taking up two texts published in

1992 that represent Elizabethan England, Charles Nicholl's history, *The Reckoning: The Murder of Christopher Marlowe,* and Patricia Finney's novel, *Firedrake's Eye,* Budra argues that the conjunction of postmodern historiography and early modern history has resulted in the paradoxical entrenchment of teleology-driven historical narrative. The result is a substitution of postmodern paranoia for early modern providence.

The remaining three chapters form the second section, "Postmodernism, Architecture, History." It opens with Kevin McNamara's "Los Angeles, 2019: Two Tales of a City," which serves as a hinge between the first and second sections, inasmuch as his piece is concerned with narrative representations of architecture in a future dystopian cityscape. On the one hand, the Los Angeles of 2019 in *Blade Runner* serves as the quintessential depthless landscape that Jameson delineates in his work on postmodern architecture; that is, the city is apparently a meaningless pastiche of styles cannibalized from urban history. On the other hand, McNamara argues that Hutcheon's sense of postmodern parody calls attention to the ideological embeddings of history-as-narrative in Ridley Scott's film; such embeddings form a critique of industrial modernity's dream of a utopian urbanism by situating architectural monuments in a degraded future through the deployment of special effects designed to shock rather than fascinate the viewer. In "Postmodern Casinos," Shelton Waldrep investigates several issues constellated around the rise in popularity of casino gambling. Focusing on the interplay between utopian impulses in the architecture of Las Vegas casinos, he explores this popular cultural phenomenon's influence on trends in family leisure, particularly as casinos relate to but differ from the Disney paradigm of theme parks. Finally, in "Postmodernism and Holocaust Memory: Productive Tensions in the U.S. Holocaust Memorial Museum," Nancy J. Peterson responds to the debates about the commodification of history in postmodernity and raises a series of questions about the proper form of Holocaust memory. Examining both the memorial's position on the Washington, D.C., Mall and its internal arrangement of space, Peterson thinks about the way the memorial simultaneously permits and inhibits historical thinking.

A version of my chapter originally appeared in a special issue of *Style* (Fall 1999) guest edited by David Gorman and titled "Postmodernism and Other Distractions: Situations and Directions for Critical Theory." Also Kimberly Chabot Davis's chapter previously was published in *Twentieth Century Literature* (Summer 1998). My thanks to the editors of these journals for permission to reprint this material here. Thanks also to Stephanie Turner for her able editorial assistance.

Mere thanks seems woefully inadequate to express my deep appreciation to Linda Hutcheon for making time to read and respond to this collection.

Troping History: Modernist Residue in Jameson's Pastiche and Hutcheon's Parody

John N. Duvall

History is unquestionably one of the most contentious areas of debate among those concerned with postmodernism. I would like to take up Fredric Jameson's and Linda Hutcheon's competing accounts of the relation between postmodernism and history not because their differences stand as a recognized debate (such as that of Jürgen Habermas and Jean-François Lyotard), but rather because their accounts of postmodern fiction seem to leave little room for compromise.[1] For Jameson, postmodern narrative is ahistorical (and hence politically dangerous), playing only with pastiched images and aesthetic forms that produce a degraded historicism; for Hutcheon, postmodern fiction remains historical, precisely because it problematizes history through parody, and thus retains its potential for cultural critique. Despite the apparent polarization of these two views, I wish to negotiate a position that acknowledges both Jameson and Hutcheon because at certain turns I find both perspectives useful—depending on the cultural texts that they scrutinize. Such a negotiation is not as daunting once one realizes that what they mean by postmodernism is not the same thing: Jameson's postmodernism focuses on the consumer, while Hutcheon's originates with the artist as producer. As a result of this different focus, Jameson and Hutcheon in many instances are speaking past each other, describing different cultural phenomena.[2] At the same time, for all their interest in defining the postmodern, both Jameson's and Hutcheon's thinking owes much to modernism, albeit differing strands: Jameson's to the Adornian tradition and Hutcheon's to the tradition of the avant garde.

Jameson—Postmodernism or Postmodernity?

Jameson makes a series of distinctions between modernization, modernism, and modernity that provide a productive insight into his work on postmodernism:

> if modernization is something that happens to the base, and
> modernism the form the superstructure takes in reaction to that
> ambivalent development, then perhaps modernity character-
> izes the attempt to make something coherent out of their rela-
> tionship. Modernity would then in that case describe the way
> "modern" people feel about themselves. (*Postmodernism* 310)

The response of art and literature to the alienating effect of modernization, as is well known, was often hostile. To invoke "modernism"
as a category is to think in the terrain of oppositional aesthetics and
poetics. But because Jameson is so interested in mapping the affect
of the contemporary moment, the way "postmodern" people feel
about themselves, when he speaks of postmodernism or the postmodern, what he means might more accurately be called—to borrow
David Harvey's title—the condition of postmodernity. Hutcheon
notes the confusion that results from Jameson's use of "the word
postmodern*ism* for both socio-economic periodization and the cultural designation," a move that deliberately collapses the distinction between postmodernism and postmodernity (*Politics* 25).
Hutcheon's postmodernism, which focuses on the intentions of artists to comment critically on their contemporary moment through
their interventions in aesthetics and poetics, is more clearly linked
than Jameson's to what he himself means by modernism; in other
words, Hutcheon's postmodernism, like Jameson's modernism, represents the arts' response to the material conditions created by modernization. Jameson's postmodernism shows his debt to both reader-
response criticism and the work of Jean Baudrillard, who as early as
Consumer Society (1970) was attempting to shift attention away from
a traditional Marxist category—the means of production—and toward a new one—the means of consumption.

In *Postmodernism, or, the Cultural Logic of Late Capitalism,*
Jameson provides a postmortem on modernist aesthetics, for he
clearly sees modernism's protopolitical projects of defamiliarization,
"with their familiar stress on the vocation of art to restimulate perception, to reconquer a freshness of experience back from the habitu-
ate and reified numbness of everyday life in a fallen world," as no
longer viable (121). Jameson groups a range of theoretical formations
into this defamiliarizing aesthetic—from Ezra Pound to the Surreal-
ists, from the Russian Formalists to phenomenology. Jameson claims
that "this remarkable aesthetic is today meaningless and must be
admired as one of the most intense historical achievements of the

cultural past (along with the Renaissance or the Greeks or the Tang dynasty)." When Jameson speaks of modernism, he retains a notion of the aesthetic formulations of its producers. Jameson's shift to the axis of consumption is signaled in his characterization of himself as a "relatively enthusiastic consumer of postmodernism" (298). Despite this characterization, his sympathies clearly lie with a lost modernist project because of its relation to Utopian thinking.

The Utopian imagination has been an important part of Jameson's thinking since *The Political Unconscious.* The "collective struggle to wrest a realm of Freedom from a realm of Necessity" (*Political* 19) signals his commitment to the political value of Utopianism as a form of praxis. Indeed, the conclusion of *The Political Unconscious,* titled "The Dialectic of Ideology and Utopia," outlines a program for cultural analysis that goes beyond the negative hermeneutic of ideological demystification vis-à-vis texts in order simultaneously to decipher "the Utopian impulses of these same still ideological cultural texts" (296). Jameson remains committed to the Marxist narrative of liberation—the end of class—even if, with Louis Althusser, he does not see the end of class as the end of ideology.

In *Postmodernism,* Jameson writes a cultural history in which the potentially political urge of postmodernism is co-opted in much the same way that the protopolitical urge of modernism is diffused and eventually institutionalized. This lost moment of postmodernism, which for Jameson is the 1960s, functions as the break that helps mark the difference between modernism and postmodernism. Jameson's sixties represent a time when the institutionalization of previously unacceptable modernism occurred. His nostalgia for the sixties emerges vividly in the figures he uses to characterize postmodernism—primarily drug use and pollution. Postmodernism is "the bad trip" of the sixties Utopian project and "the sixties gone toxic" (117). For Jameson, the sixties represent a time when an element of modernist aesthetics, fresh perception, was still possible.[3] The contradiction in Jameson's description, then, seems to be that the very moment that signals the end to modernism's position as the cultural dominant reinscribes the modernist aesthetic of fresh perception. Jameson early in *Postmodernism* states what he sees at stake: "Utopian representations knew an extraordinary revival in the 1960s; if postmodernism is the substitute for the sixties and the compensation for their political failure, the question of Utopia would seem to be a crucial test of what is left of our capacity to imagine change at all" (xvi). And it is precisely change that, for Jameson, can no longer be imagined in postmodernism, since aesthetic production has been subsumed by commodity production, thus emptying the modernist aesthetic of affect and hence of political effect. As Jameson puts it:

> In the wholly built and constructed universe of late capitalism, from which nature has at last been effectively abolished and in which human praxis—in the degraded forms of information, manipulation, and reification—has penetrated the older autonomous sphere of culture and even the Unconscious, the Utopia of a renewal of perception has no place to go. (121–22)

As Philip Goldstein has rightly pointed out, Jameson's reading of postmodernism, however much he denies it, reproduces in particular ways Georg Lukács's moralizing reading of modernism, since Jameson repeatedly chastises postmodernism's tendency to integrate culture into commodity production (158).

In marking the line between modernism and postmodernism, Jameson sets out a series of oppositions. Fueled by the demands of capital constantly to make it newer, both modernism and postmodernism attempt to respond to the processes of modernization—new technologies that modify the mode of production. Jameson characterizes the difference as follows: modernism is incomplete modernization, while postmodernism is the result of complete modernization. In incomplete modernization, one could experience the New within culture somewhat organically; in effect, the New was still new. But in the contemporary moment, the complete modernization of postmodernity, our relation to the New is more formal; now, *the New is no longer new* (310). A simple example of what Jameson means by a new relationship to the New can be found in the telephone. When the telephone first entered domestic space, its newness continually called attention to itself as an intrusion of technology. Now, of course, the phone is familiar, yet each month, it seems, we are offered a half-dozen new services, from increasingly more sophisticated ways of screening calls to giving each member of the family a different ring pattern. But these new possibilities register simply as more of the same, namely, a range of consumer choices.

Another periodizing feature for Jameson is the end of the great modernist individual styles that have been replaced by postmodernist codes. The result is that postmodernism is no longer capable of achieving the critical distance necessary for parody and ends up recombining previously articulated styles. The result is pastiche. Pastiche itself is the effect of the transformation from a society with a historical sensibility to one that can only play with a degraded historicism. "Historicism" is the name Jameson assigns to what he sees as an aestheticization of historical styles devoid of the political contradictions that those styles embodied at their particular moment. Disney's unrealized plan to construct their version of America near the site of Civil War battlefields in Virginia exemplifies the historicism Jameson deplores. Disney hoped to produce extensive simulations of American iconography—"a circle of tepees here and a quaint New England factory there; a Civil War fort looming over a peaceful Midwestern farmstead; replicas of the Statue of Liberty and Ellis Island facing a 1930s state fair (complete with Ferris wheel and ballpark) and a World War II airfield" (Silberman 26). Historian Neil Asher Silberman's embrace of Disney's America—Jameson's degraded historicism writ large—fittingly summarizes the mood of recent Republican Congresses: since all public history is mythologizing and commercialized anyway, why not privatize, have Disney do it instead of the National Parks Service? As Silberman concludes, "the depiction of history should be completely market-oriented and consumer-driven" (28). But from Jameson's perspective, such an emphasis on the consumer denudes history of its political content and creates an aestheticized space of image consumption.

For Jameson, intimately linked to this degraded historicism has been postmodernity's reshaping of subjectivity. Working from Ernest Mandel's sense of late capitalism, Jameson links the shifts from market to monopoly to multinational capital with their corresponding aesthetics—realism, modernism, and postmodernism. In the realism of the last century, novels may have told confident narratives of the individual, but in the twentieth century, the middle-class monad or unified subject has fallen away. If alienation defines and is the dominant affect of the modernist subject, recording its ruptures and tensions, then schizophrenia is Jameson's figure for what he sees as the vastly increased tendency toward the dissolution of the subject in postmodernism.

Drawing upon Jacques Lacan's description of schizophrenia, Jameson concludes that "personal identity is itself the effect of a certain temporal unification of past and future with one's present" and "that such active temporal unification is itself a function of language [. . .] as it moves along its hermeneutic circle through time" (*Political* 26–27). For Jameson, our contemporary moment, with its material production of pastiched images, erases history and thus encourages a breakdown of the temporality necessary to focus the subject and "make it a space of praxis" (*Postmodernism* 27). Jameson

insists that the schizophrenic subject is a historically specific phenomenon, a move that distinguishes his sense of the death of the
subject from that of deconstruction, which would maintain that the
subject was always already an "ideological mirage" (15).

These features that distinguish postmodernity from modernity—our relation to the New, the shift from individual styles to codes,
and the transition from the alienated to the schizo subject—all register the determining last instance of the movement from monopoly to
multinational capital.

But if the modernist aesthetic, predicated on fresh perception,
has come to the end of the road, what is to take its place? In *Postmodernism,* Jameson retools his theory of allegorical reading from *The
Political Unconscious,* now speaking of cognitive mapping. His figure
derives from his study of postmodern architecture (a field equally
important to Hutcheon), and his discussions of postmodern space
demonstrate the extent to which his conception of the postmodern
derives from his description of the visceral response contemporary
productions have on the individual as consumer.[4] Describing the
elevators and escalators in the Bonaventure Hotel in Los Angeles as a
key example, Jameson speaks of us as a generation quite literally lost
in space:

> Here the narrative stroll has been underscored, symbolized, re-
> ified, and replaced by a transportation machine which becomes
> the allegorical signifier of that older promenade we are no
> longer allowed to conduct on our own: and this is a dialectical
> intensification of the autoreferentiality of all modern culture,
> which tends to turn upon itself and designate its own cultural
> production as its content. [. . .] The descent is dramatic
> enough, plummeting back down through the roof to splash
> down in the lake. What happens when you get there is some-
> thing else, which can only be described as milling confusion,
> something like the vengeance this space takes on those who still
> try to walk through it. Given the absolute symmetry of the four
> towers, it is quite impossible to get your bearings in this lobby.
> (42–43)

If we are literally lost in a physical space that disorients us, the
"sharper dilemma," as Jameson puts it, "is the incapacity of our
minds [. . .] to map the great global multinational and decentered
communicational network in which we find ourselves caught as individual subjects" (44). Jameson's cognitive mapping is a call to artists

and theorists to provide a sense of historical orientation vis-à-vis social structures and their development—to recover a meaningful history from postmodernism's degraded historicity.

One of the great ironies of Jameson's *Postmodernism* is that even as he announces the death of modernism, and hence of its critical distance and emancipatory hopes, he reinscribes those same modernist hopes in his own writing practice. In a simple sense, Jameson's assertion of the death of the great modernist styles is undercut by his own distinctive style, which resists pastiche by its very density and difficulty; Madison Avenue will never borrow his prose for ad copy.[5] But more tellingly, his cognitive mapping remains yet another version of the modernist desire for the renewal of perception.

Jameson's maps, however, are not accessible to your typical member of AAA in part because of his own preference for the high-culture artifact rather than the textuality of a broader cultural formation. His chapter on video, for example, rather than examining the impact of MTV, focuses instead on a 1979 art school video that Jameson admits few of his readers will ever see. His intelligent close reading of this video, however, places his analysis back in the realm of the modernist valorization of the work, a problem of which he is not unaware (*Postmodernism* 79).[6] Jameson's own maps inadequately distinguish the main highways from the secondary roads in his own intellectual journey. Only in a response to a collection of essays on his work does Jameson acknowledge that cognitive mapping is "in reality nothing but a code word for 'class consciousness'" ("Afterword" 387). This coded meaning of cognitive mapping reminds us again of Jameson's debt to Lukács, for whom class consciousness rests on an understanding of "society as a concrete totality, the system of production at a given moment in history and the resulting division of society into classes" (*Postmodernism* 50).[7] As Jameson has noted elsewhere, "The project of cognitive mapping obviously stands or falls with the conception of some (unrepresentable, imaginary) global social totality that needs mapping" ("Cognitive" 356).

Jameson, then, works from an "assumption that the Marxist theory of history [as a record of class struggle] and society is unproblematically correct" (Best 363), and he remains a committed reader of postmodernism and contemporary theory. But cognitive mapping seems a problematic figure. Cognitive space knows no bounds, since cultural-aesthetic production creates more space to map. And if such production has been commodified in the fashion Jameson believes, then the power of multinational capital via advertising to colonize new cognitive space far outruns the ability of a small band of intellectuals to chart clearly where the borders of freedom and necessity lie. Jameson's totalizing and enervating sense of postmodernism must be questioned to avoid participating in his despair over the present. "If [. . .] we have lost the modernist faith in becoming," as Harvey seems implicitly to ask Jameson, "is there any way out except through the reactionary politics of an aestheticized spatiality? [. . . And] if aesthetic production has now been so thoroughly commodified and thereby become really subsumed within a political economy of cultural production, how can we possibly stop that circle closing onto a produced, and hence all too easily manipulated, aestheticization of a globally mediatized politics?" (305). These questions recall Jameson's response to a similar question asked after a lecture he gave in 1983: "I don't understand how the politics I am proposing is repressive, since I don't think I have yet even proposed a politics, any more that I have really proposed an aesthetics" ("Cognitive" 360). In *Postmodernism,* Jameson articulates an aesthetics of schizoreception but does not articulate a politics that responds to the cultural malaise he so elegantly diagnoses. Linda Hutcheon does not shy away from articulating a postmodern politics, but her political claims for postmodernism do not always easily reconcile with her postmodern poetics.

Hutcheon—Limiting Historiographic Metafiction

Hutcheon's arguments in both *The Poetics of Postmodernism* and *The Politics of Postmodernism* are often developed in direct response to Jameson, who favors modernism over postmodernism; as a result her discussion at times sounds like a polemic against modernism. Even in distancing herself from what she sees as strawman oppositions between modernism and postmodernism, Hutcheon inadvertently produces the opposition yet again. Criticizing Ihab Hassan for "creating parallel columns that place characteristics of the one next to the opposite characteristics in the other," Hutcheon decries this "'either/or' thinking" for attempting to resolve "the unresolvable contradictions within postmodernism" (*Poetics* 49). Instead of opposing modernist purpose with postmodernist play, as Hassan does, Hutcheon sees postmodernism "as a case of play with purpose. The same is true of all [Hassan's] oppositions: postmodernism is the *process* of making the *product;* it is *absence* within *presence,* it is *dispersal* that needs *centering* in order to *be* dispersal [. . .]." In other words, for Hutcheon, the postmodern partakes of a logic of "both/ and," not one of "either/or." While this move problematizes the postmodern half of Hassan's formulation, it leaves all the negatively marked terms of his left column intact. Modernism remains the essentializing foil of a more fluid postmodernism. So while seeming to transcend a binary model for thinking the difference between modernism and postmodernism, Hutcheon perhaps only adds another opposition to Hassan's list: modernism's "either-or" versus postmodernism's "both-and."[8] By saying this, I do not wish to discount Hutcheon's view of postmodernism but merely to recall that the attempt to mark difference between modernism and postmodernism necessarily involves value judgments and is never merely descriptive. From the perspective of Andreas Huyssen, Hutcheon accepts too readily the conservative New Critical/Eliotic paradigm of modernism, characterized by the terrible t's—telos, tradition, and transcendence. Like Jameson, Hutcheon equates poststructuralism with postmodernism, but as Huyssen points out, poststructuralism, "rather than offering a *theory of postmodernity*" instead provides "an *archeology of modernity,* a theory of modernism at the stage of its exhaustion" (*After* 209). The poststructuralist version is not "the modernism of the closed and finished work of art. Rather, it is a modernism of playful transgression, of an unlimited weaving of textuality, a modernism all confident in its rejection of representation and reality, in its denial of the subject, of history and of the subject of history [. . .]." For Huyssen, what makes poststructuralism simultaneously postmodern is its recognition of modernism's failed political aspirations, most notably its inability "to mount an effective critique of bourgeois modernity and modernization."

For Hutcheon, postmodernism remains historical and political precisely through its parodic historical reference; through such parodic reference, "postmodernist forms want to work toward a public discourse that would eschew modernist aestheticism and hermeticism and its attendant political self-marginalization" (*Poetics* 23). As a result of this claim, Hutcheon's postmodernism is more limited than Jameson's in the range of cultural productions that she deems postmodern. There is no poetry in her poetics (and it is difficult to imagine what her poetics could tell us about the Language poets); in fact, there is but a limited range of narratives and images that she designates as postmodern. She argues "that the term postmodernism in fiction be reserved to describe the more paradoxical and historically complex form" she calls "historiographic metafiction" (40). The terms "postmodern fiction" and "historiographic metafiction" therefore exist in a relationship of identity and describe the same set of objects: only historiographic metafiction is postmodern fiction; all postmodern fiction is historiographic metafiction. What this seems to mean then, is that, on Hutcheon's view, there is a great deal of narrative in our postmodernity that is not postmodern; in application, however, Hutcheon casts her net rather widely and is able to contain a number of apparently incommensurable narratives within her term. Historiographic metafiction blends the self-reflexivity of metafiction with an ironized sense of history; this mix foregrounds the distinction "between brute *events* of the past and the historical *facts* we construct out of them" (*Politics* 57). In doing so, such fiction draws one's attention to the problematic status of historical representation. As a vehicle for cultural critique, historiographic metafiction plays a paradoxical role because it "depends upon and draws its power from that which it contests" (*Poetics* 120). A form of cultural critique may proceed, but it is always aware of its own implication.

Although Hutcheon asserts that historiographic metafiction foregrounds the discursively constructed nature of reality "by stressing the contexts in which the fiction is being produced—by both writer and reader" (*Poetics* 40), her focus is primarily on the artist as producer. Chastising the enemies of postmodernism for claiming that its relation to history is reactionary, Hutcheon claims this position "ignore[s] the actual historical forms to which artists return" (39). Hutcheon's attention to the producer's intention reveals itself most clearly in her discussion of postmodern architecture, the area of aesthetic production that she posits as the model for postmodern fiction.

Postmodern architecture provides Hutcheon her point of entry for redefining older notions of parody to one of "repetition with critical distance that allows ironic signalling of difference at the very heart of similarity" (*Poetics* 26). For Hutcheon, "the dialogue of past and present, of old and new, is what gives formal expression to a belief in change within continuity. The obscurity and hermeticism of modernism are abandoned for a direct engagement of the viewer in the processes of signification through re-contextualized social and historical references" (32). But even here, though she appears to consider the viewer of postmodern architecture, her concern is for the architect, though this is somewhat hidden by the passive construction; it is the architect who abandons modernism, so that Hutcheon's focus still is on the producers' desire for their productions. Because of her focus on the producer, even when Hutcheon appears to engage Jameson's notion of pastiche, the confrontation turns out to be not as direct as it might initially appear:

> But the looking to both the aesthetic and the historical past in postmodernist architecture is anything but what Jameson describes as pastiche, that is "the random cannibalization of all the styles of the past, the play of random stylistic allusion." There is absolutely nothing random or "without principle" in the parodic recall and re-examination of the past by architects like Charles Moore or Ricardo Bofill. To include irony and play is *never* necessarily to exclude seriousness of purpose in postmodernist art. To misunderstand this is to misunderstand the nature of much contemporary aesthetic production—even if it does make for neater theorizing. (*Poetics* 26–27)

Here is a clear instance of the way in which Jameson and Hutcheon, although covering similar terrain, speak past each other because of their different orientation. Once we acknowledge, however, that Jameson is concerned more with aesthetic consumption in postmodernity and Hutcheon with its production, their disagreement, while not exactly disappearing, at least reveals how they might both—from within their own terms—be correct. Something else seems obvious, namely, that postmodern architects can intend their work to be a critique of the failures of the International Style, while at the same time the product of their critique—the actual buildings they design— can still be a nightmare for the users of this new postmodern space, many of whom, one supposes, do not receive the producer's intent (a critique of modernist architecture) through the mediation of the building. (Even consumers who comprehend the intended critique might find the critique inconsequential if personally inconvenienced by this new space).

A problem for Hutcheon, then, is attempting to discover a model for postmodern fiction in postmodern architecture. Postmodern architecture necessarily is implicated more fully in capitalism than postmodern literature because, while a new building might cost $25,000,000 to construct, a literary magazine costs closer to $2500 to produce. More than literature, architecture has always necessarily been more in tune with the desires of the ruling class. The desire of the aristocrat, the bourgeoisie, or the corporation to signify their hierarchical superiority almost inevitably forces architecture into an identification with high culture. This situation leads to a problem of reference: "By its doubly parodic, double coding (that is, as parodic of both modernism and something else), postmodernist architecture also allows for that which was rejected as uncontrollable and deceitful by both modernism's *Gesamtkinstler* and 'life conditioner': that is, ambiguity and irony" (30). The characterization of modernism as rejecting ambiguity and irony—the defining terms of New Criticism's version of modernist literature—would be perverse if Hutcheon were not limiting her discussion here to modernist architecture.[9] But of course she *is* referring to postmodern architecture, and her point reminds us of just how little irony and parody figured in theorizing modernist architecture. Architectural historian and critic Charles Jencks, upon whose notion of double coding Hutcheon draws, acknowledges that irony and ambiguity were "key concepts in Modern literature and Post-Modernists have continued using these tropes and methods while extending them to painting and architecture" (Jencks 329). Still, the punning that Hutcheon celebrates in postmodern architecture hardly seems startling to someone who has read Joyce or Faulkner.[10] What I wish to underscore here is the difficulty of mapping modernism in architecture onto modernism in literature. By analogy, I think the same difficulties attend a modeling of postmodern literature on postmodern architecture. The double coding Hutcheon notes, of course, is done by the architect, but what if the viewer is not a double decoder and what qualifies one to be a decoding observer? The case of postmodern architecture seems to make problematic Hutcheon's broader claim about postmodernism when she speaks of postmodern fiction: "Postmodernism is both academic and popular, élitist and accessible" (*Poetics* 44). The vast majority of the public are not attuned to the history of architecture, its terms and traditions.[11]

This issue of reference speaks directly to the problem I see in Hutcheon's modeling historiographic metafiction on postmodern architecture. What postmodernism in architecture gestures to, appropriates, and parodies largely is limited to the prior tradition of architecture. There can be no border crossings into discursive (and but few into other material) mediations of the historical. What is so postmodern here? Hutcheon's claim for postmodern architecture is that "the self-reflexive parodic introversion suggested by a turning to the *aesthetic* past is itself what makes possible an ideological and social intervention" (33; emphasis added). What is key here (and what will differ at times in her account of postmodern fiction) is the notion of reference limited to the aesthetic past. The hermetically closed text has been substituted for an equally closed tradition (the history of architecture), a move that in part could be accounted for by T. S. Eliot's conservative formulation of the relation among canonical works in "Tradition and the Individual Talent." In other words, from the perspective of literary modernism, what goes by the name of postmodernism in architecture is only now learning how to be modernist. In fact, to the extent that Hutcheon is willing to identify as postmodern those narratives that limit their parodic reference to the aesthetic past, she conflates postmodernism with a technique of avant-garde modernism. Despite this contradiction in her attempt to equate postmodernism in architecture with postmodernism in fiction, I do not want to throw the baby out with the bath water, since Hutcheon's characterization of historiographic metafiction may not need to be modeled on architectural postmodernism and carries a suggestiveness about the possibilities of contemporary narratives that escapes Jameson's totalizing view of postmodernity. But these possibilities only emerge by limiting the definition of "historiographic metafiction," so that it refers not to the aesthetic past but simply to the past and the fabrication of history. This is certainly a direction in which Hutcheon wishes to move on a number of occasions:

> Works like [Robert] Coover's *The Public Burning* or [E. L.] Doctorow's *The Book of Daniel* do not rewrite, refashion, or expropriate history merely to satisfy either some game-playing or some totalizing impulse; instead, they juxtapose what we think we know of the past (from official archival sources and personal memory) with an alternate representation that foregrounds the postmodern epistemological question of the nature of historical knowledge. Which "facts" make it into history? And *whose* facts? (*Politics* 71)

This formulation describes a trend in contemporary narrative, namely, the way a number of narratives turn one's attention away from the aesthetic past (such as literary history) and toward a more broadly conceived sense of history as textually mediated and constructed. But because Hutcheon models historiographic metafiction on architectural postmodernism, she often applies this valorizing term to narratives that—like the directed intertextuality of postmodern architecture—allude exclusively to the tradition of a particular genre. The very moment in *The Poetics of Postmodernism* that she introduces her characterization of postmodern narrative as historiographic metafiction illustrates the contradiction. She names Terry Gilliam's *Brazil* as an example of the kind of narrative that she will examine: "The postmodern ironic rethinking of history is here textualized in the many general *parodic references to other movies*" (5; emphasis added). Hutcheon goes on to list a number of such references, including the Odessa Steps sequence from Sergei Eisenstein's

Battleship Potemkin, where Gilliam's film substitutes a floor cleaner for the baby carriage in the original. However, I would deny the designation "historiographic metafiction" to any narrative in which the text's range of references or directed intertexts remain exclusively within its genre, be it literary or filmic history. And my reason would be close to Jameson's reason—how are such parodic moments experienced and who gets the reference? I recall seeing *Brazil* in graduate school with a group of bright law students. I alone marked the Eisenstein reference, and only because I happened to be taking a film course that semester. I am simply not sure how much faith one can place in such parodic allusions to disrupt the order of things.

Pastiche, Parody, and the Problem of Semiotic Regression

Jameson, however, is even more critical of Hutcheon's project; he denies efficacy to even those contemporary historical novels that attempt to engage the past in a way that might reactivate political awareness. His reading of Doctorow's *Ragtime* serves as a repudiation of Hutcheon's historiographic metafiction; he calls the novel

> the most peculiar and stunning monument to the aesthetic situation engendered by the disappearance of the historical referent. This historical novel can no longer set out to represent the historical past; it can only "represent" our ideas and stereotypes about that past (which thereby at once becomes "pop history"). [. . .] If there is any realism left here, it is a "realism" that is meant to derive from the shock of grasping that confinement and of slowly becoming aware of a new and original historical situation in which we are condemned to seek History by way of our own pop images and simulacra of that history, which itself remains forever out of reach. (*Postmodernism* 25)

This passage reflects both Jameson's Baudrillardian sense of the orders of simulacra and his Marxist belief in a scientific History.[12] But it also looks strange from so engaged a reader of poststructuralism as Jameson. Does he mean to suggest that there was a time (a mythologized moment of primitive communism?) when history was in reach, when one grasped history in some unmediated fashion? Even if Sir Walter Scott believed he was representing the historical past, the work of New Historicism revealed the illusory nature of such belief through the following inescapable logic: the past is always textually mediated and texts are always historical.

Still, Jameson's attempt to refute historiographic metafiction via *Ragtime* deserves closer scrutiny, if only because it underscores the difference between his and Hutcheon's orientation. Jameson asserts that Doctorow's novel has transparent political meaning, which he grants "has been expertly articulated by Lynda [sic] Hutcheon" (*Postmodernism* 22). The problem for Jameson is that Hutcheon's delineation of the class conflict and the recurring pattern of the working class's relation to aesthetic production creates "an admirable thematic coherence few readers can have experienced in parsing the lines of a verbal object held too close to the eyes to fall into these perspectives." Speaking from the axis of consumption, Jameson trivializes Hutcheon by making her just another formalist performing a mandarin close reading. On the one hand Jameson faults Hutcheon for belaboring the obvious—namely, that *Ragtime* has political content; on the other hand, he attacks her for attempting to articulate systematically what that political content is. In short, she is guilty simultaneously of seeing what anyone can see and of seeing coherence no normal reader would experience.

Jameson's critique of Hutcheon here, however, turns with a vengeance upon his own ideological reading. Apparently unaware of the contradiction, Jameson, after reducing Doctorow's novel to just another moment of postmodern Disneylike holographic simulation, then touts the novel as a formal experiment in style that defamiliarizes language in a fashion worthy of high modernism:

> It is, for example, well known that the source of many of the characteristic effects of Camus's novel *The Stranger* can be traced back to that author's willful decision to substitute, throughout, the French tense of the *passé composé* for the other past tenses more normally employed in narration in that language. I suggest that it is as if something of that sort were at work here: *as though* Doctorow had set out systematically to produce the effect or the equivalent, in his language, of a verbal past tense we do not possess in English, namely, the French preterite (or *passé simple*), whose "perfective" movement [. . .] serves to separate events from the present of enunciation and to transform the stream of time and action into so many finished, complete, and isolated punctual event objects which find themselves sundered from any present situation (even that of the act of story telling or enunciation). (24)

Even if Jameson is correct in his contention that the average reader does not immediately discover the thematic coherence of Hutcheon's reading, one rather suspects even fewer readers have experienced *Ragtime* as Jameson casts it. But this kind of description is necessary if he is to maintain that Doctorow's work creates "no solid historiographic formation on the reader's part." It is difficult to imagine what could ever ensure a reader's historiographic formation that Jameson requires before he will grant any political vocation to the contemporary historical novel; nevertheless, contemporary fiction that turns to history (rather than simply the aesthetic past) as its intertext opens a site wherein historical thinking becomes a *possibility.*

But only a possibility and perhaps not always the possibility Hutcheon hopes for in her understanding of the poetics and the politics of postmodernism. It is possible to raise a question about her linkage of politics and poetics through a counterexample: how from Hutcheon's perspective does one think about a novel such as John Updike's *Memories of the Ford Administration?* This novel's blurring of the boundary between history and fiction occurs through the self-conscious academic voice of a history professor, Alfred Clayton. The fictive premise is that Clayton is responding to a request from a history journal, *Retrospect,* that he provide impressions of Gerald Ford's administration. Clayton instead comments on his adulterous personal life during the Ford years, layering in his unpublished research on the administration of President James Buchanan. This premise would seem to make Updike's novel a paradigmatic example of historiographic metafiction. *Memories of the Ford Administration,* according to Hutcheon's poetics of postmodernism (the formal features that define postmodern fiction), can only be historiographic metafiction. But according to Hutcheon's politics of postmodernism (her claims regarding the cultural work of postmodern fiction), Updike's novel could never be termed historiographic metafiction. This contradiction arises because Updike's politics are conservative, while Hutcheon insists that historiographic metafiction is always politically left of center. Rather than use historiographic metafiction to dedoxify the order of things, Updike wishes to lead readers to a different orthodoxy, his version of Christian faith. What the example of Updike reveals is that to see in historiographic metafiction a politics, however compromised, is highly problematic. Despite Hutcheon's ability in *The Politics of Postmodernism* to identify a significant number of contemporary narratives that exhibit a left-leaning politics, linking any poetics to left politics may only serve as an expression of utopian desire. Whatever politics of contemporary fiction might emerge, it does not reside as an essence within the fiction but rather in the multiple possibilities of readers' engagements.

Such engagements are so complex and various, however, that even an apparently simple cultural text, the cover of a recent catalogue from a mail-order clothier (fig. 1.1), points to the difficulty of reading postmodernism exclusively through the lens of either parody or pastiche. At the same time, the catalogue cover underscores the difficulty in arguing for a politicized postmodernism on the basis of a text's parodic relation to the aesthetic past. The illustration shows how even Pop's cannibalization of consumer and media culture itself is available for appropriation. The illustration directs the knowing viewer, of course, to Roy Lichtenstein, who in the 1960s, through the medium of oil paint, pointed our attention to the formal conventions of the comic-strip panel.[13] But what is interesting here is how the image might work simultaneously for a variety of consumers who do or do not get the references to the multiple previous representations that the cover plays off. Lichtenstein's work has been reproduced on postcards. These postcards themselves have been the site of parody.

Lichtenstein frequently places a female figure in jeopardy; this figure's thoughts represented in the cartoon bubble are clichéd and stereotypical (fig. 1.2). In the 1980s, a series of parodic feminist postcards employed Lichtenstein-like images of the distressed female but replaced his bathetic words in the cartoon bubble with words that directly confront gender stereotypes and assumptions; thus, the distressed female image was represented saying things such as "My boyfriend just ran off with my best friend. . . . God, I'm going to miss her!" or "Oh my God! I think I'm becoming the man I wanted to marry!" The catalogue cover, then, interacts with all of these prior representations and can confirm the identity of a variety of consumers regardless how much or how little of the intertextual puzzle any particular viewer understands.

The image stands ready to produce pleasure—to reward the viewer for connecting with any piece of the previous system of representations upon which it depends. As a result, the image works equally well for either the middle-class housewife who enjoys the reference to newspaper comic strips or the hip academic who appreciates the bubble's shift from a Lichtensteinian bathos ("I've nothing to live for!") to the ironic ("I've nothing to wear!"). And in either case the catalogue's image might be a portion of the reason that the consumer would reach for a credit card and place an order. Certainly even for the knowing consumer of the cover's image, the parody seems more complicitous with than critical of the economic order.[14]

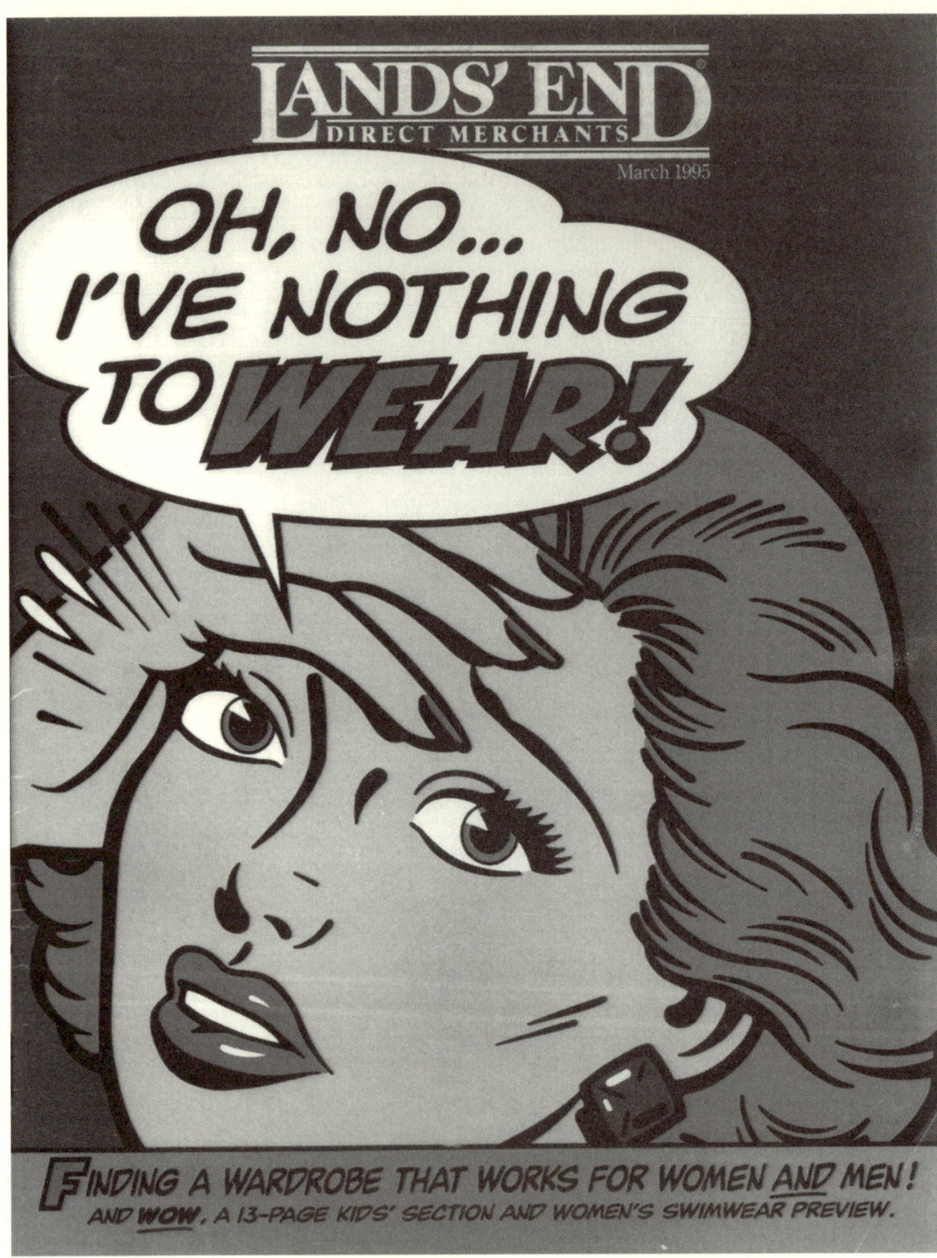

Figure 1.1 *Nothing to Wear* cover; illustration for Lands' End Catalog by Lou Brooks. Courtesy of Lou Brooks.

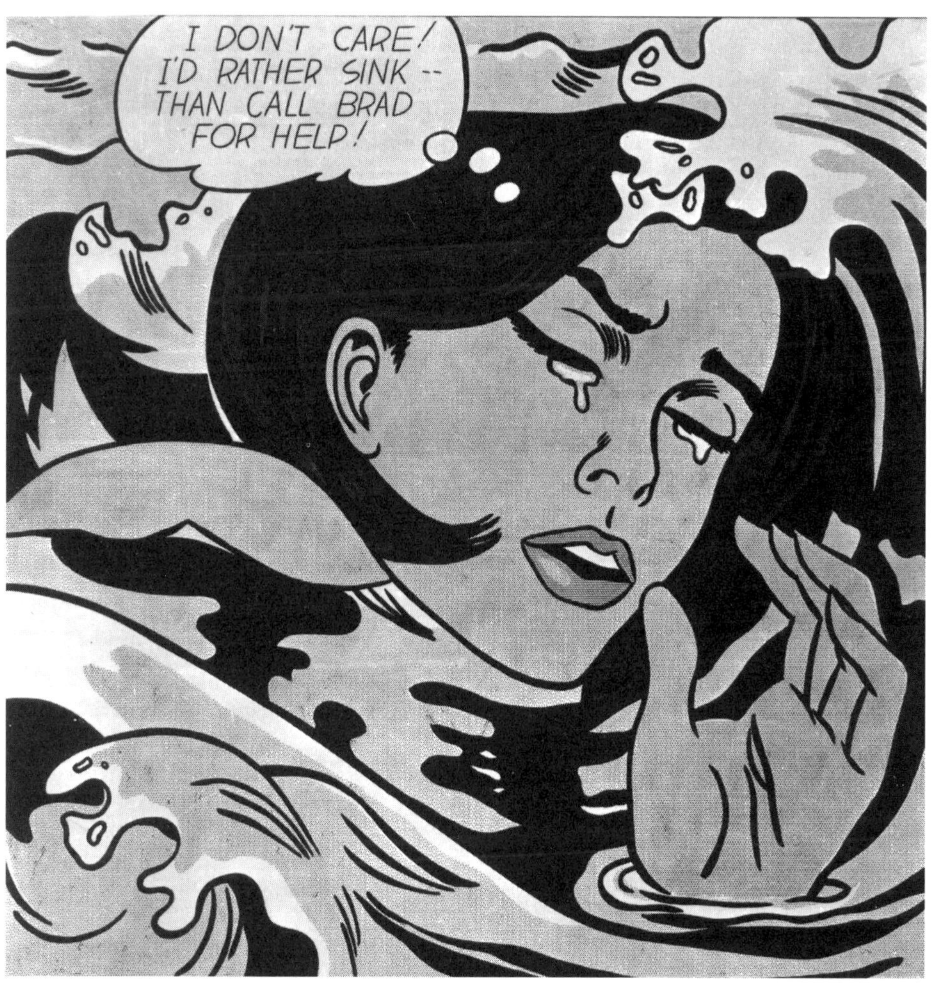

Figure 1.2 Roy Lichtenstein, *Drowning Girl,* 1963. Oil and synthetic polymer paint on canvas, 171.6 × 169.5 cm. The Museum of Modern Art, New York. Philip Johnson Fund and gift of Mr. and Mrs. Bagley Wright. Photograph © 2001 The Museum of Modern Art.

Yet it is not unimaginable that, for the uninformed viewer of this pastiched image, the catalogue cover might also provide a critical purchase on a particular enactment of femininity.

Whatever questions the above image-matrix might raise about Jameson's and Hutcheon's competing attempts to name the master trope of postmodernism, their focus on the consumer's response to pastiched images and the producer's parodic intentions remains a useful starting point for thinking about contemporary representation. Both theorists' investments in certain forms of modernism, however, render problematic their very desire to articulate the postmodern difference.

Notes

1. Clint Burnham comments briefly on the Jameson-Hutcheon impasse, dismissing Hutcheon's postmodernism as liberalism (230–32).

2. Hamid Shirvani considers the difference between Jameson's and Hutcheon's versions of postmodernism in a review-essay of Jameson's *Postmodernism, or The Cultural Logic of Late Capitalism* (hereafter cited as *Postmodernism*) and Hutcheon's *Poetics of Postmodernism*. Shirvani argues that their different accounts of postmodernism can be explained by gender differences. In Shirvani's reductive account, Hutcheon as a woman and feminist celebrates postmodern difference creating an "opportunity to promote a decentered multicultural society" (Shirvani 296) while Jameson is really a closet patriarch worried only about the disintegration of his cultural authority (293).

3. In a confessional moment, Andreas Huyssen similarly expresses his deflated hopes regarding the 1960s: "I, like many others, believed that Pop art could be the beginning of a far reaching democratization of art and art appreciation" (*After* 142). "The belief in consciousness raising by means of aesthetic experience," Huyssen notes, "was quite common in those days" (143).

4. Margaret Rose has objected that Jameson has incorrectly identified the Bonaventure Hotel as postmodern since architectural historians have called the building "either modernist or late-modernist" (76). This problem of moving between modern/postmodern architecture and contemporary narrative is even more complicated in the work of Hutcheon.

5. From Bob Pearlman's perspective, however, Jameson's parataxical style renders it more akin to pastiche (323).

6. The absence of popular culture from Jameson's field of vision is one of Burnhams's insightful focuses in *The Jamesonian Unconscious*. (See particularly Chapter 4, "The Hysteria of Mass Culture.")

7. Cornel West discusses Jameson's debt to Lukács (123–24).

8. As Astradur Eysteinsson points out, someone wishing to value modernism over realism could appropriate Hassan's list and merely substitute realism for modernism and modernism for postmodernism (129).

9. See Rose's critique of Hutcheon's use of Charles Jencks's notion of double-coding to create a parallel between literary parody and architectural postmodernism: "Despite some similarities in the functions of the dual-coded parody and dual-coded post-modern building to increase the number of 'codes' being sent out, it should be noted that parody, in contrast to postmodernism, is a device rather than a period term, and one which is to be found from ancient to 'postmodern' times." More pointedly, Rose characterizes Hutcheon's underlying argument as enacting the fallacy of the undistributed middle; that is, for Rose, Hutcheon is arguing that "all parody is dual-coded, all post-modernism is dual-coded: therefore all parody is post-modern and all post-modernism is parodic" (220–21).

10. Speaking of the Chicago Tribune Tower, Hutcheon notes, "The pun on newspaper columns is deliberate; the black and white of the building are meant to suggest print lines and, of course, the *Chicago Tribune* is red/read all over" (*Poetics* 33).

11. Hutcheon acknowledges the problem ("Like all parody, postmodernist architecture *can* certainly be élitist, if the codes necessary for its comprehension are not shared by both encoder and decoder") but optimistically believes that the quotations are usually "common and easily recognized" (*Poetics* 34).

12. McHale also examines the two theorists' readings of Doctorow. For McHale, the "superiority of Jameson's readings" is a function of his dialectical method, as opposed to Hutcheon, whose reading of *Ragtime* is yet another instance of the way "her readings end up collapsing all her texts into the same oxymoronic structure of 'complicitous "critique"'" ("Postmodernism" 26).

13. Lou Brooks, the "commercial" artist who produced this image and whose work has appeared on the cover of a number of national magazines, graciously spoke to me for forty-five minutes about his work. While acknowledging that others have noted the Lichtenstein connection, Brooks points out that he also comes to the pop culture material on its own terms. While Lichtenstein worked in oil, Brooks's work is computer-generated. He also pointed out that the

image on the catalogue cover has appeared in other noncommercial contexts.

14. The effect of Brooks's image, however, is strikingly different when it is not framed by the corporate context. To view the image in color without the commercial frame, access the Lou Brooks website (www.loubrooks.com/groundzero.html) and go to the area called "The Lou Brooks Stock Art Bar and Grill." Experiencing the image in this virtual gallery (it's the one subtitled "BOOHOO!") is nearly indistinguishable from a visit to a virtual gallery at the Museum of Modern Art's website. This different context shifts the image's emphasis, making Brooks' work more like the feminist postcards' parodic appropriation of Lichtenstein.

2

Postmodernism and History: Complicitous Critique and the Political Unconscious

Thomas Carmichael

> It seems to be easier for us today to imagine the thoroughgoing deterioration of the earth and of nature than the breakdown of late capitalism, perhaps that is due to some weakness in our imagination.
>
> I have come to think that the word *postmodernism* ought to be reserved for thoughts of this kind.
>
> —Fredric Jameson, *Postmodernism*

> The postmodern problematizing of the issue of historical knowledge is, I think, a reaction against the neoconservative appropriation of history to its own ends (a nostalgic traditionalism and a need for authority).
>
> —Linda Hutcheon, *Poetics*

At the close of *Marxism and Form,* Fredric Jameson, seeking to revitalize the work of cultural critique, calls upon literary criticism in America "to continue to compare the inside and the outside, existence and history, to continue to pass judgment on the abstract quality of life in the present, and to keep alive the idea of a concrete future" (416). Published in 1971 and containing material that first appeared in the later 1960s, the rhetoric of *Marxism and Form* is inevitably marked by what Jameson later describes as "the end of the great wave of 'wars of liberation'" and the political storm of "the brief 'American century' [1945–73]" (*Postmodernism* xx). But Jameson's occasional remarks in *Marxism and Form* also anticipate much of what will come to the fore in the cultural criticism of the last third of the twentieth century, from the recognition of "the bankruptcy of the liberal tradition" (*Postmodernism* x) to the appeal for a "postindustrial Marxism" (xix) that would address the particular problems raised by "postindustrial capitalism" (393) and the new "global class situation" (401) to a strong sense of the utter social transformation that separates the older "classical" modernism from the "new modernism" of pop art in America (413). Briefly put, what Jameson's discussions in *Marxism and Form* look forward to is the arrival of postmodernism as a cultural dominant in the vast transformation, as he later terms it, of "infrastructure and superstructures—the economic system and the cultural 'structure of feeling'" in the new world system of late capital (*Postmodernism* xxi). And one of the most striking things about this new world system of postmodernity, as Jameson himself has often observed, is the way in which its arrival collapses older categories and distinctions. Postmodernism, as Jameson reminds us, "seems to obligate you in advance to talk about cultural phenomena at least in business terms if not in those of political economy" (*Postmodernism* xxi) because in the current world system, as he so aptly puts it, culture "cleaves almost too close to the skin of the economic to be stripped off and inspected in its own right, [. . .] not unlike Magritte's shoe-foot" (xv).

I recall Jameson's remarks here not in order to recross much traveled ground, but so that I might begin with the seemingly unexceptionable observation that postmodernism presents itself most forcibly in the intersection of the practices of representation and political economy, and that this intersection finds its ideological expression most often in a concern with the codes of historical representation. This is also the logic that informs Linda Hutcheon's insistence that the "complicitous critique" she finds so characteristic of postmodernism arises from the ambivalent situation of postmodern within "economic capitalism and cultural humanism" (*Politics* 13). Although Hutcheon has expressed reservations about Jameson's symptomatic readings of postmodern culture, and Jameson, for his part, has occasionally suggested that Hutcheon has not gone far enough in describing the implications of postmodern artifacts and practices, Hutcheon's reading of the "compromised politics" (*Politics* 2) of postmodernism has much in common with Jameson's own understanding of the political unconscious and the cultural text.[1] As in the case of Jameson's work, much of Hutcheon's discussion of postmodernism turns upon the question of the relation between cultural production and the larger system or mode of production, and it is with this question that any consideration of the relationship between postmodernism and history must begin.

For Jameson, cultural production is to be apprehended on the Althusserian model as one element in a mode of production, the latter being understood as a structural totality discernible only in its effects. And like all elements in a social formation, cultural production is inescapably ideological in the sense of providing "a representational structure which allows the individual subject to conceive or imagine his or her lived relationship to transpersonal realities such as the social structure or the collective logic of History" (*Political* 30).

For the individual subject who is an effect of the social formation, there is thus no escape from ideology, and, by the same logic, there is no cultural artifact that is not social and historical. On this point, Jameson argues, Marxist criticism would concur with Northrop Frye that "all literature must be read as a symbolic meditation on the destiny of community," but in contrast to Frye's description of the fully privatized end of the literary imagination, Jameson argues that literature can never escape its social determinations, or as he puts it, "all literature, no matter how weakly, must be informed by what we have called a political unconscious" (*Political* 70). Like the mode of production itself, social determinations inevitably come before the individual consciousness in the form of determinate contradictions, whose "imaginary or formal 'solutions'" are then properly the work of the symbolic act, individual text, or cultural artifact (*Political* 79). But for Jameson, this work of the cultural text and its relation to the social totality must also be understood as passing beneath three horizons of interpretive understanding. Within the first horizon, the single narrative or cultural artifact can be apprehended as a symbolic act designed to devise imaginary resolutions to real contradictions; within the second, the artifact may be understood as partaking inevitably of a class discourse in which it assembles basic units or ideologemes in order to universalize specific class interest. Within the third horizon, all cultural artifacts are to be read as products of what Jameson calls the *"ideology of form"* (*Political* 76), or a historically situated system of semiotic production which is always part of a particular social totality defined as a mode of production (*Political* 89), as long as we admit that any social formation in history has carried with it dependent vestiges of older modes of production and anticipations of newer ones (*Political* 95).

In terms of the relation between the "antitranscendent hermeneutic model" outlined in *The Political Unconscious* and Jameson's reading of postmodern history and cultural production, it is the first and third of these interpretive horizons that will interest us most here (*Political* 23). Still, we should not pass over the notion of class discourse as an interpretive horizon without noting its contribution to Jameson's construction of the political unconscious and to his subsequent reading of postmodernism. As class discourse, the basic unit of cultural production, in Jameson's terms, is the "ideologeme," "whose essential structural characteristic may be

described as its possibility to manifest itself either as a pseudoidea—
a conceptual or belief system, an abstract value, an opinion or
prejudice—or as a protonarrative, a kind of ultimate class fantasy
about the 'collective characters' which are the classes in opposition"
(*Political* 87). But the ideologeme is more than simply a unit in some
partial superstructural expression of the dynamics of historical materialism, for if there is no escape from ideology, then every cultural
artifact is at once a representation of class interest and at the same
time, to the extent that it is socially conditioned, a representation of
some collective imagining. Moreover, Jameson persuasively maintains, to the extent that every artifact is the representation of a collective interest or fantasy, it is in its expression of that collective desire a
form of utopian imagining, if we understand, as Jameson insists, that
"[t]he achieved collectivity or organic group of whatever kind—
oppressors fully as much as oppressed—is Utopian not in itself, but
only insofar as all such collectivities are themselves *figures* for the
ultimate concrete collective life of an achieved Utopian or classless
society" (*Political* 291). Hence, all forms of cultural expression, including the most cynical instances of commercial manipulation and
political mystification, are utopian or exploit a preexistent utopian
longing, and although these representations may be found in every
mode or medium, the work they perform conforms, in Jameson's
description, largely to the dynamic of narrative.[2]

More than once in *The Political Unconscious,* Jameson insists
that narrative is "the supreme function of the human mind," (123) or
its "central function or *instance*" (13). But narrative is important in
The Political Unconscious not so much for what it may suggest about
the structures of human subjectivity, but rather for what it exemplifies with respect to the ideological function of the individual cultural artifact. And it is here, within this first horizon or interpretive
model, that we encounter the work of the political unconscious most
directly. If every cultural text is ideological and utopian, then each
individual narrative, as Jameson argues, is to be read as a formal
resolution of social antagonisms or contradictions. Although a social
antagonism or contradiction can only be resolved in the world
through praxis, it can be apprehended in the individual mind as
paradox or antinomy, or a simple contradiction that will admit of no
logical solution, but which demands, according to Jameson, "a whole
more properly narrative apparatus—the text itself—to square its circles and to dispel, through narrative movement, its intolerable
closure" (*Political* 83). As Jameson demonstrates in his Greimasian
analysis of Honoré de Balzac's *La Vieille Fille,* the power unique to

narrative is its ability to rearrange the logic of the social totality so that it might appear transformed and yet with each of its elements preserved in an unambiguously harmonious representation that at the same time mimics, more or less convincingly in its movement or working out, the dense and ceaseless circulation that is the subject's experience of the totality itself (*Political* 167).

But the horizons of interpretation do not stop there. Any single narrative, as I have already noted, is in addition an expression of what Jameson calls "the ideology of form," or the total "system of the production of signs" that is organized around a specific historical mode of production (*Political* 88). This third horizon of textual interpretation is of particular interest with respect to Jameson's later meditations on postmodern culture because it raises the question of the possibilities for any kind of oppositional cultural expression. After all, as Jameson himself acknowledges, if the mode of production is understood as something akin to the "total system," then it is difficult to conceive of "any possibility of the *negative* as such," other than an oppositional culture that is licensed by the system itself in order to confirm its own logic (*Political* 91). In *The Political Unconscious,* Jameson resolves this dilemma by insisting on the inevitable existence at the same time of several modes of production—dominant, residual, and anticipatory—so that the dominant mode at any one time is engaged in a perpetual struggle to maintain its dominance, in which "the overtly 'transitional' moments of cultural revolution are themselves but the passage to the surface of a permanent process in human societies" (*Political* 97). Culture is thus one element in an inevitably conflicted system, within which oppositional impulses (now cast as residual or anticipatory) find their own expression alongside dominant representations, and it is this understanding of the cultural text that guides Jameson's notion of a third interpretive horizon. Jameson points to generic criticism as a clear instance of how this third interpretive horizon might be worked out, in that specific historical instances of a given form can be read as expressions of residual, dominant, and anticipatory messages, which, taken together, reveal "the 'conjuncture' of coexisting modes of production at a given historical moment" (*Political* 99). But perhaps more important for the purposes of the present discussion are the implications for a critical culture of Jameson's description of the place of culture in the social totality, for the problem of the space of oppositionality would appear to evaporate when the mode of production itself is defined in advance as an agonistic network of competing modes, even though the relation between this understanding of social formations and the postmodern text remains to be worked out in Jameson's reading of the cultural logic of late capital (*Political* 148).

Jameson's assertion of the ideological and utopian nature of every cultural artifact, and of the permanence of struggle and the persistence of contradiction in any historical mode of production, shapes his reading of postmodernism. This reading is finally not all that far removed from Linda Hutcheon's less fully elaborated remarks on the role of the world system of late capital, remarks for which Jameson's own narratological and metacritical articulations will serve in this discussion as an effective gloss. Like Jameson, Hutcheon has consistently insisted that cultural production is inextricably tied to social formations and that every cultural artifact or every symbolic act is political, at least to the extent that it is engaged in the politics of representation (*Poetics* 35; *Politics* 3). And like Jameson, Hutcheon looks to Althusser for the relation between culture and the social totality. As she puts it, "the single most influential theoretical statement on the topic might well be Louis Althusser's much-cited notion of ideology both as a system of representation and as a necessary and unavoidable part of every social totality. Both points are important to any discussion of postmodernism [. . .]" (*Politics* 6). For Hutcheon, postmodern cultural production is thoroughly ideological in the sense that it is generated from the sign system of a specific social totality, but in contrast to the ways in which a utopian reading of all culture artifacts leads Jameson out of the problem of locating the space of the negative in this ideological system, Hutcheon's reading of postmodernism resolutely insists on the possibilities for oppositional discourse within the cultural dominants of late capital. Although Hutcheon concedes that "Western capitalist culture has [. . .] shown an amazing power to normalize (or 'doxify') signs and images, however disparate (or contesting) they may be" (*Politics* 7), she is firm in her opposition to what she takes to be Jameson's symptomatic reading of postmodernism. As she puts it: "The slippage from postmodern*ity* to postmodern*ism* is constant and deliberate in Jameson's work: for him postmodernism *is* the 'cultural logic of late capitalism.' It replicates, reinforces, and intensifies the 'deplorable and reprehensible' socio-economic effects of postmodernity. Perhaps. But I want to argue that it also critiques those effects, while never pretending to be able to operate outside them" (*Politics* 25). For Hutcheon, as for Jameson, it is simply axiomatic that there is no space "outside" the social totality where one might situate a critical consciousness. Postmodernism, as Hutcheon repeatedly reminds us, is "deeply implicated in the logic of bourgeois society" and (quoting Charles Newman) in its "'agencies of production, transmission, and administration of knowledge as dominant cultural institutions'" (*Poetics* 213). As a cultural dominant, it is situated "within both economic capitalism and cultural humanism," from where it engages in a mode of "complicitous critique" (*Politics* 13) in which its compromised politics both mirror and challenge the logic of the world system. In Jameson's *Political Unconscious,* the possibility of a critical postmodernism is predicated on a social totality that is itself the scene of perpetual struggle, so that without any recourse to the fantasy of an "outside," utopian projections of very different kinds might emerge from within what is understood to be a single system or mode of production, whereas in Hutcheon's reflections on what amounts to the same problem, this critique from within is best accounted for through the expression of determinate negations. As she observes at the beginning of *The Politics of Postmodernism,* postmodern culture is best characterized by its "self-conscious, self-contradictory, self-undermining statement" (1), and the aim of these practices is to "de-doxify," "to de-naturalize some of the dominant features of our way of life; to point out that those entities that we unthinkingly experience as 'natural' (they might even include capitalism, patriarchy, liberal humanism) are in fact 'cultural'; made by us, not given to us" (2). Like Jameson, Hutcheon rejects the notion that postmodernism is a politics or that it can ever address social contradictions, whose resolutions await a moment of praxis; however, what a critical postmodern can do, Hutcheon modestly maintains, "is underline the need for self-awareness, on the one hand, and on the other, for an acknowledgement of that relationship—suppressed by humanism—of the aesthetic and the political" (*Poetics* 200), or provide a critique that might anticipate and accompany the struggle for a reconfigured polity (*Politics* 100). Although Hutcheon's sense of the engine of postmodernism's ideological critique is more provisional and local than Jameson's resolute notion of a permanent cultural revolution and a perpetual struggle in the social totality, her assertion that "postmodernism is fundamentally contradictory, resolutely historical, and inescapably political" and that "[i]ts contradictions may well be those of late capitalist society" (*Poetics* 4) effectively parallels Jameson's own explication of the dynamic of mediations and differences that unites the structural elements in any mode of production, and which can here be applied to the structural relation of cultural production to the world system. In this context, and despite her occasional distancing of her work from Jameson's, Hutcheon's reading of postmodernism comes close to Jameson's own wider theory of the dynamic of textual and (more broadly) cultural production and its relation to the social totality, or, specifically, that the space of negation or oppositionality is to be found in the expression of determinate contradictions and inversions.

Within Jameson's own reading of postmodern culture, however, this space of negation is greatly overshadowed by the affirmative character of much postmodern cultural production. While he maintains that postmodernism compels us to consider culture in terms of political economy because of the ways in which anything that we might have once imagined as belonging to some semiautonomous sphere of the aesthetic has now been fully integrated into commodity production, Jameson also insists that, rather than understanding this process as an erosion, we should envision it as a "a prodigious expansion of culture throughout the social realm, to the point at which everything in our social life—from economic value and state power to practices and to the very structure of the psyche itself—can be said to have become 'cultural' in some original and as yet untheorized sense" (*Postmodernism* 48). What " 'cultural'" means in this context is of course inextricably bound up with Jameson's insistence that "capitalism is at one and the same time the best thing that has ever happened to the human race, and the worst," which in terms of late capitalism means apprehending the current world system "as catastrophe and progress all together" (*Postmodernism* 47). Thus, we are to conceive of postmodern culture as a doubly bound project, one that presents us with an infinitely expanded cultural sphere marking the final triumph of commodification over everything that might resist appropriation to a systems of pure exchanges, but which also in its various forms of euphoric compensation hints at a future in which the subject transformed by late capital might come to know new forms of collective and utopian organization.

As a symptomatic culture, postmodernism is famously characterized by Jameson as "the emergence of a new kind of flatness or depthlessness" (*Postmodernism* 9) and the often-cited "waning of affect" (*Postmodernism* 10) that together mark the eclipse of any individual style and the ascendency of "a field of stylistic and discursive heterogeneity without a norm" (*Postmodernism* 17). In the actual field of cultural commodities, the quintessential postmodern artifact for Jameson is "total flow" video (*Postmodernism* 76), or "a structure or sign flow which resists meaning, whose fundamental inner logic is the exclusion of the emergence of themes as such in that sense, and which therefore systematically sets out to short-circuit traditional interpretive temptations [. . .]" (*Postmodernism* 91–92). To the extent that "total flow" video and other contemporary cultural practices represent fairly what the postmodern feels like, they can be construed as "peculiar new forms of realism (or at least the mimesis of reality), while at the same time they can equally well be analyzed as so many attempts to distract and divert us from that reality or to disguise its contradictions and resolve them in the guise of various formal mystifications" (*Postmodernism* 49). Although for Jameson the processes of mystification are predominant in these cultural productions, his account of the dynamics of postmodern culture, as I have already hinted, does not preclude the possibility of "some effective contemporary cultural politics and [. . .] the construction of a genuine political culture," even though this possibility is only glimpsed in Jameson's reading of postmodernism (*Postmodernism* 47).

Perhaps the clearest indication of what an effective cultural politics or political culture might mean for Jameson is to be found in the unlikely pairing of his reflections on the meaning of American minimalist realism in the fiction of the 1980s and his extensive meditations on the fate of the subject in late capital. In a discussion of the mimetic spaces of postmodern architecture in *The Seeds of Time,* Jameson pauses to consider recent American minimalism, or what Bill Buford has dubbed "dirty realism," not only as the predictable contemporary representation of the commodification and simulation of both daily life and of the category of literature itself, but also, to the extent that it proclaims itself to be a kind of neoregionalism, as "a compensatory ideology, in a situation in which regions (like ethnic groups) have been fundamentally wiped out—reduced, standardized, commodified, atomized, or rationalized" (*Seeds* 147–48). In this reading, American "dirty realism" is a vast sentimentalization of a residual Fordist America in which regional codes and affiliations could coexist with, and were in fact necessary for, the success of what is now understood to be a supremely inflexible mode of commodity production. But as a specifically postmodern form of postmodern cultural production, American "dirty realism" is important to Jameson despite its nostalgic mystifications because it foregrounds the social and economic organization of a particular level of contemporary American life, and so stands as a conspicuous contemporary attempt to imagine the collective, echoing in many ways the dynamics of narrative representation that Jameson so thoroughly described in *The Political Unconscious.* However, in terms of specifically postmodern cultural production and in the context of some possibility of an effective cultural politics, "dirty realism" also stands as a conspicuously failed example, one in which the effort to sentimentalize the archaic represents a shrinking from the new and not-to-be-turned-back space of late capital. In contrast to this failed moment, Jameson then points in his discussion to Ridley Scott's *Blade Runner* (1982), and cyberpunk generally, as work of "crucial symptomatic importance in the postcontemporary political unconscious," both for the mimetic ability to represent the collective space of late capital and the power to anticipate the utopian promise in its transformations (*Seeds* 150). As Jameson puts it, "[cyberpunk's] nightmares are also on the point of becoming celebrations of a new reality, a new reality-intensification, that cannot simply be dealt with by a reactivation of the older cultural and class attitudes" (*Seeds* 150). In their utopian anticipations, these collective imaginings of cyberpunk effectively demonstrate Jameson's view of the progressive political potential in postmodern cultural production, a view that is complemented by his discussion elsewhere of the repositioning of the subject within the postmodern collective.

In *Postmodernism, or, The Cultural Logic of Late Capitalism*, Jameson draws a distinction between groups and classes: "Classes are few; they come into being by slow transformations in the mode of production [. . .]. Groups, on the other hand, seem to offer the gratification of psychic identity (from nationalism to neoethnicity)," but are ultimately governed, we might add, by the organizational logic of the market (346–47). Although a substitute and compensation for any effective experience of the collective, groups are nonetheless the basic unit of the confused social struggle of the new world system, for everyone, as Jameson reminds us, " 'represents' several groups all at once. This is the social reality that psychoanalytic currents on the left have analyzed in terms of 'subject-positions' " (*Postmodernism* 322). In terms of political culture, much turns on the relation between the subject and the collective. This is particularly true for the culture of late capital in which, as Jameson insists, the "ideology of groups comes into being simultaneously with the well-known 'death of the subject' (of which it is simply an alternate version)" (*Postmodernism* 348), a historical displacement whose markers elsewhere are the disappearance of the notion of individual style as an aesthetic sign of value, the throwing into the shadow of obsolescence older, psychopolitical affective structures, from alienation to ennui, and the end of the celebration of self-consciousness, a notion, as Jameson so aptly puts it, that "no longer seems to do the work it was thought able to perform in the past" (*Postmodernism* 244). For Jameson, the death of the traditional subject and the arrival of the schizo- or fragmented subject of late capital is in addition a crucial event in the narrative of the movement from the older Fordist mode of production of high modernism to the reconstituted cultural order of late capitalism. As he observes in *The Political Unconscious,*

> From a Marxist point of view, this experience of the decentering of the subject and the theories, essentially psychoanalytic, which have been devised to map it are to be seen as the signs of the dissolution of an essentially bourgeois ideology of the subject and of psychic unity or identity [. . .] but we may admit the descriptive value of the post-structuralist critique of the "subject" without necessarily endorsing the schizophrenic ideal it has tended to project. (125).

In Jameson's reading, the postmodern group is the means by which space is structurally organized for the newly dispersed subject of late capital, but lest we be seduced by any anti-oedipal rhetoric of liberation in this new account of subjectivity, he is quick to point out that the logic of the group carries with it a deflating moment of truth in that "although the theory and the rhetoric of multiple subject-positions is an attractive one, it should always be completed by an insistence on the way in which subject-positions do not come into being in a void but are themselves the interpellated roles offered by this or that already existing group" (*Postmodernism* 345). However, just as the ability to anticipate or hint plausibly at the possibility of an adequate political culture in the fully configured world space of late capital is the utopian content of cyberpunk's version of "dirty realism," the arrival of the dispersed subject of late capital can also be said to anticipate a new horizon within which a reconfigured collective will come into its own. As Jameson observes, "I think one cannot too often emphasize the logical possibility, alongside both the old closed, centered subject of inner-directed individualism and the new non-subject of the fragmented or schizophrenic self, of a third term which would be very precisely the non-centered subject that is a part of an organic group or collective" (*Postmodernism* 345). Elsewhere, Jameson is even more emphatic on this point, as when he affirms, "For Marxism, indeed, only the emergence of a post-individualistic social world, only the reinvention of the collective and the associa-

tive, can concretely achieve the 'decentering' of the individual subject called for by such diagnoses [. . .]" (*Political* 125). To anticipate
a new collective logic in the world space of late capitalism ("dirty
realism") and to represent a subject-position that might be adequate
to this new logic within an utterly transformed social totality ("total
flow video") is, for Jameson, the proper work of postmodern culture,
and it is only in its ability to succeed in this ultimately coherent
project that postmodernism can aspire to the logic that, Jameson insists, must ultimately govern all cultural production.

For Jameson, then, a critical postmodernism is both a collective
and a utopian field of representation, whereas for Hutcheon, postmodern representation more properly belongs with various cultural
forms of ideological critique. As Hutcheon observes of postmodern
narrative, "The premise of postmodern fiction is the same as that
articulated by Hayden White regarding history: 'every representation
of the past has specifiable ideological implications.' But the ideology
of postmodernism is paradoxical, for it depends upon and draws its
power from that which it contests. It is not truly radical; nor is it truly
oppositional" (*Poetics* 120). Still, as Hutcheon argues, to insist that
"everything is ideological" is not to invite paralysis; instead, it is to
recognize the inevitable place of all cultural production within a
specific social totality and to acknowledge that every critique is a
situated critique (*Poetics* 200).[3] As she remarks, "Rather than seeing
this paradoxical use and abuse as a sign of decadence or as a cause for
despair, it might be possible to postulate a less negative interpretation
that would allow for at least the *potential* for radical critical possibilities" (*Politics* 70). Like Jameson, Hutcheon is careful to distinguish between the symbolic act and a genuine moment of praxis.
Postmodernism, as she points out, has no effective theory of agency
(*Politics* 168), and, even though it may be said to share the unrelent-
ing hermeneutical suspicion of deconstruction, postmodern culture
often seems less convinced of the revolutionary power of self-
consciousness than the radical claims that were once made on behalf
of high French theory (*Poetics* 183). What Hutcheon describes as the
work of postmodern culture might then best be understood by what
Jameson describes in another context as a "negative hermeneutic," or
the palpable demonstration of the ideological character of all forms of
representation and the hegemonic structures at work in them, including those openly critical of the current form of social organization
(*Political* 286). But Hutcheon's postmodernism is also more canny
than this description might allow, for it equally represents a moment

in cultural history in which self-conscious comes to know its own limitations. Again, it is Jameson who offers our best gloss on what is at stake here. In *The Political Unconscious,* he observes that there is a parallel in Marxist thought to the "neo-Freudian nostalgia for some ultimate moment of *cure,*" some moment in which the unconscious would be made conscious and "somehow 'integrated' in an active lucidity about ourselves and the determinations of our desires and our behavior" (*Political* 283). In Marxist thought, this moment is envisioned as a time when an individual would become fully conscious of his or her determinations through class, and thereby would be able, as Jameson puts it, "to square the circle of ideological conditioning by sheer lucidity and the taking of thought" (*Political* 283). But this moment is an illusion never to be realized because, as Jameson points out, in Marxist thought only the collective can become conscious of itself: "the individual subject is always positioned within the social totality (and this is the sense of Althusser's insistence on the *permanence* of ideology)" (*Politics* 283). This is also the lesson of Hutcheon's postmodernism, for what her notion of complicitous critique finally represents is the dynamic and limits of a critique that necessarily transpires within the limits of a specific social totality. Whereas Jameson posits a "positive hermeneutic" that would wrest a utopian impulse in every representation, Hutcheon more clearly insists on the inescapably situated limits of any attempt to think the ideological character of the contemporary social formation and its determinate expressions.

It is this difference that carries over into Jameson's and Hutcheon's readings of the postmodern representation of history. For Jameson, history is to be uncovered as the absent cause in every symbolic act, or as he so famously puts it in *The Political Unconscious,* "History is what hurts, it is what refuses desire and sets inexorable limits to individual as well as collective praxis, which its 'ruses' turn into grisly and ironic reversals of their overt intention. But this History can be apprehended only through its effects, and never directly as some reified force" (*Political* 102). To trace this history or, more accurately, to bring into focus the political unconscious of the symbolic act is, for Jameson, to provide the only fully adequate account of what he terms "the essential *mystery* of the cultural past," which is to understand that all culture is a symbolic representation of and participation in "a single great collective story," the uninterrupted narrative of class struggle, that takes place finally within the larger horizon of the great utopian project of history, or "the collective struggle to wrest a realm of Freedom from a realm of Necessity" (*Political* 19). For Jameson this is the key to both the cultural past and the cultural present; however, in its attempt to represent history through pastiche or "the random cannibalization of all the styles of the past," postmodern culture is again largely symptomatic rather than critical (*Postmodernism* 18). Much postmodern historicism, as Jameson reads it through the examples of the nostalgia film and retro culture, simply treats the past as a subset of the codes of fashion so that any representation becomes at once fully appropriated to the depthlessness spectacle of the present. There are, however, moments when postmodern culture actually attempts to think historically, and these moments, according to Jameson, characteristically find expression in one of two forms of collective representation. The first is the conspiracy narrative, which Jameson has called the postmodern narrative form par excellence because it represents an attempt, albeit a degraded one in Jameson's terms, "to think the impossible totality of the contemporary world system" (*Postmodernism* 38).[4] The second, which for Jameson is really only a variation on the project of the conspiracy narrative, is best represented by various forms of postmodern fantastic histories, from historiographic metafiction to wild, historically encoded fabulations. Consistent with the spatialization of history itself that Jameson finds so characteristic of the frenetic and amnesiac contemporary world system, what these forms of historical projection represent for him is no more than "the symptom of social and historical impotence, of the blocking of possibilities that leaves little option but the imaginary" (*Postmodernism* 369). But even in its typically thwarted extravagance, the postmodern representation of history is still, for Jameson, really all about struggle with the determinate contradictions of late capital itself, and while it seems greatly impoverished in its confinement within the culture of fashion and the image, the postmodern version of history is in this respect nonetheless central. As Jameson himself observes, following Stuart Hall, "the fundamental level on which political struggle is waged is that of the legitimacy of concepts like *planning* or *the market*—at least *right now* and in our current situation. At future times, politics will take more activist forms from that, just as it has done in the past" (*Postmodernism* 264). To the extent that postmodern historical representations, despite their ideological overdeterminations, can be said to be engaged in this struggle or through their imaginary compensations in anticipations of it, they are, in Jameson's own terms, symbolic acts fully representative of a political unconscious at work even in the vast mystifications of the newly mutated and seemingly irrefutable world system.

On this point, Hutcheon would concur with Jameson's analysis. For Hutcheon, postmodernism is to be defined by its preoccupation at all levels with "the presence of the past," so that the dynamic of postmodern historiographic metafiction, the best example of this preoccupation, is simply paradigmatic of the logic that she ascribes to postmodern cultural production generally (*Poetics* 4). In Hutcheon's account, history and fiction are currently both deeply implicated in a contemporary crisis in representation, which, although often argued in epistemological terms, is really an ideological battle about authority and meanings, and it is this struggle that comes to the fore in postmodern historiographic metafiction (*Politics* 74). Historiographic metafiction teaches us, in Hutcheon's wry recasting of Jameson's oft-cited phrase, that "History is not 'what hurts' so much as 'what we say once hurt'—for we are both irremediably distanced by time and yet determined to grant meaning to that real pain of others (and ourselves)" (*Politics* 82). We can know history only through its traces, but, as Hutcheon points out at length, this does not mean that history is simply a discursive formation or that historical events are no more than semiotic constructs. What postmodern historiographic metafiction demonstrates instead, she argues, is an awareness of the ideological forces at work in the representation of events; it does not "in any way deny the existence of the past real, but it focuses attention of the act of imposing order on that past [. . .]" (*Politics* 67). In its relentless questioning of the authority of representation, postmodern historiographic metafiction thus takes a central place for Hutcheon among contemporary strategies of ideological critique because it is perhaps the most compelling instance, as she presents it, of a fully mimetic cultural practice that is at once the product and the adversary of the system that produces it. But the postmodern project for Hutcheon, in contrast to Jameson's claims about collective utopian anticipations, remains critical only. There is, as she once observed, no positive utopian content in Woody Allen's *Zelig*. Nonetheless, Hutcheon is insistent that this essentially negative project of ideological critique not be underestimated. As she maintains of postmodern culture more broadly, the installing and subverting strategies that we find in postmodern historiographic metafiction do not reflect an irresponsibility toward history, nor do they represent a cultural imaginary simply spinning its color wheels in a world system that seems for the time being, at least, to be beyond reproach. Rather, the postmodern representation of history is the scene of a symbolic struggle, part of a broader contesting of meanings and authority, which presses on us urgently and inescapably at the present moment, as we collectively try to come to terms with a vast new reconfiguration of the global mode of production. Here Hutcheon and Jameson shake hands most vigorously and here postmodern culture comes to know its true place—not as the inflated and belated logic of some thoroughly commodified avant garde, but as the last chance for ideological critique before the past is swept away utterly.

But even if we are tempted to understand postmodernism as a critical culture hauled out in some ritual fashion to attend the celebratory unveiling of a shiny new world system, we should finally keep in mind Jameson's suggestion that the postmodern might well represent "little more than a transitional period between two stages of capitalism" (*Postmodernism* 417). Although this view implies, as Jameson puts it, that "we ourselves are still in the trough, however, and no one can say how long we still stay there" (*Postmodernism* 417), it also suggests that transformation and upheaval, rather than the iron logic of the total system, are the order of the day and that therefore collective utopian representations might yet come to know the logic of their unfolding or, as Hutcheon would term it, ideological critique might yet prove the "deconstructive first step" in the struggles about to be played out. It is this symbolic struggle that postmodernism and history might be said to represent and to enact, not as opposition after the fact nor as imaginative compensation, but as an expression of newly reconfigured political unconscious.

Notes

1. For Hutcheon's observations on Jameson's reading of postmodern culture, see her *Politics* 2, 25. Jameson's remarks on Hutcheon's work can be found in his *Postmodernism* 22, 340.

2. The notion that all cultural expression is both ideological and utopian leads Jameson elsewhere to insist that his position "affirms the Utopian character of all collective experience (including those of fascism and the various racisms) but stresses the requirement of an existential choice of solidarity with a specific concrete group: on this nonformalist view, therefore, the social solidarity must precede the ethicopolitical choice and cannot be deduced from it" (*Seeds* 43–44). But even with the Sartrean qualification, this descrip

tion still doesn't really answer the problem of how to distinguish between utopian collectives and the pathological group formations that can be so easily enlisted to perpetrate any number of mass atrocities. Jameson himself notes that the solution to this problem is often, as in existentialism, a Kantian one.

3. Brian McHale's critique of the logic of Hutcheon's account of postmodernism in terms of an anxiety about master narratives overlooks the importance of ideology critique in Hutcheon's reading of postmodern culture, but it is precisely here that we might locate the real force of Hutcheon's postmodern poetics ("Postmodernism" 22–23).

4. For his extended reflections on postmodern conspiracy narratives, see Jameson's *The Geopolitical Aesthetic.*

Postmodernism, Fiction, History

3

A Mother (and a Son, and a Brother, and a Wife, et al.) in History: Stories Galore in *Libra* and the Warren Commission *Report*

Stacey Olster

If you research the life of Jesus, you see that Mary mother of Jesus disappears from the record once he is crucified and risen. Where is the mother who raised the boy?
>   —Marguerite Oswald in *Libra* (DeLillo 1988)

And we have stories galore, believe me—with documents and everything.
>   —Marguerite Oswald, Hearing Before the President's Commission
>   on the Assassination of President Kennedy (1964)

Composed by two juxtaposed story lines that converge in Dallas on 22 November 1963 at the novel's conclusion, and punctuated by the account of CIA analyst Nicholas Branch's attempts to write the secret history of the assassination of John F. Kennedy years later, Don DeLillo's *Libra* subverts all semblance of totalizing structure in the composition of history.[1] It also subverts all notions of complete originality, for the cumulative text that Branch is supposed to be writing only calls attention to the text of the Warren Commission *Report*—and its lone gunman master narrative—that DeLillo's work both inscribes and repudiates.

That recovering the past is a matter of examining the texts in which traces of that past reside is by now a critical commonplace. Just how much inscription involves critical interrogation, however, remains a matter of some debate. Locating in postmodern intertextuality "the history of aesthetic styles displacing 'real' history," Fredric Jameson laments "a new and original historical situation in which we are condemned to seek History by way of our own pop images and simulacra of that history, which itself remains forever out of reach" (*Postmodernism* 20, 25). As Linda Hutcheon points out, though, saying that the past is known to us through textual traces does not imply, as some forms of poststructuralism contend, that the past itself is only textual: "This ontological reduction is not the point of postmodernism: past events existed empirically, but in epistemological terms we can only know them today through texts. Past events are given *meaning,* not *existence,* by their representation in history" (*Politics* 81–82). And that *meaning,* according to Hayden White, derives from viewing narrative as a dialogic "process of decodation and recodation" in which assumptions canonized by time and convention are continually reviewed and reinterpreted with respect to the new contexts within which they are cast (*Tropics* 96). Thus, as Hutcheon asserts, "A literary work can actually no longer be considered original; if it were, it could have no meaning for its reader. It is only as part of prior discourses that any text derives meaning and significance" (*Poetics* 126).

Such a conception of dialogic interchange is particularly relevant when examining *Libra:* the Warren Commission *Report* that functions as prototext for the novel has as its own foundational texts the fifteen volumes of testimony and eleven volumes of 3,154 exhibits that comprise the Warren Commission *Hearings.* Within those twenty-six antecedent volumes, moreover, Lee Harvey Oswald, the central figure of the work DeLillo once considered calling "Texas School Book" (DeCurtis 55), only acquires presence through the reconstructions in other people's testimony and the autobiographical documents reprinted as part of the exhibits, texts within texts, one more representational step removed from those witnesses who got to testify in person. Represented in the first as an inveterate watcher of movies, television, and commercials, Oswald as American consumer defines his role in history with respect to the formulae proffered by visual media. Represented by the latter as artistic producer, Oswald grows up believing that posterity is to be found in print. Because so many others in the historical drama—Oswald's brother, wife, and, most of all, mother—shared similar authorial yearnings, DeLillo's Oswald in many ways acts as a traditional historical type. Once he shifts from producer to object of consumption in order to achieve stardom through visual media, however, the kind of figure he typifies belongs exclusively to the postmodern period. From the social misfit we all avoid, he becomes the celebrity manqué we all are.

At first, ironically, it would seem that the self that is Lee Oswald does not exhibit enough of a unified form to cast in any role, illustrating as he does the end of the bourgeois ego or monad, as critics have noted.[2] As devised by Win Everett in the alternating chapters that portray the CIA's plan to stage a "spectacular miss" on the life of the President (51), the lone gunman that Lee Oswald is to incarnate is a fictional construct, a "character" Win creates with the most banal items of consumer culture, "household things, small and cheap" (50, 145), Q-tips, razor blades, his daughter's school eraser, held together by nothing stronger than Elmer's Glue-All, for which Oswald later will supply a vehicle of transmission: "a name, a face, a bodily frame they might use to extend their fiction into the world" (50). Comprised by "the contents of a wallet" (50)—driver's license, credit card, address book, passport, Social Security card, in short, "pocket litter," "ordinary dog-eared paper" (28, 50)—Everett's Oswald exists purely as documentation, a function of letters on a requisite number of pages. Even the model intended to wear Everett's paper wardrobe realizes this when musing on one of his aliases: "Take the double-*e* from Lee. Hide the double-*l* in Hidell. Hidell means hide the *L*. Don't tell. White ideograms" (90).

But as the fact of Oswald's alias also suggests, Lee Oswald is in the process of constructing himself, with the same kind of cheap implements that Everett employs, in his case, a ninety-eight-cent stamping kit, and with respect to the same kinds of paper artifacts: draft cards, passports, vaccination certificates, committee membership cards. To the extent that this evidence of Oswald's efforts testifies to a reality of the man Win cannot deny, forcing him to acknowledge Oswald as a "fiction living prematurely in the world" (179), Everett the conspirator feels panic. To the extent that the sloppiness of Oswald's work contrasts with the precision of Win's own efforts, Everett the craftsman experiences the more jarring feeling of having been "displaced" (179), for the ease with which Oswald creates his multiple selves testifies to the ease with which identity defined by paper can be constituted. Oswald thus understands full well why he does not need the approval of the Fair Play for Cuba Committee to open a branch office: "He had his rubber stamping kit. All he had to do was stamp the committee's initials on a handbill or piece of literature. [. . .] This makes it true" (313). The corollary of such easy paper construction, of course, is an equally easy destruction. "She knew exactly what Ruby was thinking," conspirator Larry Parmenter's wife Beryl thinks when watching Oswald's death replayed on television. "He wanted to erase that little man" (446). To put it another way, in a world that can "make Stalin disappear" by blowing up his statue (207), how hard can it be to get rid of someone represented in far less durable matter? "How many letters do you have to lose before you disappear?" Parmenter's wife wonders after her husband is issued a new badge with a diminished number of letters around its edges (118).

Viewed from one perspective, this portrayal of literary characters as alphabetical characters might suggest a literature of aesthetic detachment, as typified, for example, by a novel like Gilbert Sorrentino's *Mulligan Stew* (1979), composed purely of documents and populated by characters whose names derive from earlier works of fiction (*The Great Gatsby, The Glass Key, Lolita, At Swim-Two-Birds*), none of which is ascribed with any more consistency from work to work than any letters grouped upon a page demand. As indicated by the one character whose name, Martin Halpin, derives from a mere footnote in James Joyce's *Finnegans Wake,* "In a way, I *was* the letters, no more" (25). And DeLillo's earlier fiction is replete with passages that anticipate *Libra*'s reduction of character to linguistic configuration.[3] In *The Names,* for instance, "character" is shown to derive from a Greek word for "brand" or "pointed stake." "This is probably because 'character' in English not only means someone in a story but a mark or symbol," James Axton observes, the similarity of which his son immediately grasps: "Like a letter of the alphabet" (10). Such a conception of characterization obviously corroborates Victor Burgin's denotation of "the 'post-modernist' subject" as an "'effect of language'" (49). As a character in both historical fiction and the actual past, however, Oswald occupies a dual position, as both "object of history," or "referent of the proper name," as well as "object of perception," or "empirical, once alive" person, to quote Hutcheon's paraphrasing of Jean-François Lyotard (*Poetics* 145). Thus, *The Names* also asserts that those letters of the alphabet that now may appear as formal codings proposed by humans to make sense of the world around them through pattern and repetition in fact originated in ancient times as "pictographs" intended to represent that world around them in all its chaotic imperfections (116). Those in the book who would forget those origins and use linguistic codings to assuage "the terror in our souls" with systematization, as the cultists do who match the initials of their victims to the place names in which they are killed, embark on a mission DeLillo views as both unnatural and unsuccessful—by the end of the book, the number of fractured cells indicates that "the cult was nearly dead" (290). As Andahl, the renegade cultist with whom Axton meets, admits, "Numbers behave, words do not" (208).

The contrast that Andahl draws is not altogether accurate, of course, for in DeLillo's work numbers often prove as unstable as letters—in *Libra,* Nicholas Branch may begin thinking of the date of the Kennedy assassination as 11/22, but using "strictly numerical terms" to understand the events he is investigating affords him little help in mastering the data the CIA curator keeps sending him (377). Yet just how much words misbehave in *Libra* is illustrated by the fact that neither Everett's nor Oswald's written script is directly responsible for the death of President Kennedy in DeLillo's novel. If plot in narrative, as White has argued, endows the individual events that comprise it with "a meaning by being identified as parts of an integrated whole" (*Content* 9), the components in the conspiracy to kill the President are drained of meaning as the plot that encloses them disintegrates into process. So many permutations does Everett's original plan undergo after it leaves the confines of his enclosed basement (and passes from Everett to Parmenter to T-Jay Mackey to shooters Raymo and Vásquez), and so many personae does Oswald sketch for himself (A. J. Hidell, O. H. Lee, H. O. Lee, D. F. Drictal, to name a few), that it finally is only a large degree of coincidence that brings together the two men's scenarios.[4]

Everett, whose distinctly postmodern collages of information only hint at "secret symmetries in a nondescript life" (78), in fact admits the workings of chance into his plan by recognizing the necessity of withholding causal connections from his audience: "You have to leave them with coincidence, lingering mystery. This is what makes it real" (147). Oswald, in contrast, accepts no such dictum. Portrayed as a would-be author, quoted as having listed "*To be a short story writer on contemporary American life*" as his vocational interest when applying to Albert Schweitzer College in Switzerland (134), Oswald structures the script of his life according to much more traditional narrative principles—as the "word-blindness" from which he suffers dictates that he must (166). Because the inability to "clearly see the picture that is called a word" also leaves him unable to "get a grip on the runaway world" (211), he suffers a form of disorientation that proves particularly debilitating, living as he does in a world DeLillo anachronistically defines in terms of "curved space," devoid of all "plane surfaces" (164), a "postmodern hyperspace," to recall Jameson's term, that "transcend[s] the capacities of the individual human body to locate itself, to organize its immediate surroundings perceptually, and cognitively to map its position in a mappable external world" (*Postmodernism* 44). Oswald therefore commits words to paper "to explain himself to posterity" (211), presuming that committing his story to paper will authenticate, organize, and—by extension—ascribe agency to his life: "It validated the experience," he thinks of his "Historic Diary," "as the writing of any history brings a persuasion and form to events" (211).

True, he takes his cues for action from events that are staged in visual media, as befits someone who also is presented as an inveterate watcher of movies and television. "I believe I shot myself," he says after shooting himself in the arm while in the navy. "Bushnell studied the perfect little scene. He thought Ozzie's remark sounded historical and charming, right out of a movie or TV play" (91). And he shapes those events with respect to plots that derive from visual media formulae, *I Led Three Lives, Red River, Suddenly, We Were Strangers* being just four of the artifacts DeLillo cites. But when Oswald acts as the performing self that DeLillo depicts him as being, conscious of the representation of his acts at the time of their perpetration, he does so as artistic producer, assuming that the road to posterity is to be found in print.[5] He attempts suicide in Russia and imagines what he will and will not say for publication (152). He writes a "Historic Diary" in which he sees himself relating his story for *Life* or *Look,* in whose waiting rooms he sees himself sitting with a leather manuscript folder—"What is it called, morocco? (206)—in his lap. He writes "The Kollective," and appends to it a forward and a sketch entitled "About the Author" (212–13).

Unlike the script devised for Oswald by the CIA Bay of Pigs veterans, which reflects a real political agenda—namely, making the attempt on Kennedy's life appear to come from Cubans in retaliation for plots against Castro, and thereby squelch any reconciliation between the United States and Cuba—none of the scripts that Oswald imagines for himself is motivated by any belief in organized politics one way or the other. This, as it turns out, is quite consistent with the apolitical roles in which the actual Oswald tended to cast himself in those writings he composed while in Russia. It also is consistent with the schizophrenic self that permeates those autobiographical pieces included as exhibits in the Warren Commission *Hearings,* for if subjectivity requires a teleological sense of history for its support, Oswald's refusal to commit himself to any ideological belief left him as decentered in his own (self-)representation as he would later be in DeLillo's. The "Historic Diary" portrays him more as licentious (or, depending on the woman, languishing) Lothario than lumpen proletariat: "Rosa about 23 blond attractive unmarried Excellant English, we attract each other at once" (XVI: 99); "A growing lonliness overtakes me in spite of my conquest of Ennatachina a girl from Riga" (XVI: 101); "I am introduced to a girl with a French hair-do and red-dress with white slipper [. . .] Her name is Marina. We like each other right away" (XVI: 102).[6] Two self-questionnaires alternate between the expatriate living the good life—"I had plenty of money, an apartment rent-free lots of girls etc. why should I leave all that?" (XVI: 436)—and the tourist frustrated at having to deal with bureaucratic red tape—"almost 1 year was spent in trying to leave the country. thats why I was there so long not out of desire!" (XVI 439)—in explaining the reasons for his two-and-a-half-year stay abroad. Even the "New Era," political in nature in that it proposes no choice to exist between Russian Communism and American capitalism as "[b]oth offer imperilistic injustice, tinted with two brands of slavery" (XVI: 429), concludes by advocating "stoical readiness" (XVI: 430) as the vaguely defining trait of the equally vague pose of "radical futurist" (XVI: 425) that Oswald adopts.

In DeLillo's novel, this lack of political motivation is, in part, a function of Oswald's being a Libran, "sitting on the scales, ready to be tilted either way" (319). And, as Jack Ruby will later recognize, it also is a function of Oswald's not having enough of a personality, his being "a complete nothing, a zero person in a T-shirt" (421), to maintain deeply held convictions of any sort. It is primarily the need to assuage the dreadful loneliness from which he suffers, almost a throwback to modernist alienation, that causes Oswald to affiliate himself with organized politics, an affiliation that notably begins with Oswald's early reading of Marxist books that "made him part of something" (41), since political movements offer him the prospects of ending his isolation by "merging" with history (101). The particular movements with which he opts to effect this merger vary with whatever movement seems to promise the greatest hope of community at any one time. Yet not only do all the movements he samples frustrate his desire for community, they expose how ineffectual his attempts to define identity in terms of printed materials are. Feeling himself "a zero in the system" (106) of American capitalism, Oswald emigrates to the Soviet Union, thinking he will be "a man in history now" (149), only to discover he is a "zero in the system" (151) there too. Not even considered for Soviet citizenship, Oswald is a figure of state bureacracy, assigned "Identity Document for Stateless Persons Number 311479" (167). Presuming that "[d]ocuments are supposed to provide substance for a claim or a wish" because a "man with papers is substantial," he takes his papers to the Cuban embassy in Mexico City, and once again "the system floats right through him [. . .] He is a zero in the system" (357). While Oswald's felt absence of self recalls that of another "true life novel" killer, Gary Gilmore, who described his personality as "[s]lightly *less than bland*" (Mailer,

Executioner's 674), the violence through which he ultimately tries to fill that void springs from an altogether different motive. The suggestiveness of his remarks prior to shooting two bullets into Max Jensen's head notwithstanding ("This one is for me," "This one is for Nicole" [227]), Gilmore's killing of two young men resonates as more than simple rage directed away from himself and his girlfriend. "I'll bet a nickel he knew those boys were Mormon before he killed them," a family friend wagers (456), so framing Gilmore's actions as reactions to a history of imprisoning American theocracies, the most recent of which is incarnated in Utah. Oswald's real motivating desire, by contrast, is not to merge with history, but to stand apart from history. As David Ferrie accurately points out, "I think you've had it backwards all this time. You wanted to enter history. [. . .] What you really want is out. Get out. Jump out. Find your place and your name on another level" (384). In Marxism, after all, the individual is subservient to economic/historical processes; likewise, the CIA system that Oswald later seeks to penetrate "perpetuate[s] itself" (22).

For someone like Oswald who feels himself a zero in system after system, the only "other level," to recall Ferrie's words, on which he will find a "place and name" of sufficient compensation is a marquee. Suspicions that the U.S. Marine Corps manual "had been written just for him" (42), that the navy brig "was invented just for him" (100), that the Office of Naval Intelligence's false defector program "was written with him in mind" (162), that the television networks showing movies about assassination plots "were running this thing just for him" (370), in short, that "[t]hey had plans for him, whoever they were" (329) reflect far less Oswald's paranoid fears than they do his yearnings for centrality. Not surprisingly, the easiest way for anyone to enlist Oswald's support is to tell him how important he is. "You're an interesting individual," says George de Mohrenschildt, when approaching Oswald about talking to the CIA. "I'm sure they would very much like to learn about your contacts in the Soviet Union" (238). "You're an interesting fellow" (247), repeats CIA agent Marion Collings, with whom de Mohrenschildt sets up a meeting, only to have his flattery topped by Agent Batemen of the FBI, who attempts to secure Oswald's services for his own organization: "You're an interesting fellow. Every agency from here to the Himalayas has something in the files on Oswald, Lee" (311).

Such insinuating remarks only reinforce the message continually sent by the one medium, television, that encourages the zero person to believe that he truly has exceptional value. Television frustrates the poverty-stricken Oswald in that the life of consumer fulfillment it promises is repudiated by the life in small rooms that he and his mother have been forced to live. Marguerite gets fired from a salesperson's job at Lerner's "because they said she did not use deodorant," DeLillo writes. "This was not true because she used a roll-on every day and if it didn't work the way it said on TV, why should she be singled out as a social misfit?" (38). Nevertheless, television's presence in DeLillo's work is treated ambivalently. On the one hand, television remains the only medium that dissolves those differences in social class that separate people. In *White Noise,* popular culture lecturer Murray Jay Siskind argues that television "welcomes us into the grid" (51). On the other hand, the grid into which it welcomes everyone also imprisons everyone, symptomatic as it is of the dominant mass media that no person can escape, as Oswald and his Russian wife experience one evening when they stop to look at a television set in a department store window and see "the most remarkable thing": "It was the world gone inside out. There they were gaping back at themselves from the TV screen. She was on television. Lee was on television, standing next to her, holding Junie in his arms. [. . .] She didn't know anything like this could ever happen" (227). Having thus discovered the "world inside the world" he has sought for years in the very medium he has watched since childhood (13), Oswald shifts from words to pictures, and concomitantly from artistic producer to object of consumption, as a means of ensuring his place in posterity. He poses in his backyard with rifle, revolver, and radical literature and imagines himself on the cover of *Time* magazine, entering "the frame of official memory" as "[t]he Castro partisan with his guns and subversive journals. [. . .] The man who shot the fascist general. A friend of the revolution" (279, 281), or, more simply, as DeLillo has stated in interviews, "almost the poor man's James Dean" (qtd. in DeCurtis 56).

In this desire to be a media celebrity, DeLillo's Oswald is not the disaffected American, as the role of lone gunman would suggest, or even the lunatic American, as his prolonged habitations in small rooms would imply, but every American.[7] Such typicality, in fact, was exactly the point that Oswald's mother stressed in those interviews with Jean Stafford in which she tried to vindicate her place as "a mother in history" (98): portraying her son's childhood as defined by "regular trend[s]" (19) like chess, stamp collecting, comic books, and Monopoly, she refused to see "anything abnormal about any part of his life" and defended the Oswald family as "an average American family," despite the fact that one "regular trend" in which her son engaged was prolonged truancy and the fact that the history of her own matrimonial misfortunes, as Stafford noted, "shoots off at a forty-five degree angle from the norm" (25–26). Yet even those Warren Commission counselors with less at stake personally contributed, however inadvertently, to the impression of Oswald's representative status through questions (often leading) posed to witnesses about how "typical" or "normal" Oswald was. "Your family was always a typical, loyal American family?" his brother Robert was asked (I: 375). "And Lee had what you would describe as a normal interest in firearms?" (I: 296), "And it is your opinion [. . .] that they [Lee and Marina] led a reasonably normal married life?" (I: 414), all of which elicited answers in the affirmative. "Would you say that the course of conduct of Lee Oswald was normal, having in mind the problems he was facing?" (VIII: 7), childhood acquaintance Edward Voebel was made to recall. "And you don't think Lee was an outstanding student [. . .] You think he was more or less average, is that right?" (VIII: 13); affirmative on all counts once again. The difference—and it is crucial—is that DeLillo ironizes the protagonist as the type from which the traditional historical novel generalized, since his portrayal of the outsider Oswald as typical suggests that all of us are marginalized figures now.

DeLillo reinforces that representative status of Oswald with respect to the myriad characters who parade through his book, taking their cues for action from the various films that have left on them the greatest impressions. Wayne Elko hires himself out as a mercenary in order to act as a masterless *Seven Samurai* warrior (145). Parmenter stages Caribbean CIA invasions with "[c]ryptic messages from spy movies of the forties" (127). And so similar to Oswald is the figure of Jack Ruby introduced in the second half of the novel that he functions as Oswald's mirror image. A "nothing person" by his own admission whose present domicile resembles "a lost-and-found" and whose past dwelling in hotel rooms recalls the isolated lives in small rooms that Oswald and his mother have led (342); a Jew in Texas who inhabits a decentered space "off to the side" (350) despite his club ownership making him "a known face, with ads in the paper, as only America can turn out" (344); and a fragmented self, as suggested by the Mafia emissary who shows how "not outfit" he is with a reference to Ruby's not being "*connected*" (256), Ruby the avenger must be "piece[d] together," as the epigraph to Part II of the novel indicates (215), much like the figure of the lone gunman and from the same kind of movie scenarios. "You killed my President, you rat," the actual Ruby recalled himself exclaiming, à la James Cagney, at the moment he pumped lead into Oswald's body (V: 200). It is no wonder, then, that DeLillo describes the scene of Oswald being shot in the Dallas police station as a stage lit with spotlights and TV cameras, with Ruby "seeing everything happen in advance" (437), for Ruby, no less than Oswald, is acting as performing self-seeking celebrity status at the point of a gun. "I am Jack Ruby," he said after the deed was done. "You all know me" (V: 200).

Which is not to say, of course, that Oswald's end brings to an end the impulse toward celebrity that he typifies. All that changes is the means by which notoriety is achieved as the celebrity performer is replaced by the celebrity author. "I will write books about the life of Lee Harvey Oswald," his mother states to the Warren Commission in the final pages of DeLillo's novel (449), so echoing the aspirations that permeate the remarks entered into the actual transcribed document. "It is my story that some day I hope to write," Marguerite Oswald announces to the Warren Commission (I: 222), having already whetted its appetite with the "stories galore" she plans to narrate prior to beginning the "speaking tours" (I: 163) for which she is—pun intended—"booked" (I: 236). Aware from the start that "[t]his is my life and my son's life going down in history" (I: 182), and having already obtained the committee's word that "you will let me have my life story from early childhood and Lee's life story from early childhood" (I: 196), she proceeds to relate the most minute details of her life since childhood—such as the fact that she wore a pink dress to her grammar school graduation and sang "Little Pink Roses" at the ceremony (I: 252)—and transform those relating to Oswald's to the degree that they affect her own. Hence, her dismissal of any objections her son has had to an earlier book she has planned to write of his defection: "It has nothing to do with you and Marina. It is my life, because of your defection" (I: 132). Not to be outdone, wife Marina writes the "story of my life from the time I met him [Oswald] in Minsk up to the very last days" (I: 3). Brother Robert begins a diary with the statement: "Dated December 6, 1963, for the history of the past 2 weeks as seen through my eyes, and heard with my ears, and felt with my body, I write for future reference for myself and for the future members of the family" (I: 341).

If DeLillo then characterizes the Warren Commission *Report* and its accompanying twenty-six volumes as "the megaton novel James Joyce would have written if he'd moved to Iowa City and lived to be a hundred," containing as they do "a poetry of lives muddied and dripping in language" (181), it is because the witnesses in them jump at the chance to testify and elevate to public prominence the otherwise trivial details of their ordinary lives. Presuming that "[e]ventually somebody would have to be coming after me," the man who shares Ruby's apartment comes before the committee of his own volition and shares insider information about the meals he cooks for Ruby: "After all, I was his roommate," George Senator states (XIV: 246). The woman with whom Marina lives from September 1963 until the assassination insists on introducing into the public record a letter she wrote her mother because, as Ruth Paine asserts, it shows how ordinary Oswald was from her privileged perspective as "one of the few people who can give it" (II: 509).

And with the passage of time enabling them to supplement the discovery of their prominence as witnesses with the discovery of their prominence as participants, the tragedy of the dead king itself is replaced by differently emplotted productions in which each has played a major role, much like Tom Stoppard's Rosencrantz and Guildenstern. Robert concludes that the assassination is the product of sibling rivalry, of Lee's "realization that I had been lucky enough to achieve what he wanted and would never achieve" (Oswald 240) because he notices that his brother's "most reckless acts" occurred on "dates which had particular significance in my life" (his birthday, the birthday of his son, and his wedding anniversary) (232). Marguerite, who earlier has reminded Lyndon Johnson in *Time* magazine "that he is only President of the United States by the grace of my son's action" (I: 242), starts publicizing the history of her own contributions to the history of the Oval Office. As she pointedly reminds Stafford, "After all, I *am* responsible for two Presidents" (62). Ably assisted by the disbursements that the media awards them, of course, these people have every reason to believe in the value of those details about their own lives that they proffer: movie and television rights to Texitalia Films and World-Wide, photo rights to *Life* and the *London Daily Mirror,* serial and article rights to *Stern* and *This Week* magazines, and world book rights to Meredith Press net Marina $132,350 in contract fees (I: 496), in addition to $7,500 plus expenses for each filmed appearance and $1,500 plus expenses for each personal appearance (II: 23). So thoroughly implicated are they that any complaints that arise concern less the fact of the media's scrutiny than they do the division of the media's spoils. "This whole thing seems to me like I have been kind of made a patsy," whines James Martin, who has quit managing motels to manage Marina's business affairs, after Marina cancels their ten-year contract and his 15 percent cut (I: 491). Similarly humiliated by the paltry $900 she has received from charitable donors in contrast to the $35,000 mailed to Marina, Marguerite instructs the Secret Service men opening envelopes, "I definitely want my share" (I: 176), and takes sterner measures with respect to the media: "if we are going to have the life story with Life magazine [. . .] I would like to get paid" (1: 145).

The more immediate problem they face, however, stems from the distance between ambition and composition, for while quite willing to pose as celebrity authors, few are willing to do what Oswald himself did and proceed with the task of actually putting words on paper. Nowhere is that disparity between whim and work more trenchantly displayed than in Marguerite Oswald's attempts to get Jean Stafford to write the numerous stories she has available to tell. That Mrs. Oswald is a veritable well of authorial potential she quickly establishes for Stafford at the start of their first interview: the book she intends to write, alternately entitled *One and One Make Two* or *This and That,* is to be the first of three or five projected books Marguerite could write "on what I know and what I have researched" (11–12). But it is not until Stafford returns to Mrs. Oswald's home for their final interview and discovers Marguerite calmly eating her lunch while listening to her one-hundred-eighty-word-a-minute voice blare out the "Mother's Day Epistle" (Stafford's term) she has earlier that day fed into a tape recorder—a wonderful image of communications loop—that the full extent of the older woman's authorial yearnings becomes completely clear (85). Certain by this time that she has enough material for a series of books, enough, at the very least, to run "for two or three years every month in a big national magazine, and after that as a sort of a soap opera on radio or even on TV" (101), Marguerite makes her a cappella pitch after the tape runs out: "Couldn't you take the summer off and come on down and rent the other side of the house so we could write it all up?" (102). As her next remarks indicate, though, the "we" she envisions is no authorial sorority, for underlying the added inducements of "a discount house where you could get a hot plate cheap" and a back porch on which the two can work in housecoats is a division of labor that hardly qualifies as joint composition: "I mean, I would give of my time and voice and let you see the work I've done and we could split the proceeds" (102).

DeLillo attributes Marguerite's rhetorical inability to move from orality to literacy to a narrative fixation with chronology and causation: "I cannot enumerate cold," she tells the Warren Commission in his novel. "I have to tell a story" (455). Yet as the picture of Nicholas Branch struggling to formulate any finished prose illustrates, it is virtually impossible to tell a story about the assassination of John F. Kennedy in the traditionally realist manner that Marguerite requires.

All one *can* do, in fact, is enumerate or list the pieces of data that surround the event, as Branch does with the data the curator continues to send him, and *not* draw any connections among them, however provocatively they call out for assemblage, as Branch observes when listing the various deaths of those connected, however loosely, to the events of 22 November, and as DeLillo substantiates by the scattered presentation of those details throughout his text (58, 378–79, 442–43). If, as White contends, the demand for closure is a demand for moral meaning (*Content* 21), the relinquishing of the former implies the futility of uncovering the latter.

In the pre-Oprah 1960s, moreover, no appropriate visual forum exists for the assassination's authorial wannabes to hawk the instant literary wares they project, and so, like most performances by actors and actresses in supporting roles, they get consigned to virtual oblivion.[8] None is awarded by the Academy that middle name, which—if not Oscar literally—serves to confer on its recipient equivalent celebrity status. "Once you did something notorious, they tagged you with an extra name, a middle name that was ordinarily never used," DeLillo's Oswald realizes in Russia when confronted with the imprisoned Francis Gary Powers. "You were officially marked, a chapter in the imagination of the state" (198). Oswald himself is so catapulted in *Libra* after the assassination of the President who, having run for office as a box office star, according to Norman Mailer, had been reconstituted as a media simulacrum of three names as early as 1960 ("Superman" 38). "After the crime comes the reconstruction," Oswald thinks in prison. "People will come to see him, the lawyers first, then psychologists, historians, biographers" (434–35). Ruby, who never gains that third name, continues to feel himself "a nothing person" (443), without ever understanding why. "All he knows for sure is that there is a missing element here, a word that they have canceled completely" (445). That word is "Leon," Ruby's middle name.

As Frank Lentricchia has noted, "The question, who or what is responsible for the production of *Lee Harvey Oswald* (or *John Fitzgerald Kennedy*), is inseparable from the question of where DeLillo imagines power to lie in contemporary America" ("*Libra*" 203–204). In the words of Marguerite Oswald's personification, "TV gave directions and down he went" (452). Therefore, the celebrity crossover that grants Oswald the singular self for which he strives, that "single clear subject now, called Lee Harvey Oswald" (435), gives him a self that he is incapable of recognizing. "It sounded extremely strange," he thinks when hearing his official name on radios and televisions. "He didn't recognize himself in the full intonation of the name. [. . .] It sounded odd and dumb and made up. They were talking about somebody else" (416). Whereas he previously has imagined his sense of destiny in terms of "a network of connections" in which "the private world" of miniature rooms in which he has been locked would expand "out to three dimensions" (277), being encased in the black box that is network TV ends up reducing him to two dimensions, thereby imprisoning him in what, in effect, serves as the smallest of the small rooms in which he has been trapped throughout his life. Only now he is both literally and figuratively flattened and devoid of all depth, a postmodern subject defined by what Jameson views as "the supreme formal feature" of all postmodern art (9). "It was a process that drained life from the men in the picture, sealed them in the frame," Beryl Parmenter realizes when watching the footage of Oswald's death replayed on television (447). As such, Oswald ends up a "victim of a total frame" (418) in more than the one way he means when the police first apprehend him, for the frame that victimizes him comes as much from a photograph as it does from the CIA, just as the shot that kills him comes as much from a camera as it does from Jack Ruby's gun, as DeLillo's description of the replayed footage of his death indicates: "He is commenting on the documentary footage even as it is being shot. Then he himself is shot, and shot, and shot, and the look becomes another kind of knowledge" (447).[9]

Reviewing the Kennedy assassination in an essay written for *Rolling Stone* two decades after it occurred, DeLillo saw Oswald as presaging all those media-saturated young men who took guns into their hands and committed acts of political violence for reasons other than politics: Arthur Bremer, John Hinckley, James Earl Ray ("American Blood" 24, 27).[10] Two years later, he could portray the type as cultural cliché. Tommy Roy Foster, the imprisoned killer with whom Jack Gladney's son plays chess in *White Noise,* cares for his weapons obsessively, has an arsenal stashed in a "shabby little room off a six-story concrete car park," makes tapes of his voice asking forgiveness of loved ones, hears voices on TV telling him "to go down in history," and goes out to kill six people in Iron City from a rooftop sniper's position (44). Tommy Roy Foster forgets, unfortunately, that Iron City is the one place in the country that has no media. "He now knows he won't go down in history," Gladney's son says ruefully. And Gladney, ever the empathic parent, responds with the most appropriate truism possible under the circumstances: "Neither will I" (45).

Notes

1. Critical approaches to DeLillo's portrayal of history have employed a variety of theoretical paradigms in their presentations: John Johnston invokes Gilles Deleuze's concepts of "intensive system" and "internal resonance" ("Superlinear"); Joseph Kronick investigates the "grammaticality" of historical events with respect to Paul de Man's theories of reading; and Christopher Mott joins Hayden White's narratological duplicity to Michel Foucault's epistemological skepticism.

2. See, for instance, O'Donnell 6–11 and Thomas 111–19.

3. DeLillo's remarks in interviews contribute to the temptation to read his novels as advocacies of modernist aesthetic detachment, as illustrated by his description of writing as "trying to make interesting, clear, beautiful language" and his depiction of *Ratner's Star* in particular as "naked structure" (qtd. in LeClair 82, 86). Complicating the issue are other remarks of DeLillo that repudiate a pose of complete aesthetic disengagement: "I've always had a grounding in the real world, whatever esoteric flights I might indulge in from time to time" (qtd. in DeCurtis 62). For a representative sampling of the variety of critical positions taken with respect to this issue of aesthetic detachment, see Kucich 334–41; Johnston, "Generic" 262–63; and Molesworth 147–51.

4. For a discussion of the way in which coincidence is the means by which chance and necessity are reconciled in *Libra,* see Kronick 120, 116–17, 125–26. For a discussion of the contingent as anchoring the conspiratorial, and the way that astrology resolves the antimony between the two, see Willman, "Traversing" and "Art" 630–37.

5. Almost every critic of *Libra* has recognized this element of Oswald's performing in considering DeLillo's fictional protagonist. See, for instance, Cain 279 and Civello 48–52. To the extent that the novel's Oswald initially seeks his place in history through the medium of print, however, he complicates these earlier critical readings of his intentions.

6. Parenthetical citations to volumes designated by Roman numerals refer to the twenty-six volumes of testimony and exhibits that comprise the *Hearings before the President's Commission on the Assassination of President Kennedy.* Grammatical infelicities and misspellings of words duplicate those in the original documents.

7. For earlier critical commentary on this point, see, for instance, Goodheart 129 and Lentricchia, "*Libra*" 205.

8. DeLillo's two-act play *Valparaiso* (1999), provides a remedy for this pre-Oprah omission in its portrayal of the cultural role of the television talk show. See Duvall 559–61.

9. For a discussion of the televised killing of Oswald as forging a national collectivity around the collapse of public and private spaces, see Green 585–93.

10. DeLillo's portrait of Oswald also presages his portrait of the fictional Texas Highway Killer in *Underworld.* For a discussion of the Highway Killer's frustrated attempts to control his own image, see Walker 460–61.

4

Donald Barthelme and the President of the United States

Michael Zeitlin

Late Fascism

In 1950 Theodor Adorno et al. published *The Authoritarian Personality,* an empirical study of "the rise of an 'anthropological' species we call 'the authoritarian type of man'" (ix). This new man embodied a historically specific network of contradictions. Able to function efficiently within a technologically advanced and highly industrialized society, he was also susceptible to profoundly "irrational or antirational beliefs" (ix). He considered himself enlightened and yet behaved superstitiously. He was proud to be a unique individual, yet lived "in constant fear of not being like all the others" (ix). Most significantly, he celebrated the ideology of independence yet was "inclined to submit blindly to power and authority" (ix). For Adorno and his Frankfurt School colleagues—Jewish refugees from Hitler's Europe—this new, postwar version of "authoritarian man" bore too many uncomfortable similarities with the old-style fascist with whom they had become familiar in Nazi Germany.

Indeed, the fear of the reemergence of fascism, and hence the need for a certain vigilance against that possibility, did not strike Max Horkheimer as absurd in 1950: "Mankind has paid too dearly for its naive faith in the automatic effect of the mere passage of time; incantations have really never dispelled storms, disaster, pestilence, disease or other evils; nor does he who torments another cease his torture out of sheer boredom with his victim" (v). And though Jews have perhaps learned to breathe a bit easier in the past fifty years, war and genocide in Yugoslavia, Cambodia, Rwanda, and elsewhere have shown that death camps, charismatic leaders, and mass psychology are not yet antiquated, historical, or obsolete; nor is the world experiencing a shortage of those to play the part of the Jews in the new cleansing campaigns of the last two decades. Contrary to the claims of a good many people, it does not always feel as if the fight against fascism and mass psychology is now a "historically superseded protest" (Huyssen, *After* x), even though the resistance to fascistic tendencies "needs rethinking precisely in the context of late capitalism" (Hutcheon, *Politics* 28).

For Herbert Marcuse, in his psychoanalytic understanding of the problem, the subversion of the autonomy of the individual subject or ego prepares "the ground for the formation of *masses.* The mediation between the self and the other gives way to immediate identification" (235) with outside forces and figures. In the postmodern version of this scene, the contours of the would-be concrete individual subject or ego have become even more ambiguous, uncertain, blurry. That is, with the famous dying away of the old modernist or bourgeois individual, a traditional unit of cultural analysis fades into something wider and more amorphous: the whole contemporary sign-sprawl as endlessly produced, reduplicated, and overdetermined by a global web of corporations, ad agencies, Hollywood production studios, radio and television networks, Internet providers, and publishing companies. The waxing of the public image-world thus coincides with the waning of the traditionally valorized private subject who might be thought capable of resisting its seductions. And as my citations of Adorno, Horkheimer, and Marcuse are meant to suggest, this postmodern loss of critical distance with respect to "the totality" should not be understood as being wholly unprecedented.

The persistent power of the psychoanalytic tradition lies in its effort to zero in on the individual subject as that psychosomatic place where forces converge, where the action of absorption by or opposition to "the system" or "the machine" or "the totality" occurs. The "interface" still has an unmistakable psychological dimension, here to be understood as the problem of the subject's "susceptibility" (Adorno et al. 1 and passim) or resistance to mass culture's "total flow" (Jameson, *Postmodernism* 70), which spreads outward only to draw the mass gaze inward toward certain significant consumer images and objects, including the radiant faces of central figures of eros and authority (for example, Princess Diana, President Clinton, Kenneth Starr, Monica Lewinsky).[1]

In opposition to such images projecting from myriad flat, luminous surfaces, the gazing subject who has a psychology still has to remain very much in focus precisely because he is supposedly fading into a nostalgically remembered past. As Marcuse put it in an important essay, "The evolution of contemporary society has replaced the Freudian model by a social atom whose mental structure no longer exhibits the qualities attributed by Freud to the psychoanalytic object" (233). If the Freudian subject has become "obsolete" in the postwar world of monopoly capitalism and its interlocking technical, cultural, and political mechanisms of social control (Marcuse 235), this is a situation to be lamented and mourned, though in a politically urgent way. Insofar as the Freudian tradition insists on the primary authority of the individual biological and creative individual,

> [t]hat which is obsolete is not, by this token, false. If the advancing industrial society and its politics have invalidated the Freudian model of the individual and his relation to society, if they have undermined the power of the ego to dissociate itself from others, to become and remain a self, then the Freudian concepts invoke not only a past left behind but also a future to be recaptured. [. . .] (Marcuse 246)

It may be interesting to note that one encounters the same theme in a significant liberal-humanist document of the early Cold War period, Lionel Trilling's *Freud and the Crisis of Our Culture*.[2] Here Trilling, in tones classically composed, describes a situation which brings out the Jeremiah, as we shall see, in Jean Baudrillard:

> One does not need to have a very profound quarrel with American culture to feel uneasy because our defenses against it, our modes of escape from it, are becoming less and less adequate. One may even have a very lively admiration for American culture, as I do, and yet feel that this defenselessness of the self against its culture is cause for alarm. [. . .] We must, I think, recognize how open and available to the general culture the individual has become, how little protected he is by countervailing cultural forces, how unified and demanding our free culture has become. (49–50; 53–54)

In this description of the individual's "openness" to his surrounding general culture, one may recognize what Linda Hutcheon has termed "the paradox of postmodern complicitous critique" (*Politics* 9) and its attendant "danger (for the critic) of the illusion of critical distance" (15). The problem now as it was in earlier periods of the past century concerns the impoverishment of the resistant ego from which something like genuine privacy, creative resistance, and praxis (whether personal or collective) might be said to flow:

> The shrinking of the ego, its reduced resistance to others appears in the ways in which the ego holds itself constantly open to the messages imposed from outside. The antenna on every

house, the transistor on every beach, the jukebox in every bar or restaurant are as many cries of desperation—not to be left alone, by himself, not to be separated from the Big Ones, not to be condemned to the emptiness or the hatred or the dreams of oneself. (Marcuse 235)

What Marcuse called this "immediate, external socialization of the ego, and the control and management of free time—the massification of privacy" (238) has come to signal, for Baudrillard, not merely "the weakening of the 'critical' mental faculties: consciousness and conscience" (Marcuse 237) but their complete annihilation in the technological nightmare of schizophrenia, that everyday postmodern pathology which has displaced all the old, "bourgeois" pathologies.[3] Postmodern schizophrenia signals the final dissolution of the border between the private and the public spheres. The individual subject exists without boundaries, limits, or insulation. He is radically exposed in a historically unprecedented way:

> No more hysteria, no more projective paranoia, properly speaking, but his state of terror proper to the schizophrenic: too great a proximity of everything, the absolute proximity, the total instantaneity of things, the feeling of no defense, no retreat. It is the end of interiority and intimacy, the overexposure and transparence of the world which traverses him without obstacle. He can no longer produce the limits of his own being. [. . .] He is now only a pure screen, a switching center for all the networks of influence. (Baudrillard, "Ecstasy" 132–33)

As the postmodern communicational apparatus, in its very efficiency, extends and reduplicates itself by means of the television set and the computer screen, it comes to "penetrate the older autonomous sphere of culture and even the Unconscious itself" (Jameson, *Postmodernism* 122). Yet if even this last domain of interiority has now been colonized by the forces of an imperializing exteriority (though postmodernism—by definition as it were—deconstructs this binary), how are we to imagine the place from which postmodern culture may be judged, rejected, or transformed? "For it seems plausible that in a situation of total flow, the contents of the screen streaming before us all day long without interruption (or where the interruptions—called *commercials*—are less intermissions than they are fleeting opportunities to visit the bathroom or throw a sandwich together), what used to be called 'critical distance' seems to have become obsolete" (Jameson, *Postmodernism* 70).

Yet in the actual everyday scene of this proximity or fusion of human individual and machine, one suspects that the evacuation of "the interior" is perhaps not so absolute. Inherent in the watcher's entanglement with what Don DeLillo, in his novel *Players,* has termed "the mesh effect of television" (17),[4] there remains enough evidence of the survival of "older" forms of subjectivity—fantasy, dependence, addiction, mourning, depression—which themselves signal a kind of latent protest, if not an involuntary romantic survival, of that older, modernist self-as-alienated. That is, the older Freudian metapsychology (of id, ego, superego, unconscious, dreams, phantasy, oedipus, group psychology, sexuality, biology, perversion,) and its human subject/object are still quite meaningful, if only in a transitional or even nostalgic sense. In the words of Baudrillard, "In a certain way all this still exists, and yet in other respects it is all disappearing" ("Ecstasy" 126).

In what follows, I shall focus on this historically transitional problem of the relation between the individual and the television image, and for this purpose I shall turn to a much-neglected dark gem of Donald Barthelme, his short story entitled "The President," which was originally published in the September 5, 1964, issue of *The New Yorker.* A psychoanalytic reading of this narrative will allow me to focus the metapsychological dimension of a real-enough contemporary problem—the mysterious power of authority, its roots in "the irrational," the seductiveness of the image. Given the current aura of "the president" as a television image, I shall contemplate the extent to which, in our current situation, there are certain residual survivals of an older, but by no means antiquated or superseded, problematic: the authority of the father-image/imago. In its role as fetish, as the mark and the veil of that something wider that cannot (yet) be adequately represented, the father-image/imago also signifies the decentered yet interlocking and overlapping networks of late capitalism, or the "whole new economic world system" itself (Jameson, *Postmodernism* 6).

Donald Barthelme's "The President"

Barthelme's story is post-JFK in its understanding of the intensity and the depth of the internalization of the image of the President of the

United States as an object of mass fascination, love, guilt, mourning, and unconscious fantasy. The President may be nothing but an image inseparable from the technology that projects it, but this does not prevent the image from assuming a powerful, personal, intimate proximity, indeed from taking up residence in the agitated souls of those whose lives, as a consequence, unfold in perpetual relation to it. If, as Guy Debord claims, "'the image has become the final form of commodity reification'" (qtd. in Jameson, *Postmodernism* 18), the commodity is there not so much to be consumed as to be *dreamed over:* "To consume in America is not to buy; it is to dream" (Delillo, *Americana* 270). Indeed, Barthelme's essential narrative mode is oneiric. It stages a series of fascination scenes signifying the agency of that domain of psychic life over which the subject has no control. Relevant here is a set of Lacanian themes: the subject as trapped "in a fictional direction" (Lacan 2) by his narcissism, by his mirror images, by the "impossible" objects of his desire, by the impossible-to-fulfill demand for recognition by the impossible object, and so on. Equally, one encounters in Barthelme's narrative the operation of a more properly Freudian set of motifs: The President, as a focus of psychic and affective ambivalence, is an image to be "worked over" in the turbulent currents of idealization and disrespect that spring from the dark Sophoclean heart of the great Freudian parricidal tradition.

That is, the key question here has an important metapsychological dimension: it's not so much what the president is, or even whether he *is* ("real") or not, or whether there is an "original" President to cash the check of the simulacrum.[5] Rather, the question is, Where does the President exist, and how do all these overlapping fields in which he appears traverse and entangle the human subject?

In Barthelme the encounter with the President is staged as a personal one; "individualistic residues, sentimentality" (Adorno, "Culture" 131), and pathos cling to it:

> "When he rides in his black limousine with the plastic top I see a little boy who has blown an enormous soap bubble which has trapped him. The look on his face—" [. . .] I speculated about the President's mother. Little is known about her [. . .] She must be pleased that her son is what he is—loved and looked up to, a mode of hope for millions. [. . .] I could tell you about his mother's summer journey, in 1919, to western Tibet—about the dandymen and the red bear, and how she told off the Pathan headman, instructing him furiously to rub up his English or get

out of her service—but what order of knowledge is this? [. . .]
The new President must have certain intuitions. I am convinced
that he has these intuitions (although I am certain of very little
else about him; I have reservations, I am not sure). [. . .] The
President stepped through the roaring curtain. We applauded
until our arms hurt. (151–54)

The President is more than an object of curiosity; he's an enigma to be
pored over, a site of overdetermined complexity and contradiction, a
sphinx who refuses to speak, an object of uncanny repulsion and
fascination. His strange magnetic/repellant power suggests not so
much a static image as the dynamism of an unconscious scene. In the
psychoanalytic understanding of "the absurd," the turbulent or
strange "work" of narrative imagination (whether dream or artistic
production) signals the presence of a "particularly embittered and
passionate polemic" (Freud, *Interpretation* 436). The weird, parodic,
and comic elements of Barthelme's treatment (with its chronological
archaisms and juxtaposed absurdities) help weave an affective texture of ambivalence, muted protest, and deep unconscious mistrust:

> I am, as I say, not entirely sympathetic. Certain things
> about the new President are not clear. I can't make out what he is
> thinking. When he has finished speaking I can never remember
> what he has said. There remains only an impression of strange-
> ness, darkness. . . . On television, his face clouds when his
> name is mentioned. It is as if hearing his name frightens him.
> Then he stares directly into the camera (an actor's preempting
> gaze) and begins to speak. One hears only cadences. Newspaper
> accounts of his speeches always say only that he "touched on a
> number of matters in the realm of. . ." (Barthelme 152)

If the mystery, obscurity, and opacity of the image represent a demand on interpretation, interpretation implies, in turn, some sort of
"depth" encounter, not so much with the repressed contents of the
unconscious as with the internalized institution of the censorship.
As Freud notes in *The Interpretation of Dreams,* the agency of the
censorship is observed in the effects of distortion, condensation, and
displacement produced in the dialectical struggle between the Primary and the Secondary processes. By definition, as it were, and
despite its best efforts, the text cannot give explicit, conscious expression to that which is split off from itself, that is, the repressed. All

it can do, rather, is insist, compulsively, that there is something "strange" about the president, even as the effects of this "strangeness complex" are to be "acted out" in scenes of mass fainting:

> I am not altogether sympathetic to the new President. He is, certainly, a strange fellow (only forty-eight inches high at the shoulder) [. . .] "He is a *strange fellow,* all right. He has some magic charisma which makes people—" She stopped and began again. "When the band begins to launch into his campaign song, 'Struttin' with Some Barbecue,' I just . . . I can't . . ."
>
> The darkness, strangeness, and complexity of the new President have touched everyone. There has been a great deal of fainting lately. (Barthelme 150)

Simulacrum, mirage, fetish, father-imago, "strange fellow," heart-throb: the collective speculation and dreaming over this image are indices of the "work" of mass interpellation, the forming of the Imaginary of the masses through participation in a grand public spectacle. What Barthelme is describing in this sense is the mass "who have put one and the same object in the place of their ego ideal" (Freud, *Group* 116) and who, in fixing the image as their central point of libidinal extension and attachment, are able to find its appropriate level of abasement.

Yet who, after all, is this President if not a functionary, in Marcuse's words, of the "higher authority which is no longer embod-ied in a person: the authority of the prevailing productive apparatus which, once set in motion and moving efficiently in the set direction, engulfs the leaders and the led—without however, eliminating the radical differences between them, that is, between the masters and the servants" (241). Barthelme hints in the direction of this invisible, "off-camera" puppet master: we cannot help but project an anthropo-morphic image even as we know enough now to grasp its obsoles-cence as a formulation for that "inconceivable financial system," that "combination of abstract wealth and real power in which all of us also believe, without many of us ever really knowing what that might be or look like" (Jameson, *Postmodernism* 128):[6] "When he has fin-ished speaking he appears nervous and unhappy. The camera credits fade in over an image of the President standing stiffly, with his arms rigid at his sides, looking to the right and to the left, as if awaiting instructions" (Barthelme 152).[7]

If we see Barthelme's President as a symbol of the mystification of the realities of postmodern power and the repressed truth of social relations, the narrative's oneiric inability to fix the ontological plane on which the president exists becomes more properly intelligible. The president is the imaginary totem which is proof of the Real, that is, an unconscious and inaccessible target, that "[t]otality [which] is not available for representation, any more than it is accessible in the form of some ultimate truth (or moment of Absolute Spirit)" (Jameson, *Postmodernism* 55): Yet "even the most complex, the most objective, impersonal social and political control must be 'embodied' in a *person*—'embodied' not in the sense of a mere analogy or symbol but in a very literal sense: instinctual ties must bind the master to the slave, the chief to the subordinate, the leader to the led, the sovereign to the people" (Marcuse 240).

The anthropomorphic image is there to give point and focus to our struggles. Will Special Prosecutor Kenneth Starr succeed in "getting" President Clinton? Did President Clinton actually do *that* with, or allow *that* to be done by, Monica Lewinsky? (Yes! But he's still up in the polls.) Does this president know that I care about him, personally, deeply? Will he be able to salvage his presidency with a heroic bombing campaign in Iraq or against the world's most dangerous terrorist, Osama bin Laden? These were pressing questions in 1998– 1999. Such questions always constitute the scene that deludes me and the mass to which I belong with "false conflicts which [we] are to exchange for [our] own" (Adorno, "Culture" 133).

The President is a signifier in this sense of the endurance of something we might recognize as a form of modernist "depth integration" (Jameson, "*Ulysses*" 175): "one begins to wonder whether there is not some deeper correlation between these Western 'myth' figures and their technical function as a means of holding together and unifying large quantities of disparate raw material" (Jameson, *Ideologies* 7).[8] The President suggests in this sense a general communal failure to "test" reality successfully and thus to transcend the imaginary realm in which the mass remains immured by virtue of its unconscious investment: with his blurred face and shadowy figure, he is a piece of distorted memory, a walking piece of *das unheimliche* itself. He is an incubus, interposing himself between and interfering with personal relations, even as the space he postulates magnetizes the lines of force that hold the group together. Like Jessie Weston's Fisher King, the primal father of Freud's *Totem and Taboo,* or the Name-of-the-Father of Lacanian psychoanalysis—the signifier of the group's erotic relation with an essentially absent yet strangely potent figure of proscription and authority—the President (like Barthelme's Dead Fa-

ther) diffuses himself throughout the culture's complex of social relations, and presides over the field of erotic competition:

> "The President!" I said to Sylvia in the Italian restaurant. She
> raised her glass of warm red wine. "Do you think he liked me?
> My singing?" "He looked pleased," I said. "He was smiling." "A
> brilliant whirlwind campaign, I thought," Sylvia stated. "Win-
> ning was brilliant," I said. "He is the first President we've had
> from City College," Sylvia said. A waiter fainted behind us.
> Other waiters carried the waiter who had fainted out into the
> kitchen. (Barthelme 151)

That is, the President is also uncanny in the more properly Freudian
sense of the father-imago, a disturber of the relations of love. Oedipus
is the not-so-hidden mode of the President's relation to the mass, the
larger imaginary scene which overlays the people—or rather which
lays them out:[9] "At Town Hall, I sat reading the program notes to 'The
Gypsy Baron.' Outside the building, eight mounted policemen collapsed en bloc. The well-trained horses planted their feet delicately
among the bodies. [. . .] The President was smiling in his box. At the
finale, the entire cast slipped into the orchestra pit in a great, swooning mass" (154–55). The theme of fainting encodes the theme of
masochism and submission, of what Freud has called "the craving for
authority" and the "unruly piece of homosexual feeling [that lies] at
the root of the matter."[10] As he writes in his essay, "The Future
Prospects of Psycho-Analytic Therapy":

> I need not say much to you about the importance of authority.
> Only very few civilized people are capable of existing without
> reliance on others or are even capable of coming to an indepen-
> dent opinion. You cannot exaggerate the intensity of people's
> inner lack of resolution and craving for authority. The extraordi-
> nary increase in neuroses since the power of religions has
> waned may give you a measure of it. The impoverishment of the
> ego due to the large expenditure of energy on repression de-
> manded of every individual by civilization may be one of the
> principal causes of this state of things. (146)

For Barthelme writing in 1964, on the eve of America's full-scale
escalation of the war in Vietnam, some version of an American
fascism-in-readiness is the political unconscious of his narrative, in
whose final scene the capitulation of "the sphere of the ego" and "the

agency of critical resistance" is dialectically linked to a kind of "orgiastic transaction" (Sontag 92) between the magnetic leader and his joyful followers: "The President stepped through the roaring curtain. We applauded until our arms hurt. We shouted until the ushers set off flares enforcing silence. The orchestra tuned itself. Sylvia sang the second lead. The President was smiling in his box. At the finale, the entire cast slipped into the orchestra pit in a great, swooning mass. We cheered until the ushers tore up our tickets" (155).

In a classic essay, "Fascinating Fascism," Susan Sontag gives us the materials for a compelling gloss on this scene, in which we may well be willing to find what she calls "the transformed thematics of latter-day fascism" (88). Indeed, we may be tempted to link the scene point for point with Leni Riefenstahl's *Triumph of the Will*. All the structural elements of a "fascist dramaturgy" are here: the massing of groups of people "under the gaze of the benign Super-Spectator" (Sontag 87); "the dissolution of alienation in ecstatic feelings of community; the repudiation of the intellect; the family of man (under the parenthood of leaders)" (Sontag 96); "The expression of the crowds in *Triumph of the Will* is one of ecstasy; the leader makes the crowd come" (Sontag 102).

If Barthelme's little narrative feels the sway of this longing and implicates us all, it also makes the entire scene available for analysis and reflection. It also suggests that literary production and representation remain an important basis from which to launch a critique of our surrounding culture. As Trilling put it in 1955, "[t]he function of literature, through all its mutations, has been to make us aware of the particularity of selves, and the high authority of the self in its quarrel with its society and its culture. Literature is in that sense subversive" (33). Insofar as Barthelme's story conveys a strong sense of the latent dignity and resistant authenticity of the individual subject, it contributes in its way to the restoration of private autonomy and rationality, from which critical and creative resistance might spring.

Notes

1. The September 1998 Internet release of Kenneth Starr's report to Congress on the Clinton/Lewinsky affair should be enough to suggest the staggering dimensions of this mass interest in the private life of the president of the United States. Such enormously popular and profitable films as *The American President, Independence Day,* and *Air Force One* would also appear to feed off the same complex of

fantasies: the president as a human character with whom it is possible to have an intimate personal or sexual or imaginary relation; American technological, military, moral, and ideological superiority (the threats to Saddam, the cruise missile attack on Osama bin Laden's suspected hideouts, the bombing of the pharmaceutical factory in Sudan); and "the vertigo before power" (Sontag 87).

2. This publication is based on Trilling's Freud Anniversary Lecture of 1955, the fifth of the annual lectures established by the New York Psychoanalytic Institute and Society to mark the day of Freud's birth (6 May 1856).

3. "The end of the bourgeois ego, or monad, no doubt brings with it the end of the psychopathologies of that ego" (Jameson, *Postmodernism* 15).

4. See also DeLillo's first novel, *Americana:* "Sitting that close all I could perceive was that meshed effect, those stormy motes, but it drew me in and held me as if I were an integral part of the set, my molecules mating with those millions of dots. I sat that way for half an hour or so" (43).

5. "[G]one is the Benjaminian 'aura' with its notions of originality, authenticity, and uniqueness" (Hutcheon, *Politics* 35); what we are dealing with, instead, is the aura of the simulacrum: "the culture industry is defined by the fact that it does not strictly counterpose another principle to that of aura, but rather by the fact that it conserves the decaying aura as a foggy mist" (Adorno, "Culture" 131). But sometimes the foggy mist glows like neon.

6. "Yet conspiracy theory (and its garish narrative manifestations) must be seen as a degraded attempt—through the figuration of advanced technology—to think the impossible totality of the contemporary world system" (Jameson, *Postmodernism* 38).

7. The president is unreal and uncanny in precisely the sense first isolated by E. Jentsch in Freud's famous essay "The Uncanny." For Jentsch, whom Freud cites as having preceded his own researches into the subject, the sense of the uncanny pertains to "'doubts whether an apparently animate being is really alive; or conversely, whether a lifeless object might not be in fact animate'": and he refers in this connection to the impression made by "waxwork figures, ingeniously constructed dolls and automata" (226).

8. "Why is it that, in the depthlessness of consumer society, the essential surface logic of our world of simulacra—why is it that the mythic ideal of some kind of depth integration is no longer attractive and no longer presents itself as a possible or workable solution?" (Jameson, "*Ulysses*" 175).

9. "The dynamic of the Oedipus situation is not only the hidden mode of every father-son relationship but also the secret of the enduring domination of man by man—of the conquests and failures of civilization" (Marcuse 234). See also DeLillo's *Libra:* "She wondered how many women had visions and dreams of the President. What must it be like to know you are the object of a thousand longings? It's as though he floats over the landscape at night, entering dreams and fantasies, entering the act of love between husbands and wives. He floats through television screens into bedrooms at night. He floats from the radio into Marina's bed. There were times when she waited for him, actually listened late at night for a few words of a speech or a news conference recorded earlier in the day, waited for the voice of the President, the radio on a table near the bed" (324).

10. This is from Freud's letter to Ernest Jones describing his fainting spells in Jung's presence. See Gay 275–76.

5

"Postmodern Blackness": Toni Morrison's *Beloved* and the End of History

Kimberly Chabot Davis

When they asserted that our postmodern society has reached the "end of history," theorists Fredric Jameson, Jean Baudrillard, and Francis Fukuyama launched a compelling debate that has persisted for over a decade. They argue that we no longer believe in teleological metanarratives, that our concept of history has become spatial or flattened out, and that we inhabit a perpetual present in which images of the past are merely recycled with no understanding of their original context. In short, they think postmodern culture has lost a sense of historical consciousness, of cause and effect. Jameson, in particular, sees literary postmodernism as a byproduct of this new worldview. Such a controversial stance has, of course, provoked numerous antagonists to speak out; Linda Hutcheon, for example, has written two studies of "historiographic metafiction," suggesting that much of postmodern fiction is still strongly invested in history, but more importantly in revising our sense of what history means and can accomplish. My project is to examine how Toni Morrison's acclaimed historical novel *Beloved* (1987) enacts a hybrid vision of history and time that sheds new light on issues addressed by Jameson and Hutcheon in their theories of the postmodern—topics such as the "fictionality" of history, the blurring of past and present, and the questioning of grand historical metanarratives. I argue that while the novel exhibits a postmodern skepticism of sweeping historical narratives, of "Truth," and of Marxist teleological notions of time as diachronic, it also retains an African American and modernist political commitment to the crucial importance of deep cultural memory, of keeping the past alive in order to construct a better future. Morrison's mediations between these two theoretical and political camps—between postmodernism and African American social protest—enable her to draw the best from both, and make us question the more extremist voices asserting that postmodern culture is bereft of history.

Since the term "postmodern" has been at the center of many highly charged cultural debates, I am aware that describing *Beloved* as such, even as a "hybrid" postmodern novel, is a gesture that might draw criticism. Clearly, the novel's status as part of the African American tradition of social protest, and Morrison's investments in agency, presence, and the resurrection of authentic history seem to make the novel incompatible with poststructuralist ideas at the root of postmodernism. Morrison herself has spoken out against a postmodernism that she associates with Jameson's terms. In my view, however, Morrison's treatment of history bears some similarity to Hutcheon's postmodern "historiographic metafiction," but her relationship to this discourse is affected by her aim to write "black-topic" texts. Morrison acknowledges that history is always fictional, always a representation, yet she is also committed to the project of recording African American history in order to heal her readers. Instead of a playful exercise in deconstructing history, Morrison's *Beloved* attempts to affect the contemporary world of the "real." While the novel should not simply be assimilated into the canon of postmodernism, Morrison's work should be recognized as contributing a fresh voice to the debates about postmodern history, a voice that challenges the centrism and elitism of much of postmodern theory. *Beloved* reminds us that history is not over for African Americans, who are still struggling to write the genealogies of their people and to keep a historical consciousness alive.

The relationship of African American writers and their work to the discourse of postmodernism has been hotly contested, and has unfortunately reified a dichotomy that I would like to question. This relationship has become even more vexed since the Nobel Prize committee bypassed postmodern guru Thomas Pynchon to select Toni Morrison as their 1993 literature winner; Morrison claimed her prize as a victory particularly for African Americans.[1] Black critics such as Barbara Christian continue to argue that Morrison's work must be understood as an expression of African American forms and traditions, and are concerned that "the power of this novel as a specifically African American text is being blunted" as it is being appropriated by white academic discourse (6). I too share her suspicion of the increasingly popular move to read Morrison's fiction through the lens of postmodernism, poststructuralism, or "white" academic theory, a tactic which underestimates the crucial importance of Morrison's black cultural heritage to any interpretation of her works.

While we must question the tactics of critics like Elliott Butler-Evans, who simply and somewhat blindly plot poststructuralist and postmodernist theory onto Morrison's "black-topic texts," we should be equally wary of concluding that postmodernism is a "white" phenomenon. Any claim that the lives of black people have nothing to do with postmodernism ignores the complex historical interrelationship of black protest and liberal academic discourse. As Andreas Huyssen, Kobena Mercer, and Linda Hutcheon have noted, racial liberation movements of the 1960s and 70s (as well as the feminist movement) contributed to the loosening of cultural boundaries, a change that is seen as characteristically postmodern.[2] White liberal theorists of postmodernism and African American critics often share an oppositional relationship to the bourgeois state or to the universalizing "objectivity" of some humanist intellectuals. A rigid demarcation between postmodern texts and African American texts merely perpetuates a false dichotomy of academic theory and social protest, ignoring that they emerged in response to a similar set of lived conditions.

I do not seek simply to join the fray of critics who unequivocally claim Morrison's novel *Beloved* for one side or the other (postmodernist or "antipostmodernist" social protest) while leaving the text's ambiguities and ambivalences unexplored. Deborah McDowell, arguing that the theory/practice hierarchy equates theory with men and marginalizes black women to the realm of social protest, calls for a "counterhistory [. . . that] would bring theory and practice into a productive tension that would force a reevaluation of each side" (256). I am attempting here to enact that counterhistory, to investigate how Morrison's fiction speaks to postmodern theory and, more importantly, allows us to reevaluate this discourse. I do not aim to measure *Beloved* against the authority of these theorists, but rather to examine how each has represented the specter of history differently and to suggest the difference that race can make.

In her novels, interviews, and essays, Morrison has expressed opinions and agendas that resound with the concerns of both critical camps—both postmodernist theorists and African American and feminist critics seeking social agency. Feminist and African American critics have often dismissed postmodernism's philosophical questioning of foundationalism and essentialism as being incompatible with their sociopolitical criticism (Fraser and Nicholson 20–21). Morrison herself acknowledges and occasionally reifies this rift by defining herself in interviews as an antipostmodernist author of black-topic texts, written to pass on agency to her black readers ("Living" 11). Certainly, Morrison's works seem to be defined by the prefixes "pre" or "re" rather than "post"; in *Beloved,* she is more concerned with origins, cycles, and reconstructing agency than with decadence and self-parody. Both *Beloved* and *Jazz* are set in time periods of birth and regeneration—the age of Reconstruction after the Civil War and the Harlem Renaissance of the 1920s.[3]

Despite her reluctance to associate her work with postmodernism, I believe that Morrison has produced the kind of hybrid cultural work that socialist feminist Donna Haraway calls for. In *Simians, Cyborgs, and Women,* Haraway writes: "Feminists have to insist on a better account of the world. [. . .] So, I think my problem and "our" problem is how to have *simultaneously* an account of radical historical contingency for all knowledge claims and knowing subjects, a critical practice for recognizing our own 'semiotic technologies' for making meanings, *and* a no-nonsense commitment to faithful accounts of a 'real' world" (187). Haraway underscores the urgent need for new and better "her-stories" that might empower women but that are still informed by poststructuralism's denaturalizing critique and for narratives that attempt to approximate "true history" while remaining aware of the limits and impossibility of truth or of any historical metanarrative. Morrison's work can be compared to Haraway's in its recognition of this dual process—although Morrison demystifies master historical narratives, she also wants to raise "real" or authentic African American history in its place. She deconstructs while she reconstructs, tapping the well of African American "presence."[4] As Anthony Hilfer has suggested, Morrison's novels offers a "both-and," dialectical, indeterminate character, a doubleness that Hutcheon would argue is itself a distinctly postmodern strategy (Hilfer 91).

Despite the indeterminacies of her fiction, Morrison's *Beloved* can be read as an overt and passionate quest to fill a gap neglected by historians, to record the everyday lives of the "disremembered and unaccounted for" (*Beloved* 274). Rejecting the artificial distinction between fiction and history, Morrison considers artists to be the "truest of historians" ("Behind" 88). In "The Site of Memory," Morrison explicitly describes the project of writing *Beloved* as one of fictional reconstruction or "literary archeology" (112), of imagining the inner life of the slave woman Margaret Garner, her source for Sethe. While working on *The Black Book* (1974), a collection of cultural documents recording African American "history-as-life-lived," Morrison discovered a newspaper clipping about Garner, a runaway slave who had murdered her children at the moment of capture. Like Denver's efforts to reconstruct the past through storytelling, Morrison's narrative has succeeded in "giving blood to the scraps [. . .] and a heartbeat" to what had been merely an historical curio (*Beloved* 78). The desire to uncover the historical reality of the African American past fuels Morrison's fictional project of literary archeology: "you journey to a site to see what remains were left behind and to reconstruct the world that these remains imply" ("Site" 112). Working to fill in the gaps left by the constrained slave narrative genre, she attempts "to rip the veil drawn over 'proceedings too terrible to relate' " (110) in order "to yield up a kind of a truth" (112).

Although this last phrase suggests that Morrison pursues authenticity in her historical renderings, I will argue that she accepts the poststructuralist critique of the idea of a single totalizing Truth or History. While she sees herself as a creative historian who reconstructs, Morrison also works to deconstruct master narratives of "official history" in *Beloved.* Mae Henderson describes the novel as a counternarrative to the "master('s) narrative," one example of which is the newspaper account of Garner's deed, a document which reappears in the novel as a harsh official alternative to Sethe's emotional interpretation of events (Henderson 79). In this novel, the appearance of the newspaper clipping is one of the few intrusions of the dominant culture's process of historical documentation. Morrison drops only a few references to historically recognizable "encyclopedia" events of the period; for example, the Fugitive Slave Bill, the historical fact that provokes Sethe's infanticide, is mentioned only in parentheses (171). Even more striking is her rendering of the Civil War, the apocalypse of American national history, as a minor, inconsequential event in the lives of these former slaves. As Denver lovingly remembers the gift of Christmas cologne she received as a child, she mentions offhandedly that she received it during "one of the war years" (28). Paul D's haunting memory of the chain gang in Alfred, Georgia, outweighs the significance of his participation in the war, of which we learn only in the last few pages of the book. The private realities of persecution and daily survival matter more to Sethe and Paul D than any dates or public documents worthy of note in a history textbook. Paul D recognizes that prejudice and racism certainly did not end with the Emancipation Proclamation or the surrender of the Confederate Army: "The War had been over four or five years then, but nobody white or black seemed to know it" (52). Marilyn Sanders Mobley suggests that the fragments of recognizable history in *Beloved* "punctuate the text and [. . .] disrupt the text of the mind which is both historical and ahistorical at the same time" (196).[5] While I agree that these historical facts appear as interruptions, I would argue that the minds of Sethe and Paul D are never "ahistorical." Rather, Morrison attempts to redefine history as an amalgamation of local narratives, as a jumble of personal as well as publicly recorded triumphs and tragedies.

Morrison's commitment to historical remembering arises from her concern about the ignorance of and even contempt for the past that she sees in both contemporary African American and postmodern culture. In an interview in 1988, she remarked: "the past is absent or it's romanticised. This culture doesn't encourage dwelling on, let alone coming to terms with, the truth about the past" ("Living " 11). While working on *The Black Book* in the early 1970s, Morrison expressed disdain for the Black Power movement's creation of new myths and their retreat to ancient African myths of the "far and misty past" ("Behind " 87). More relevant to the process of liberation, she felt, was knowledge of the three-hundred-year history of African Americans. In the 1988 interview, Morrison applauded the emergence of a new body of historical fiction by black writers, and she found it ironic "that black writers are descending deeper into historical concerns at the same moment white literati are abolishing it in the name of something they call 'post modernism.' [. . .] History has become impossible for them" (11). Morrison seems here to accept Jameson's negative portrayal of postmodernism—a definition contested by Hutcheon and others—as historical "depthlessness" and "a consequent weakening of historicity, both in our relationship to public History and in the new forms of our private temporality" (Jameson, *New Left Review* 58). Back in 1974, Morrison also expressed concerns that would be echoed by Jameson, a concern that real history was being replaced by historicism—the textualizing of time as a mere representation, as a simulacrum (to use Baudrillard's formulation). Sounding rather Marxist, Morrison bemoaned the "shallow" myths of the black liberation movement's Afrocentrism, "because our children can't use and don't need and will certainly reject history-as-imagined. They deserve better: history as life lived," which Morrison was attempting to record in *The Black Book* ("Behind" 88).

Although in 1974 Morrison sounds like a Jamesonian precursor, criticizing contemporary literature's historical travesties, in *Beloved* she has offered a different conception of the relationship between history and fiction, acknowledging that all history is "imagined," and that all knowledge of the past is derived from representations, such as *Beloved* itself. As Haraway seeks better scientific stories, Morrison attempts to draw a historical portrait closer to "life lived," but she recognizes that no totalizing truth can ever be reached.[6] Morrison's fictional works offer a different theory of "postmodernist history" than does Jameson, and critics who try to read Morrison's work through Jameson's lens end up misreading the novels. Butler-Evans uses scanty textual support to argue that *Tar Baby* is postmodern (in Jameson's definition) because it offers "a displacement of history by 'historicism,' in which the past is reread and reconstructed in the present" (152). As Hutcheon has pointed out, the fundamental problem with Jameson's formulation is his rigid distinction between authentic history and inauthentic historicism. Jameson describes our postmodern society as one "bereft of all historicity, whose own putative past is little more than a set of dusty spectacles [. . .] the past as 'referent' finds itself gradually bracketed, and then effaced altogether, leaving us with nothing but texts" ("Postmodernism" 66). For Morrison, history and "historicism" are one and the same, and her work offers a necessary correction to Jameson's theories, precisely because she questions the assumption that there is a knowable reality behind the inauthentic simulation or representation.

Moments of self-reflexivity in her text remind the reader that Morrison is also constructing a textual representation of the past, just as historians did before her. When Paul D is confronted by the newspaper account of Sethe's deed, the reader is made aware that textual documents often—or always—fail to capture life exactly as it is experienced. Although he cannot read, Paul D finds the representation of Sethe's face to be inauthentic: "that ain't her mouth" (154). While Paul D is wrong in denying the truth of Sethe's infanticide, his reaction to the picture of Sethe makes the reader aware of the difference between a real live original and any simulation, either photographic or textual. At the same moment, however, the possibility of distinguishing between the real and the reproduction is rendered unstable, and the very concept of authenticity is put into question as Paul D doubts both the white culture's representation and his own knowledge of the real woman, Sethe. In this scene, Morrison seems to be revising her previous belief that the documents collected in *The Black Book* could offer authentic history as life lived; now she suggests that a fictional account of the interior life of a former slave might be more historically "real" than actual documents, which were often written from the perspective of the dominant culture. While Morrison reminds us of the slippage between signifier and signified in the scene with the newspaper clipping, she also calls attention to the fact that the past is only available to us through textual traces, such as *Beloved* and *The Black Book*. Newspapers—as a figure for discourse itself—make one other appearance in the novel. They are stacked in a pile in the woodshed, the pivotal space in which Sethe kills her baby, and where the resurrected Beloved lures Paul D to have sex; the printed words of the newspapers are metaphoric spectators to the "real" action of this fictional story. This metaphor allows Morrison simultaneously to point out the gap between representation and reality and to suggest that we can only know the past through discourse. She seems to concur with the poststructuralist view that reality is a function of discourse, yet does not let this point pacify her into accepting the representations that exist—the voyeuristic news accounts and the constrained slave narratives. I would argue that Morrison's sociopolitical project is the idea that new representations can change our perceptions of historical reality.

Morrison's choice of epigraphs also reflects her dual response to the representation/reality dialectic. Hutcheon argues that the inclusion of paratextual materials, such as epigraphs, serves both to "remind us of the narrativity (and fictionality) of the primary text and to assert its factuality and historicity" (*Politics* 85). Morrison's choice of two epigraphs underscores this dialectic; one points to the historical "fact" of the Middle Passage, the other to a text (the Bible) that has often been received as fact. While the scriptures themselves blur the boundary between fact and fiction, the "60 million and more" statistic is an estimation gleaned from historical records. Although the Middle Passage was a horrific historical reality, the estimated number is not a verifiable fact because the deaths of slaves were often deemed unworthy of recording. All the lives lost can never be accounted for because our access to history is always limited by words, and by those who have control of textual production. Thus, in beginning her novel with these epigraphs, Morrison seems both to ground her fictional work in historical reality and also to question the possibility of ever finding the historical referent outside of or preceding representation.

As an artist, Morrison places a great deal of faith in the power of representation to determine our perceptions of reality. For her, the character of Beloved has become a piece of living history—words made into flesh. According to Morrison, she drew Beloved as a composite of the dead child of Margaret Garner, and of a "dead girl" from a Van der Zee photograph—a girl who had been murdered by a jealous ex-lover ("Conversation" 583–84). Morrison remarked passionately in an interview: "bit by bit I had been rescuing her from the grave of time and inattention. Her fingernails might be in the first book; face and legs, perhaps, the second time. Little by little bringing her back into living life. So that now she comes running when called [. . .] she is here now, alive" ("Conversation" 593). Morrison's commitment to resurfacing the dead and paying tribute to black Americans of previous generations has made her works particularly poignant to African American readers. With the novel's newly acquired place in the canon of American literature, Morrison's representation has helped to contribute to the historical consciousness of Americans, just as the television miniseries *Roots* did in the 1970s. The popularity of *Beloved* and the healing power of its representation may have enlarged our culture's understanding of black women's history and of the history of the Civil War and Reconstruction era.

To ground my argument that Morrison's fiction has much to contribute to a postmodern theoretical debate about history and representation, I will turn to a close reading of the novel and suggest that its thematic interest in temporality relates to larger concerns about history. If Morrison's career reveals both a desire for "authentic" history-as-life-lived and the postmodernist realization that history is a fictional construct, the plot of her novel *Beloved* is marked by a parallel dialectic—the mind's struggle between remembering and forgetting the past. *Beloved* is a novel about the traumas and healing powers of memory—or "rememory" as Sethe calls it, adding a connotation of cyclical recurrence. Sethe's ambivalent relationship to her cruel past creates a kind of wavelike narrative effect, as memories surface and are repressed. On the one hand, "Sethe worked hard to remember [. . .] as close to nothing as was safe. Unfortunately her brain was devious," offering her memories of the beauty of Sweet Home rather than of her children (6). Painfully aware that she lacks control of her memory, Sethe also attempts to repress, to "start the day's serious work of beating back the past" (73). The ghost child Beloved represents the "return of the repressed" past that demands to be worked through and not forgotten. Although the novel proves Sethe wrong in her belief that "the future was a matter of keeping the past at bay" (42), the text also contends that neither must the past consume us. With Beloved's entrenchment at 124 Bluestone, Sethe's life begins to ebb away, her strength sapped by the swelling ghost daughter, a figure for the threatening past. Morrison suggests that dwelling on one's own past, or the collective past of the slaves, can strangle your present as Beloved nearly strangles Sethe in the Clearing.

Morrison's novel endorses neither a Marxist obsessive, teleological historical remembering nor a "postmodernist" forgetting of the past, suggesting instead that both processes are necessary to move into the future.[7] The simultaneity of remembering and forgetting is evident in Sethe's state of mind after Beloved's return: "her mind was busy with the things she could forget" (191). At the end of the novel, the ambiguity of the repeated phrase "It was not a story to pass on" also enacts the simultaneity of moving forward and looking back, since "passing on" has two meanings—sharing the tale with future generations and walking on by and forgetting the story. Thus, although Morrison promotes a delving into the historical past, she realizes that the past must be processed and sometimes forgotten in order to function in the present and to "pass on" to the future. Her earlier statements, when working on *The Black Book,* about the crucial need for knowledge of recent history have been qualified in *Beloved,* which teaches that a historical memory also has its costs, resulting often in the reopening—rather than the healing—of old psychic wounds.

One way to free oneself from the horrors of the past is to reenact and reconfigure the past in the present, as Sethe does with an ice pick at the end of the novel, attacking the white man Bodwin (whom she perceives as a reincarnation of her slave master Schoolteacher) rather than her own children. Henderson argues that this reconfiguration of the past delivers Sethe, who "demonstrates her possession *of* rather than *by* the past," and thus exorcizes Beloved (80). While Henderson rightly asserts the importance of a "mediation between remembering (possession) and forgetting (exorcism)," she seems to grant more subversive powers of agency to Sethe than the close of the novel actually suggests (82). After this attempt to reenact "the Misery," Sethe is hardly healed, whole and "reborn," as Henderson argues, but has resigned herself to die rather than live as a "bleak and minus nothing" (*Beloved* 270). Sethe admits that "something is missing [. . .] something more than Beloved" (270). While Henderson celebrates her as a subversive heroine and revisionist historian who has achieved the power to change the past, she ignores the fact that Sethe is still haunted by her complicity with whites at the end of the book, as she recalls that she compliantly "made the ink" that allowed Schoolteacher to delineate her "animal" characteristics (271). Morrison, I believe, presents a more balanced and postmodernist view by acknowledging both Sethe's complicities and her subversions, and recognizing that Sethe has limited power to revise or erase the past.

Many critics have read the ending (and the phrase "pass on") as an indication that Sethe is healed and Beloved put back in her place, but I find that the last chapter denies such a simplistic closure. Morrison ends the novel with the word "Beloved," suggesting that the past is a lasting presence, waiting to be resurrected: "Down by the stream in back of 124 her footprints come and go, come and go. [. . .] Should a child, an adult place his feet in them, they will fit" (275).

Although the ending suggests partial healing, the specter of the past remains, waiting to resurface. I find *Beloved*'s ending similar to Hutcheon's description of the postmodern historiographic novel: "the past is not something to be escaped, avoided, or controlled. [. . .]. The past is something with which we must come to terms and such a confrontation involves an acknowledgment of limitation as well as power" (*Politics* 58).

While Henderson's analysis is often insightful, I find her view to be one-sided because she ignores the novel's postmodernist suspicion of coherent and logical historical narratives that attempt to smooth over the disorder of lived experience. I disagree with her suggestion that this novel creates coherence out of the dismembered lives created by slavery; she writes: "If dismemberment deconstitutes the whole [. . .] then re-memory functions to re-collect, re-assemble, and organize into a meaningful sequential whole through [. . .] the process of narrativization" (71). Henderson uses words like "cohesive" to describe Sethe's narrative, an adjective that seems inappropriate for a novel that rejects closure and facile narrative solutions. In opposition to Henderson, Emily Miller Budick cogently argues that gaps left by a tragic past are not easily filled or smoothed over in this work: "recovering the missing [child. . .] reconstituting in the present what was lost in the past, will not, this book insists, restore order and logic to lives that have been interrupted by such loss" (131).

I would argue along with Budick that Morrison's novel does not aim to fill in all the gaps of the historical past; the result of her literary archeology is not a complete skeleton, but a partial one, with pieces deliberately missing or omitted. Because the reconstruction is not total, the reader is engaged in the process of imagining history herself. Although Morrison's historical project is to unveil the "unspeakable thoughts, unspoken" (*Beloved* 199), many things nevertheless remain inaudible or buried in the novel, and these gaps can be read as characteristically postmodern.[8] When Paul D confronts Sethe with the newspaper clipping about the murder of her child, Sethe is unable to give voice to the unspoken: "she could never close in, pin it down for anybody who had to ask" (163). Of course, she continues to try to pin it down throughout the rest of the novel, and the process of putting some of her memory into words, rather than a complete and seamless product, is stressed here.

Rather than the "meaningful sequential whole" that Henderson finds, I see a text with many holes and gaps, a testament to the incoherence of "life lived," especially the life of a freed slave.[9] For example, the novel begins with Howard and Bugler, but we never learn their fate, or that of their father Hale. Who was the girl whose red ribbon Stamp Paid finds attached to a raft? This novel never forgets or underestimates the difficulty of representing the lives of the disremembered and unaccounted for, "the people of the broken necks, of fire-cooked blood and black girls who had lost their ribbons" (181). The Middle Passage, in which "sixty million and more" slaves died, is another significant gap that looms on the horizon, and it can only be obliquely alluded to in the novel's epigraph, in Sethe's buried memories of her mother's story, and in Beloved's postmodern fragmented narrative which blends the historical past and present. Beloved's disjointed narrative, composed of phrases with no punctuation, calls attention to the visual spaces on the page, a metaphor for the gaps in the storytelling. In Beloved's narrative, "it is always now" (210), and Morrison combines imagined scenes of life on the slave ships with details from Beloved's and Sethe's stories: "the little hill of dead people [. . .] the men without skin push them through with poles   the woman [Sethe] is there with the face I want   the face that is mine [. . .] the woman with my face is in the sea   her sharp earrings are gone" (211–12). Christian has written of *Beloved* as a novel giving voice to this "unspeakable event" of the Middle Passage, an event almost erased from American cultural memory (6). Although I agree that Morrison has attempted to imagine this "terrible space" in American history, the gap cannot be completely bridged, and the psychic trauma on the slave ships can only be narrated elusively.

Unlike a traditional novelistic development of teleological, "sequential and meaningful" narration, Morrison's narrative technique stresses the fact that black Americans, particularly freed slaves, did not experience time or history as an ordered and linear sequence of events. Morrison's narrative techniques are echoed in the novel by Denver, who weaves stories, constructing "out of the string she had heard all her life a net to hold Beloved" (76). Both Morrison and Denver weave a porous net with their storytelling, leaving gaps to allow some of the mysterious and unspeakable past to escape narration, to flow on through. Morrison recognizes the important healing powers of narration, yet also understands the limits of representation and of the storytelling process. Hutcheon finds this dual response to narration to be postmodern: "A plot [. . .] seen as a narrative structure [. . .] is always a totalizing representation that integrates multiple and scattered events into one unified story. But the simultaneous desire for and suspicion of such representations are both part of the postmodern contradictory response to emplotment" (*Politics* 68).

This indeterminacy and double movement contributes to the richness of Morrison's text, enabling it to engender a plethora of critical interpretations, often at odds with one another.

As I have suggested, Hutcheon clearly finds Morrison to be a postmodernist writer with a dialectic quality and a deconstructive political project—to write new "ex-centric" definitions of history from the margins. Working with a more generalized concept of postmodernism than does Hutcheon, Hilfer presents an important warning to critics who view Morrison's work as a response to, or derivative of, academic postmodernism: "Morrison derives her indeterminacies not from French postmodernism nor from the new, oddly dematerialized forms of Marxism but from the center of African American culture [. . .] jazz" (93). In an interview with Nellie McKay, Morrison remarked, "Classical music satisfies and closes. Black music does not do that. Jazz always keeps you on the edge. There is no final chord. And it agitates you. [. . .]. I want my books to be like that" (McKay 429). Although it is significant that Morrison finds the sources of her indeterminacies in jazz, and not in theories of the postmodern developed by white academics, their similarities arise out of shared conditions of urbanity and the chaos of modern life. Morrison herself acknowledges this similarity: "Black women had to deal with 'post-modern' problems in the nineteenth century and earlier [. . .] certain kinds of dissolution, the loss of and the need to reconstruct certain kinds of stability" ("Living" 11).

Although Morrison seems to stand against postmodernism and poststructuralism by claiming to write an "authentic" African American history of slavery that aims to reconstruct a stable sense of self for her characters, Morrison's narrative strategies nonetheless share some affinities with postmodern fiction as described by Hutcheon. But I do not mean to suggest that Morrison's work can be grouped comfortably alongside postmodern writers such as Milan Kundera or Thomas Pynchon. Hutcheon herself is guilty of marginalizing African American writers in her books; after extended readings of texts by white men, she merely refers to Morrison and Ishmael Reed as participants in the same postmodern historiography. Butler-Evans runs into this problem when he simply attempts to graft Jameson's criteria for postmodern fiction onto Morrison's novel *Tar Baby,* which he claims exhibits "pastiche and collage as structuring devices; the emergence of a schizophrenic textual structure; a displacement of history by 'historicism'" (152). Although Morrison's work contains strong doses of irony, *Beloved*'s overwhelmingly serious tone and overt political project make it difficult to describe as parody or playful pastiche. Nothing less than the reconstruction of the erased history of the African American people motivates Morrison, rather than playful exercises in form, however politically subversive these aesthetic innovations may be. In my view, race signifies more than Butler-Evans and Hutcheon acknowledge. Hutcheon locates the politics of postmodernism in its aesthetics but ignores agency and the subversive political content that Morrison and other African American novelists aim for. I argue that the politics of Morrison's texts can be found both in her aesthetic strategies and in the kind of historical consciousness that her characters enact as they struggle with their own temporality.

The critical commentary about Morrison's decision to develop a circular, nonlinear narrative technique offers a useful case study of the competing trends in the critical reception of *Beloved*. Many critics cite the following passage, in which Sethe's concept of time becomes clear as she evades Paul D's questions about the newspaper clipping: "Sethe knew that the circle she was making around the room, him, the subject, would remain one. That she could never close in, pin it down for anybody who had to ask. [. . .] Because the truth was simple, not a long-drawn-out record of flowered shifts, tree cages, selfishness, ankle ropes and wells" (163). Deconstructionist critics read this passage as a rejection of "long-drawn-out" linear and teleological historical narratives, in favor of a circular experience of time without a center. For example, Catherine Rainwater argues that Morrison's circular patterns are postmodern because they are never completed (Sethe "could never close in") and thus deny traditional narrative closure (101). Barbara Hill Rigney has found Morrison's circular narrative to be an example of Julia Kristeva's concept of "woman's time" as circular (nonphallic) and cyclical, reflecting the natural cycles of reproduction and the seasons (76). In answer to poststructuralist critics, Christian notes that in African cosmology, time is nonlinear, and thus Morrison's and Sethe's circling finds root in an ancestral worldview rather than in the work of Jacques Derrida (13). Feminist and poststructuralist readings that celebrate the nonlinear narrative forget that circles are also laden with ominous symbolism in an African American context, since they recall the circles of iron (and nooses) surrounding the necks of slaves, particularly the "neck jewelry" that Paul D was forced to wear. Thus, while all of these critics agree that Morrison uses a circular narrative technique to subvert a linear reading of time and history, each attributes her motives differently.

Placing questions of authorial intent aside, I believe that the text itself portrays circularity in both a positive and a negative light, as both an accurate reflection of the mind's "rememory" process, but also as a treadmill from which one must escape in order to move forward in time. Rejecting a linear time consciousness, Sethe expresses her belief that time is spatial and operates like a wheel, and that past events are waiting to recur: "I was talking about time. It's so hard for me to believe in it. Some things go. Pass on. Some things just stay. [. . .] Places, places are still there. [. . .] The picture is still there and what's more, if you go there—you who never was there—if you go there and stand in the place where it was, it will happen again" (35–36). The belief that "nothing ever dies" haunts Sethe, as she tries desperately to protect Denver from reliving the events of her past. Sethe attempts to subvert this recurring cycle by creating a kind of "timeless present" in her home, where she hopes the past can no longer hurt Denver or Beloved (184). Sethe wants to "hurry time along and get to the no-time waiting for her" at 124, where her infanticide has been erased by the miraculous return of Beloved (191). Morrison accompanies Sethe's discovery of Beloved's true identity with a textual shift from the past tense (which dominates the novel before this point) to the present tense: "this day they are outside" (120). Although Sethe hopes that her timeless world has put a stop to the cycle in which the past can return to haunt, 124's no-time represents a different kind of vicious circle—with the past, present, and future collapsed into one.

Both Sethe's concepts of a timeless present and the spatial time from which she wants to escape are echoed in Jameson's discussion of postmodernism. In an interview, Jameson summed up the thesis of his book *Postmodernism, or, the Cultural Logic of Late Capitalism* with the remark "time has become a perpetual present and thus spatial" in postmodern culture (qtd. in Stephanson 46). Retaining a Marxist desire for teleology and linearity, Jameson regrets the postmodern flattening of time, arguing that it deprives people of a "true" sense of history, of cause and effect, of "deep phenomenological experience" (*Postmodernism* 134). He is nostalgic for the "the great high modernist thematic of time and temporality, the elegiac mysteries of *durée* and memory [found in the works of Faulkner. . . .W]e now inhabit the synchronic rather than the diachronic" (*Postmodernism* 16). Morrison is more willing than Jameson to entertain the possibility of spatial time as an authentic experience rather than a loss or a mere "simulacrum." In her essay "The Site of Memory," she uses the metaphor of the archeological site to refer to memories of the past, as if they were a place that one could visit to mine for bits of history. As Mobley has argued, Beloved's narrative, lacking punctuation, suggests the "seamlessness of time, [and] the inextricability of the past and present, of ancestors and their progeny" (196). The concept of history in *Beloved* is not flattened but rather takes on extra volume to contain the cultural memories of ancestors, to which we can have access only through imagination.

Rather than exhibiting "historical depthlessness," Morrison's works may be seen as modernist (in Jameson's terms) because they respect the importance of deep memory and explore the relationship between the past and the present. On the other hand, her novels also exhibit a postmodern skepticism of teleological narratives and of the modernist myth of forward progress espoused by Marxists. Because she rejects a modernist diachronic view of history, Morrison explores the idea of a more synchronic, spatial experience of time.[10] Her spatial sense of time can be read not only as a postmodern form of temporality, but it could also be viewed as an expression of the temporal experiences of African Americans, who are often denied a future and are therefore haunted by or retreat to the past. Sethe is clearly frustrated and "boxed in" by time; she cannot construct an ordered timeline of her life, so she attempts her experiment of living only in the present, as do many hopeless inner-city youth.

Although Morrison embraces a more synchronic concept of time than does Jameson, she concurs with him in rejecting the *timeless* world of 124 Bluestone, a timelessness which both identify—wrongly, I think—with postmodernism. While she suggests that time need not be perceived as linear, it nevertheless must be respected and dealt with. From his experience on the chain gang, Paul D learned that living only in the present moment is like not living at all, because life means "caring and looking forward, remembering and looking back" (109). Although Sethe believes she has created an idyllic no-time at 124, Stamp Paid finds the house to be encircled by strange "voices that ringed 124 like a noose" (183). The timeless circle must be broken or Sethe and Denver will be strangled, their future erased. I disagree with Mobley, who reads the last dialogue in which the voices of the three women merge as the final word and concluding message of the text, a message that "the past, present, and future are all one and the same" (Mobley 196). This reading of time as wholly synchronic ignores the text's attempt to preserve some temporal boundaries (however permeable) and to prevent the swirling eddy around 124 from turning into a black hole. Morrison's theoretical conception of temporality is best expressed through the figure of the wheel—of a circle rolling forward (or occasionally backward) through time, while continually kicking up the dust of the past. Although wheels are circular, I do not believe that Morrison pursues a sense of wholeness that her circular narrative strategy might suggest, because the circles are never completed, the center never reached, and the "rememory" process always unfinished. The figure of the wheel can instead be translated into a progressive temporal strategy for a postmodern society—a strategy of learning from the past but not being paralyzed by its lessons, of forging a loose and flexible synthesis out of the fragments of history, of reaping the benefits of both a diachronic and a synchronic sense of time.

The lessons about history and temporality offered by Toni Morrison in her masterwork should and must be critically discussed in relationship to academic discourses about postmodernism. Postmodern theories need to be modified to accommodate texts like *Beloved* with an overt political agenda of social protest, and to recognize these fictions as contributions to a theoretical discourse of contemporary life. As bell hooks argues in her essay "Postmodern Blackness," there is a crucial need for black-topic texts to be read in light of poststructuralist and postmodernist theory and its indeterminacies, while maintaining attention to the texts' specific messages for black readers. Like hooks, I believe that such a culturally powerful discourse as postmodernism should not be left in the hands of the elite few. Although many postmodern theorists emphasize "difference," the literary category is often used by critics to refer to a sealed set of texts, usually produced by white men. I would like to see postmodernism continue to be a site of contestation for meaning, cultural power, and political change. *Beloved* poses a challenge to neat theories because it balances on the cusp between two worldviews, rupturing the dichotomy between African American social protest (based on a modernist ideology) and a postmodernist questioning of metanarratives about history and time. It is precisely the ambivalences of this novel which make it "beloved" by so many critical groups, but these indeterminacies themselves seem to resist the many and varied critics who have tried to claim Morrison for their very own. I believe that it is more important to explore what her representations have to offer to all of us, simultaneously.

Notes

1. See William Grimes, as well as "Nobel Prize in Literature" in *Jet* magazine. Morrison told *Jet:* "Winning as an American is very special—but winning as a Black American is a knockout" (34).

2. See Andreas Huyssen, *After the Great Divide,* 191, 194, and 199; Kobena Mercer 424–25; and Linda Hutcheon, *A Poetics of Postmodernism,* 62.

3. The term "Harlem Renaissance" is itself a construction of literary historians and somewhat of a misnomer. How could the African American literary tradition have been experiencing a rebirth, some argue, when it hadn't yet established itself? The term served to reinvent a past in order to forge a present and a future, and this move is strikingly similar to the projects of many postmodern historical novelists.

4. In "Behind the Making of *The Black Book*," Morrison writes: "It has what I believe may be the only mythic quality unique to Black people: presence" (89). She made this statement in 1974 before Derrida's critique of the metaphysics of presence won over the American academy, but I think she would concur today.

5. Mobley's formulation echoes that of Friedrich Nietzsche in his seminal essay "On the Uses and Disadvantages of History for Life."

6. See Barbara Hill Rigney's *The Voices of Toni Morrison,* which analyzes her mythmaking as a view of history that isn't totalizing.

7. I use Jameson's false dichotomy between Marxism and postmodernism here purposefully to show that Morrison ruptures this binary opposition.

8. Andrew Levy makes a similar argument in "Telling *Beloved,*" 114–23.

9. Robert Grant sees similar absences in *Sula.*

10. Morrison's relationship to Modernism is obviously dependent on one's definition of this heterogeneous body of literature and on one's choice of central texts. Many literary critics have argued that modern poetry is also spatial—see Joseph Frank's essay "Spatial Form in Modern Literature." T. S. Eliot, in his essays and his poems, presents a conception of history that is both synchronic and diachronic (narrative) simultaneously. I would argue that the central difference between Morrison and Eliot is that Morrison would challenge his elitist view of literature as a series of monuments. Her investigations of time and historical consciousness are also more directly linked to her progressive politics. Eliot may be concerned with spatial form (in poetry) and a spatial sense of literary history (in "Tradition and the Individual Talent"), but he does not share Morrison's interest in the possibility of spatial memory for every individual, even those of the masses.

6

Historiographic Metafiction and the Celebration of Differences: Ishmael Reed's *Mumbo Jumbo*

W. Lawrence Hogue

Ishmael Reed's *Mumbo Jumbo* works out of a critical matrix akin to the philosophical project of deconstruction. Using Jacques Derrida's *Of Grammatology* and his seminal essay from *Writing and Difference,* "Structure, Sign, and Play in the Discourse of the Human Sciences," I wish to suggest how Reed's novel shares some of the same suppositions as deconstructive thought. In linking deconstruction and *Mumbo Jumbo,* I hope to illustrate the way Reed's fictional practice confirms Linda Hutcheon's sense of postmodern fiction as historiographic metafiction while simultaneously questioning Fredric Jameson's totalizing version of postmodernism.

Derrida's persistent claim that the heritage of Western philosophy effaces alterity harmonizes with Reed's assessment of the Atonist/Wallflower Order, a secret society that symbolizes western civilization in *Mumbo Jumbo.* The Atonist/Wallflower Order is an example of what Derrida calls "logocentrism," which is "the most original and powerful ethnocentrism, in the process of imposing itself on the world" (*Of* 74). Reed critiques Atonism's logocentric values in Western society (both black and white) by overturning binaries and undermining hierarchies, suggesting a postmodern or dispersed way of defining history and reality. In *Mumbo Jumbo* Jes Grew, the feared pandemic that makes whites embrace black cultural identity, is the very phenomenon of postmodernism.

In "Structure, Sign, and Play," Derrida describes the mechanism of logocentrism and explains that the inherited concept of a coherent, totalized structure containing a stable, organizing center is merely that, a *concept:*

The concept of structure and even the word "structure" itself are as old as the *episteme*—that is to say, as old as Western science and Western philosophy—and that their roots thrust deep into the soil of ordinary language [. . . The] structure [. . .] has always been neutralized or reduced, and this by a

> process of giving it a center or of referring it to a point of pres-
> ence, a fixed origin. The function of this center was not only to
> orient, balance, and organize the structure [. . .] but above all
> to make sure that the organizing principle of the structure
> would limit what we might call the play of the structure. (*Writ-
> ing* 278)

This critique of the center usefully describes the structure and content of *Mumbo Jumbo* and its critical take on the novel as a genre. The
traditional novel emerged in eighteenth-century England with the
rise of Enlightenment rationalism and the belief in progress, both of
which are pressed into service to prop up notions of middle-class
respectability. Novels of this period conventionally assume that the
world is linear; that the world has a beginning (origin), middle, and
ending; and that it wills a truth through the mastery of knowledge.
The traditional novel (or detective story) represents itself as a closed
system, as a categorical reality, as an essential truth. It represents
itself as a coherent, totalized structure containing a stable, organizing
center. And in not exposing its signifying practice, the traditional
novel naturalizes itself.

Reed deconstructs the traditional novel and certain naturalized
belief systems of Western civilization. He wants the reader to know
that the traditional novel is not innocent, that it is a construct, and
that it belongs to Western metaphysics. "I think that the Western
novel is tied to Western epistemology," the novelist states in an interview with John O'Brien, "the way people in the West look at the
world. So it is usually realistic and has character development and all
these things that one associates with the Western novel" (31). The
statement suggests three of the strategies Reed employs in *Mumbo
Jumbo,* which involve challenges to novelistic convention, notions of
absolute truth, and linearity.

To take up the first strategy, Reed violates the conventional
reader's expectations by juxtaposing many texts and genres not traditionally associated with the novel. The reader does not know whether
Mumbo Jumbo is a novel, a history, a spell, or a Voodoo narrative. "Of
course," says Reed, "the book has all kinds of styles. There are naturalistic passages and there are some which are not naturalistic. There
are some passages which do what painters do, using peripheral information to explain an event, meshing the factual and the imaginative"
(qtd. in O'Brien 18). *Mumbo Jumbo* mixes romance, necromancy,
hagiography, Egyptology, Voodoo theory of history, movie techniques, American civilization, Western history, black dance, as well

as science fiction and fantasy, with the detective story. The novel opens like a film: the action starts before the title page. As Carol Siri Johnson points out, "Only after the initial reports of the spontaneous epidemic, Jes Grew, do we get the title, publisher, date, epigraph and dedication. Then, like a film, it returns to the story" (27). The movement from chapter to chapter mimics the movement in what Joe Weixlmann calls "quick-splice scene changes" (2).

Throughout *Mumbo Jumbo* a "metafictional impulse plays lightly," "an exuberant parody abounds," and a "purposeful anachronism penetrates its reader's defenses" (Weixlmann 2). Reed's literary canon is permeated by his "unique blend of the verbal and visual, prosaic and poetic, old and new, fictive and factual, serious and satiric, African and American, traditional and popular" (Weixlmann 2). The text, a pseudoacademic system of quotes, footnotes, and even a bibliography, is a mixture of the fictive, or mythical, with the historical. In the very midst of a kidnapping, the text is interrupted to provide—as the motive for the kidnapping itself—the long myth of Osiris. Reed gives the reader a kind of panoramic linguistic "disruption" of the traditional novel through his play with a number of its conventions.

Regarding Reed's second strategy, *Mumbo Jumbo* constantly challenges the reader through exaggeration, as a way of undermining the notion of an absolute truth. He gives enough facts and materials to make *Mumbo Jumbo* sufficiently plausible that the reader cannot reject it. But he also makes the telling of the story so outrageous and fantastic—usually through parody, mimicry, and exaggeration—that the reader cannot accept the text completely. When Reed tells us that sixty-one lynchings occurred in 1920 alone and that sixty-two occurred in 1921, he is referring to historical facts, or at least something that can be verified in the standard annals of history. On the other hand, Reed mixes these verifiable historical events with fictional ones. Reed presents a kind of alternate mythical history concerning Moses, Egyptian gods and goddesses, an ageless Knights Templar, and a mysterious ship from Haiti. This history is pure mythology. While in the invented Osiris myth Moses's visit to Isis may not have the same truth claim as the reference to lynchings, we are certainly left with the question of where exactly we can draw the line between truth and falsity, since the two seem so intertwined. In what sense is history myth and myth, conversely, history? In this nonhierarchical juxtaposition of fact and fiction, *Mumbo Jumbo* allows the reader only to accept a provisional, or a "suspect," truth.

Finally, Reed's third strategy involves an undermining of linearity. At its simplest level, this challenge can be seen as part of his continual assault on novelistic convention. "I think the linear novel is finished," Reed remarked in 1978. "As a matter of fact, I don't think we're going to call [such books] 'novels' anymore—that is a name that is imposed on us. [. . .] I would call mine 'work'" (qtd. in Weixlmann 2). In *Of Grammatology,* Derrida argues that the problem of linearity is that it is part of the metaphysics that contributes to the idea of an absolute, total history. All times are measured in relation to the present; this "linearist concept of time is therefore one of the deepest adherences of the modern concept of the sign to its own history" (72).

Mumbo Jumbo further demonstrates that the concept of linear temporality is "part of the metaphysics that contributes to the idea of an absolute, total history" and that linearity is *only* one of many forms of speech. Therefore, to expose and deconstruct the linear form of speech, Reed violates the expected linear sense of time both by presenting simultaneous narratives and by presenting sequences in non-chronological order. The story of Jes Grew develops simultaneously with the story of Buddy Jackson. Buddy Jackson, who is "noted for his snappy florid-designed multicolored shoes and his grand way of life" (18), is a part of the gang warfare of New York. Because he is a "race man," he acquires boats and ships for Berbelang's operation. He assists in LaBas's arrest of Hinckle Von Vampton. Biff and the white gangs are out to kill Jackson, but they fail. The effects of Jew Grew occur prior to its first trace. Reed appropriates a variety of media such as graphics, pictures, photographs, drawings, posters, anagrams, newspaper clippings, dictionary definitions, symbols, and signs—many of them improvisationally placed in the text and, at times, lacking direct correspondence to the narrative of the text—that function not to illustrate scenes from the plot, as in a traditional novel, but to reinforce visually messages, feelings, and images. And dispersed improvisationally throughout *Mumbo Jumbo* are photographs of people dancing, marching, singing, being alive—obviously as signifiers and representations of Jes Grew. These appropriated organizational modes undermine the notion of linearity and the idea of an absolute, total history.

In undermining closure or mastery through interpretation and language, Reed plays with linguistic refusal, which becomes fundamental to the text through its pervasive signifiers of "Jes Grew." Jes Grew is at the core of *Mumbo Jumbo;* it is its impetus, its raison d'être, its organizational common denominator. But at the same time, Reed withholds Jes Grew. As much as a modern reader may desire a referent for Jes Grew and believe to have "uncovered" it, the text does not have one. Derrida uses the term "trace" to connote signification, which has no referent or origin. In *Mumbo Jumbo* there is, to use Derrida's terms, no "originary presence" of Jes Grew. Jes Grew cannot be "summed up in the simplicity of a present" (*Of* 66). We have only Jes Grew's traces in jazz, ragtime, the storefronts, the band on the Apollo stage, in blues, and in the Creole band. We have only its evidence in the epidemic "acute crisis" it is causing. Jes Grew refuses definition and, therefore, also refuses the typical signifier/signified relationship. But in the text it is never mastered through interpretation and language; it is never successfully labeled and classified.

Furthermore, Reed's novel problematizes certain hegemonic, naturalized Western or American myths, concepts, and beliefs, historical representations that have given the illusion of being essential truths. First, Reed goes back to the decade of the 1920s as a historical period that has many interpretations. Is this decade best defined in the political terms of a Republican presidency as the Age of Harding, or is the legalistic designation Age of Prohibition more accurate? Reed chooses to emphasize the period culturally as the Jazz Age. To represent the 1920s as the Jazz Age is not to say that this representation is better than the others. However, it is to say that, in Reed's case, there is no "natural" way to represent the 1920s, and that representing this decade as the Jazz Age is more appropriate for him because he wants to focus on the realm of cultural—rather than racial— expression. Reed problematizes the whole idea of historical representation by giving a different definition of the 1920s.

Second, this idea of giving a different definition/representation to naturalized cultural referents, thereby problematizing representation and making truth provisional, is again nicely illustrated when Reed renames, and therefore refigures, what we ordinarily refer to as art museums. In *Mumbo Jumbo,* art museums are "pirate dens" or "Centers of Art Detention." By renaming museums in this fashion, Reed reinterprets the referent. The naturalized concept "museum" suggests an innocent, harmonious unification of objects. To use Roland Barthes' notion of naturalized myth, it is "not read as a motive," or as having motivation, "but as a reason": "The adhomination of the concept [museum] can remain manifest without however appearing to have an interest in the matter" (129). In this way, the idea of a museum becomes "frozen into something natural," whereas the terms "Centers of Art Detention" or "pirate dens" suggest struggle, power, and the execution of control over a resisting subject. In calling the museum a center of art detention, Reed refers to the general tendency of Western societies to seize, incorporate, and exploit cultural materials from Africa, Latin America, and Asia. Reed's renaming of museums is part of his larger desires to show how representations are naturalized and to unmask the illusion that meaning can be mastered through interpretation and language. For Reed, the meaning of a sign is the product of motivation with multiple meanings.

The novel's title itself, *Mumbo Jumbo,* presents the problem of meaning, interpretation, and truth. The term "mumbo jumbo" suggests white notions of black gibberish, a recitation of meaningless syllables, especially those connected with such discredited religious practices as Voodoo (Gates 703). But Reed provides an etymology, presenting the terms as having derived from "mandingo" or as evoking a "magician who makes the troubled spirits of ancestors go away" (11). What appears to be "mumbo jumbo" from one perspective may be perfectly meaningful from another.

In addition, the novel itself may appear to be a kind of "mumbo jumbo" in containing a wealth of diverse details, genres, and texts that are all seemingly "jumbled" together. Compared to a traditional novel, such as James Weldon Johnson's *The Autobiography of an Ex-Coloured Man* (1912), which is the archetypal canonical African American novel, *Mumbo Jumbo* has considerable "disorder." The various stylistic devices used by Reed to undermine the conventions of the novel remind the reader of the arbitrariness of conventions, especially of novelistic conventions. In *Mumbo Jumbo,* the reader is constantly forced into the role of the critic, examining the nature and assumptions of various institutions, including the institution of the novel itself. The reader is aware that Reed's work has been "made" by someone and that it is "fictive." In this sense, Reed's fictional practices confirm Hutcheon's sense of postmodern fiction as historiographic metafiction.

Yet despite the novel's seeming disorder, arbitrariness, and undermining of conventions, *Mumbo Jumbo* is organized by a rather complicated and meaningful plot. But the novel's content, like its form, ultimately advocates the values of diversity and spontaneity, which are brought on by the disruptive influences of Jes Grew. The main dramatic action in *Mumbo Jumbo* revolves around the conspiratorial efforts of the Atonist Path's Wallflower Order of the Knights Templar to adulterate Jes Grew, to neutralize its force. Sensing Hamid Abdul's reassembling of its text, Jes Grew breaks out in New Orleans—the charming city that is an amalgam of Spanish and French and African cultures. After spreading throughout the south, from Pine Bluff, Arkansas, to Saint Louis, Missouri, Jes Grew moves north. When it finally reaches Chicago, an epidemic is declared. Jes Grew, the life force that infects its host with black oral/aural culture, is en route to New York in search of its written text.

When Jes Grew initially breaks out in New Orleans, the mayor and his cronies think that it is a plague. Believing that "the local infestation area [is] Place Congo," they "put [. . .] antipathetic substances to work on it, to try to drive it out; but it start[s] to play hide and seek with [them], a case occurring in 1 neighborhood and picking up in another" (4). As the mayor's poker partner tells him, "it's not 1 of those germs that break bleed suck gnaw or devour. It's nothing we can bring into focus or categorize; once we call it 1 thing it forms into something else. No Man. This is a *psychic epidemic*" (4–5). Jes Grew is not a plague; it is an "anti-plague" (6). And although no one knows what it is, everyone knows its effects. Jes Grew *"enliven[s] the host [. . .] Jes Grew victims said that the air was as clear as they had ever seen it and that there was the aroma of roses and perfumes which had never before enticed their nostrils [. . .] Jes Grew is electric as life and is characterized by ebullience and ecstasy[. . .] Jes Grew is the delight of the gods"* (6).

As Jes Grew makes a turn in Chicago for New York, while causing attacks as far away as Europe, the Atonist Path devises strategies to contain it. The Atonist Path does not allow for difference, contradiction, diversity, or heterogeneity. Its mind is one that seeks "to interpret the world by using a single loa. Somewhat like filling a milk bottle with an ocean" (24). Like logocentrism, the Atonist's order is rational and linear. It believes in destiny and progress and, like Western civilization, for the last two thousand years it has attempted to make an orderly world. Its institutions and apparatuses guard the status quo, repressing the Other—the instinctual, the different, and the animal. The poker partner tells the mayor of New Orleans, "if this Jes Grew becomes pandemic it will mean the end of Civilization As We Know It" (4). Although Reed makes the African American Jes Grew's host the United States, he makes it quite salient that it is not *essentially* African American. It exists everywhere; it is a part of everyone's history. It existed in the Europe before the Age of Reason. He defines the United States as "a Protestant country ignorant even of Western mysteries" (30). According to *Mumbo Jumbo*, the Atonists "wiped out the Greek mysteries" (50).

Through its secret society, the Wallflower Order, the Atonist Path maintains order: *"Only they could defend the cherished traditions of the West against Jes Grew"* (15). The Wallflower Order attempts to meet the psychic plague by installing an anti-Jes Grew president, Warren Harding. It decides that it must get its "hands on Jes Grew's hunger. That text" (64). Therefore, the Atonist Hierophant 1 kidnaps Hinckle von Vampton and puts him in charge of finding the text and creating a Talking Android—which entails "creating a 'spokesman' who would furtively work to prepare the New Negro to resist Jes Grew and not catch it" (190). After meeting with his top aides, Attorney General Harry M. Daugherty goes before the camera to read "recommendations in a bill to be sent to Kongress. A way of allaying the Jes Grew crisis which threatens our National Security, survival and just about everything else you can think of" (93). And as President Harding looks on, raids are made of Washington speak-easies. "NO DANCING! signs of huge black letters and exclamation points are posted throughout the city" (93–94).

Struggling to contain Jes Grew, the Atonists attack PaPa LaBas because they know that he is in contact with Jes Grew. They launch a long series of annoyances against him. There is harassment from the police, constant inspections of his Mumbo Jumbo Kathedral by the fire department, and reviews of his tax records. An endorsement of one of his techniques by Irene Castle causes the "vicious campaign aimed at him" to abate. But when she moves to the right of Jes Grew and begins "consulting the Goverment on the Epidemic," the hostility and harassment against LaBas are renewed.

Adding to the complicated plot of *Mumbo Jumbo,* various characters such as Papa LaBas, Hinckle Von Vampton, and Berbelang encounter various problems and resistances. Some of these characters are heroic and others villainous, but none are presented uncritically. PaPa LaBas, who is from a long line of Jes Grew carriers, runs the Mumbo Jumbo Kathedral, a center for Voodoo practice, in Harlem. He is the detective who is trying to find Jes Grew's text. "People trust his powers. They've seen him knock a glass from a table by staring in its direction; and fill a room with the sound of forest animals" (24). He is intuitive; he rejects "empirical evidence," preferring to understand and interpret phenomena through dreams, feelings, and his "Knockings." He is in a continual struggle with the Atonist Order to maintain his practice.

Meeting Fuentos and Yellow Jack in an Art History class at City College, Berbelang enters into a "pact" and organizes with them, along with Thor Wintergreen, the multicultural *Mu'tafikah* whose objective is to "return the plundered art to Africa, South America and China, the ritual accessories which had been stolen so that [they] could see the gods return and the spirits aroused." They want "to conjure a spiritual hurricane which would lift the debris of 2,000 years from its roots and fling it about" (87–88). The task is quite dangerous because the contents of these centers of art detention are guarded by a powerful Atonist system. Nevertheless, the *Mu'tafikah* raid museums throughout Europe. The reader follows Berbelang and the *Mu'tafikah* as they attempt to liberate the four-and-one-half-ton Olmec head from Biff Musclewhite's Center for Art Detention and return it to Central America. Finally, there is Hinckle Von Vampton, who is released from his job at the New York *Sun* for printing information about Jes Grew that white authorities prefer to keep from readers. Brought before the Atonist leader, Hierophant 1, Hinckle pledges his support to the Atonist cause and begins his own newspaper, the *Benign Monster,* which is ostensibly devoted to the black arts movement; in fact, the paper's true purpose is to authenticate white Western civilization and to assist in the controlling of Jes Grew. The narratives of LaBas, Berbelang, and Von Vampton are told simultaneously as *Mumbo Jumbo* charts the journey of Jes Grew, informs the reader of the mythical history of Osiris, and tells us the stories of other characters, such as Hamid Abdul, Earline, Nathan Brown, Woodrow Wilson Jefferson, and Charlotte. Thus, *Mumbo Jumbo* has a complicated but clearly defined plot.

As Jes Grew comes within sixty miles of New York, Atonist Hierophant 1 thinks, "Things look hopeless. It has been an interesting 2,000 years but this is the end of the road. 2,000 years of probing classifying attempting to make an 'orderly' world so that when company came they would know the household's nature and would be careful about dropping ashes on the rug. 2,000 years of patrolling the plants. He would miss the daily species count" (153). Hierophant 1 senses the end of two thousand years of Atonist rule. As he is about to commit suicide, the red button on the Jes Grew board lights up and Walter Mellon of the Wallflower Order in America informs him that he has "made it." Again, Jes Grew fails to find its text and therefore bring about the end of Western civilization "As We Know It." As a solution to the institutional spread of Jes Grew, Mellon offers to take money out of circulation so that people will not be able to support the appendages of Jes Grew, "the cabarets the jook joints and the speaks" (154). Mellon suggests replacing these appendages of Jes Grew by subsidizing "the 100s of symphony orchestras across the country," having "government-sponsored Waltz-boosting campaigns," and dispersing "the art from the Art Detention Center so that if the *Mu'tafikah* strike again all of the pillage won't be in 1 place" (154–55). This move precipitates the Depression.

The "desire for a center" is the compulsion of Atonists such as

Hinckle Von Vampton, Hierophant 1, Biff Musclewhite—who is described as "the man who tamed the wilderness" (107)—and others to locate themselves as a center, a fixed nucleus, in order to encompass and order the play of mutable elements of history. Their Atonist narrative schema produces a particular representation of the world they have ruled for the last two thousand years. The organizing principle of their narrative—in this instance, Western, rational, Judeo-Christian, white male desire—limits the play of Western civilization. Since Jes Grew threatens "civilization in the West as we know it," the Atonists must destroy or neutralize it. And in this two-thousand-year-old civilization, the Atonists confess to stand on solid grounds simultaneously at the center of, and external to, history, creating boundaries specifically designed to circumscribe the contents of history, and above all, to limit the scope of their play. For the last two thousand years, the plurality, heterogeneity, and diversity of history die at the hands of the Atonists. By shrinking the fabric of history and by creating a center that orients, balances, and organizes Western civilization, Reed's Atonists find themselves its masters.

The Atonist Path's narrative is built on what Derrida terms the "deception that the center [is] sheltered from play" (*Writing* 296). In assuming mastery over language, the Atonists (like Jameson) locate themselves as sturdy points of presence where no permutation occurs. They assume a position of subjective sovereignty consistent with a humanistic Western metaphysical, logocentric worldview.

Crucially, it is this very dynamic of delimiting as a means of controlling and assuring privileged selfhood that informs the Atonists' relationship with and representations of Jes Grew, African Americans, and the non-Atonists throughout the text—a fact that for Reed has violent, exploitative consequences. *Mumbo Jumbo* views history-making narratives that propose to represent the past—viewing language as a simple means of transcribing supposedly inevitable realities—as what Derrida calls "motivated repressions" (*Positions* 6) and "calculated effacements" (*Of* 142) that serve to dominate Jes Grew and its practitioners and to minimize their prospective subject position. The Atonists represent individuals and cultures that embody creative, instinctive, and anarchic impulses as Other. But in exposing the strategies of their various institutions and apparatuses, Reed shows how Western history is not "natural" but is a construct, the product of a signifying practice. He shows how it is the product of motivation, of a "force of desire."

To establish a framework to discuss how *Mumbo Jumbo* exposes Western metaphysics and its notion of a totalized history and thereby offers a postmodern or plural way of defining history, I want to summarize the Jameson-Hutcheon debate. In *Postmodernism, or, The Cultural Logic of Late Capitalism,* Jameson offers his characterization of postmodernity in socioeconomic terms. As the title of his book indicates, Jameson intends to demonstrate that a fundamental global economic shift has caused a new social era to emerge. Jameson identifies the new area of commodification for multinational capitalism as preeminently representation itself. He defines the production, exchange, marketing, and consumption of cultural forms as a central focus and expression of economic activity. If cultural forms are economically based, how does one go about analyzing a situation that is deterministic? In the loss of history, the dissolution of the centered subject, and the fading of individual style, it becomes immensely difficult for Jameson to specify the nature and direction of postmodernity.

Hutcheon, on the other hand, in critiquing Jameson, argues that postmodernism, in possessing a parodic impulse, is capable of performing social critique. Historiographic metafiction includes those "well-known and popular novels which are both intensely self-reflexive and yet paradoxically also lay claim to historical events and personages. [. . . It] incorporates all three of these domains: that is, its theoretical self-awareness of history and fiction as human constructs [. . .] is made the grounds for its rethinking and reworking of the forms and contents of the past" (*Poetics* 5).

Mumbo Jumbo operates as an example of Hutcheon's historiographic metafiction, for Reed works within the traditional conventions in order to subvert them. And in the subversion, Reed offers a social critique of oppressive and violent social, racial, and economic structures in the West, such as the linear, singular, closed narrative of the Atonist Path and its totalized, unified, and coherent narrative of history. Unlike Jameson, Reed would interpret any totalized reading of history as a repression of history's endless play of differences, as a subduing of history's plurality and heterogeneity. Reed, to use Hutcheon's words, does not believe that history is obsolete, but is "being rethought—as a human construct" (*Poetics* 16).

The struggle in the 1920s between the Atonist/Wallflower Order and the followers of Jes Grew has its origin in an invented myth of Osiris. Reed uses this myth along with historical figures and facts not only to undermine the notion of a singular, centered history but also to show history as a dispersed, human construct. According to Theodore O. Mason, Jr., Reed rewrites the Egyptian myths of Osiris and Set in order to establish a mythic, transhistorical opposition between two kinds of consciousness: the psychologically liberated and the mechanically inhibited. In PaPa LaBas's account of the myth, it is a parody of the two kinds of consciousness in Western civilization that are located within the Osiris-Set conflict. In fact, Reed constructs his myth so that Moses of the Old Testament becomes a disciple of Set and continues his destructive practices (101). The influence of Set leads to Christianity's fundamentally repressive theology. This mythic, transhistorical opposition is reduplicated in Reed's 1920s. The descendents of Set are the members of the Wallflower Order, which comprises forces tending toward social and psychological rigidity. The descendents of Osiris, on the other hand, are the followers of Jes Grew.

Mixing historical and fictional events and characters, *Mumbo Jumbo* refigures a history in which—from the Emperor Constantine, the medieval papacy, Milton, and Cromwell, through Freud, Wilson, Coolidge, and Hitler—the Atonists have repressed the instinctive, the mystical, and the rhythmic. But even Western historical figures have contributed to the Atonist status quo. Karl Marx and Friedrich Engels's objective scientific research repressed or ignored alterity, denying its mystery. Sigmund Freud, who created the psychoanalytical framework for twentieth-century Western civilization, was an Atonist. He did not know the Work, the mysteries. As an Atonist, he is a *"part of Jealous Art which shut out of itself all traces of animism"* (45).

Unlike the Atonists, who totalize history, the Voodoo practitioners, or the followers of Jes Grew, symbolize forces of oppressed freedom, flexibility, diversity, and spontaneity. They are contesting, in Hutcheon's terms, the Atonists' power to "control history" (197). They embody Jes Grew, which cannot be rationally labeled, classified, or categorized. "It knows no class no race no consciousness. It is self-propagating and you can never tell when it will hit" (5). In describing the theological dimension of Jes Grew, Reed refers to "the ancient Vodun aesthetic: pantheistic, becoming, 1 which bountifully permits 1000s of spirits, as many as the imagination can hold. Infinite Spirits and Gods" (35). The idea of infinite spirits puts a positive twist on the idea of mumbo jumbo as a collection of many different things. These varied elements do not represent mumbo jumbo negatively. Rather, they take on meaning in terms of assertion; they take on meaning in terms of the celebration of life, as the "delights of the gods."

But in deconstructing Atonism as a closed, repressive system that limits the play of differences, Reed is not countering with another totalizing, rational system. Instead, Reed's Voodoo is an undogmatic system, infinitely adaptable to new ideas, new truths, new forms and methods.[1] A new loa can be added at any time. The way Reed presents Voodoo in *Mumbo Jumbo* is less as a religious orthodoxy with rigid rules, norms, and conventions than as a way of living in the world that values flexibility, adaptability, heterogeneity, and individual creativity.

The always elusive "text" that Jes Grew is seeking promises an articulating ordering of discontinuous experiences and a bringing together of all the separate variations of African American experiences. "So Jes Grew is seeking its words. Its texts. For what good is a liturgy without a text" (6). The unifying verbal articulation of Jes Grew (finding its own text) promises a greater power, one that can threaten the Wallflower Order and one that the Wallflower Order wants to keep from African Americans. If Jes Grew reaches New York and "cohabits with what it's after [, t]hen it will be a pandemic and you will really see something. And then *they* will be finished" (25). Yet while Reed and the practitioners of Jes Grew yearn for this power, and may in some sense embody it provisionally in *Mumbo Jumbo,* Reed wants to preserve the power and the value of individual difference. He wants to acknowledge discontinuous African American experiences. "*Individuality. It couldn't be herded, rounded-up; it was like crystals of winter each different from one another but in a storm going down together. What would happen if they dispersed, showing up when you least expected them; what would happen if you couldn't predict their minds?*" (140). If Jes Grew were to find its text, it would become just another rational, predictable, categorized, Atonist system.

From the outset, *Mumbo Jumbo,* through its play with representational constructs and playful representation of Jes Grew as a driving yet undefinable force, wishes to undermine the construct of a unified text. In spite of this, the novel also appears to construct a clear binary; in fact, it seems to construct the most typical Western binary of division between the Atonists, on the one hand, and the followers of Jes Grew, on the other. Throughout much of *Mumbo Jumbo,* Reed appears to confirm the work of Berbelang and the *Mu'tafikah,* PaPa LaBas and the Mumbo Jumbo Kathedral, and Black Herman. Since Reed consistently places himself on Jes Grew's side by declaring its ability to liberate its followers, the binary that emerges is the righteousness of the Jes Grew followers contrary to the egregiousness of the Atonists.

But even with this most basic binary that emerges from *Mumbo*

Jumbo, Reed finds ways to undermine it. First, Atonists are not monolithic; they have differences. In Reed's invented myth of Osiris, the Atonists are not represented as monolithic. The Knights Templar, one of the military Christian orders during the Crusades, were killed by the Teutonic Knights because the Templars had attained too much power and were threatening the power of the hegemonic Teutonic Knights. As Battraville explains to LaBas and Black Herman, "there are many types of Atonists. Politically they can be 'Left,' 'Right,' 'Middle,' but they are all together on the sacredness of Western Civilization and its mission. They merely disagree on the ways of sustaining it" (136).

Reed illustrates this diversity among the Atonists best with Biff Musclewhite and Thor Wintergreen. In his decision to include Thor Wintergreen in the multicultural *Mu'tafikah,* Berbelang takes a big risk. Defining Western history in terms of the Faust myth, Berbelang claims that the real point of the story is that Faust is a charlatan, a *bokor.* Berbelang's interpretation of the Faust myth, argues Peter Nazareth, is that "perhaps deep down, Western man *knows* that he has been stealing the art and creativeness of non-Western and *knows* he is a fake" (221). Responding to Berbelang's interpretation of the Faust myth, Thor says, "I'm just 1 man. Not Faust nor the Kaiser nor the Ku Klux Klan. I am an individual, not a whole tribe or nation" (92). "That's what I'm counting on," replies Berbelang. "But if there is such a thing as a racial soul, a piece of Faust the mountebank residing in a corner of the White man's mind, then we are doomed" (92). But Thor is weakened by an appeal to his race, class, and tribe. "Son," says Biff Musclewhite, "this is a nigger closing in on *our* mysteries and soon he will be asking *our* civilization to 'come quietly.' This man is talking about Judeo-Christian culture, Christianity, Atonism whatever you want to call it" (114; emphasis added). Thor tearfully unties Musclewhite, who proceeds to kill Berbelang, Charlotte, and finally Thor himself.

But between the two, Thor is considered better than Biff. As Biff says, "I know you look down on me because I come from one of the European countries under domination by stronger Whites than my people. We were your niggers; you colonized us and made us dirt under your heels" (111–12). Here, Reed is defining Atonist history not only as one of dispersion, but also one that has been represented by hegemonic Atonists as unified. A close scrutiny of Atonist history shows oppositions, binaries, and hierarchies. It also shows a fictive schema that neutralizes the play of differences. Earlier, I discussed the (Atonist) Teutonic Knights oppressing the (Atonist) Knights Templar. Here, Biff, the supposed representative of the oppressor in the Atonist/Jes Grew binary, becomes the oppressed in the Thor/Biff binary. He is the Other within a white schema. He too has suffered under the Atonist domination in the West.

Reed also defines African American history and culture as one of dispersion. He is responding to those African American scholars, particularly the makers of the canon of African American literature who attempt to impose a single interpretation on African American differences. Reed seems to be saying that African Americans do not constitute a monolithic group, but instead, a multiplicity of responses to a commonly perceived situation: racial oppression and otherization. Reed points to the diversity of African American experiences, critical of those African Americans who would try to unify those experiences as *only* one thing. For example, Woodrow Wilson Jefferson, who must be "saved" by his backwoods preacher father, has an unfortunate leaning toward the values of Atonism and a unifying singular. Woodrow Jefferson leaves Rē´-mōte Mississippi "to quit the farm and hit the Big City" (New York) because he wants to "make something out of himself" and to "abandon this darkness for the clearing" (29). While in New York, he enters the office of the New York *Tribune* because he wants to meet Karl Marx and Friedrich Engels (75). He likes the journalistic style of Marx and Engels, evident in the articles they had written for the *Tribune* of the mid-nineteenth century. Jefferson is especially enamored of Marx and Engels's "objective, scientific [approach], the use of the collective We, Our" (29).

Abdul Hamid, as representative of Black Muslim Nationalism, also serves as a vehicle for Reed's critique of overly unifying, dogmatic approaches to problems facing African Americans. Abdul, a noted magazine editor who "wears a bright red fez and a black pinstriped suit and a black tie emblazoned with the crescent moon symbol" (33), is translating an "anthology that's really going to shake them up" (39). He assembles the Jes Grew text and even translates the Book of Thoth from the hieroglyphics. However, because he is completely ignorant of the text's value, he burns it. Hamid's monotheism parallels that of the Eurocentric Christians and is opposed to many of the same values of difference, creativity, and spontaneity as they are.

Despite his monotheism, Reed allows even Abdul a certain validity. Abdul also advocates plurality. He states:

> This country is eclectic. The architecture the people the music the writing. The thing that works here will have a little bit of jive talk and a little bit of North Africa, a fez-wearing mulatto in a

> pinstriped suit. A man who can say give me some skin as well as Asalamilakum. [. . .] Perhaps I will come up with something that will have a building shaped like a mosque, the interior furnishings Victorian, the priests dressed in Catholic garb, and soul food as offerings. What of it as long as it has popular appeal? (Reed 38)

His eclecticism is positive. Hamid Abdul may be complimented insofar as his approach is creatively adaptable. But Abdul dies at the end of the text. Reed seems to think that his cult of personality leans toward the values of the unifying singular.

Even Papa LaBas fails to embody completely Reed's heterogenous Voodoo system. Despite the fact that LaBas is a direct descendent of the carriers of Jes Grew to the United States and that he has devoted his life to the loas, Reed uses Abdul to critique LaBas, who is due some criticism for being too rigid and insulated. Abdul exposes LaBas's and Black Herman's inability to adjust to current times. He believes that they "have something. Something that is basic, something that has been tested and something that all of our people have, it lies submerged in their talk and in their music and you are trying to bring it back but you will fail. It's the 1920s, not 8000 B.C. These are modern times" (38). "Maybe what you say is true about the nature of religions which occurred 1000s of years ago, but how are we going to survive if they have no discipline?" (37). (And from what we learn about LaBas in the 1920s and 1960s, Abdul's prediction comes true.) After the conversation with Abdul at the Rent party, LaBas asks Black Herman, "Do you think we're out of date as he said?" (40). At the end, Jes Grew dies out and LaBas, who has naturalized his version of Jes Grew, is last seen speaking to a black studies class in the 1960s and being considered a relic of the Jazz Age.

Nathan Brown, like Papa LaBas, embodies Reed's idea of diversity. But Brown, too, has limitations. He is a New Negro poet "whose work commingles Death and Nature in haunting ways" and has published a collection of poetry called *Dark Crepuscule,* which is "solidly in the Western tradition" (116). Brown is also a Christian. PaPa LaBas thinks the poet is "serious about his Black Christ, however absurd that may sound, for Christ is so unlike African loas and Orishas, in so many essential ways, that this alien becomes a dangerous intruder in the Afro-American mind, an unwelcome gatecrasher into Ifé, home of the spirits" (97).

But Nathan Brown is able to use materials from both European and African cultures. "I have been educated in both cultures and so I use the advantage of both" (117), he says. This double influence is to be used in Harlem schools to counter the negative influence of such people as the nefarious Hinckle Von Vampton. He rejects Von Vampton's notion of a singular "Negro Experience," refuting the idea that "all Negroes experience the world the same way. In that way [Von Vampton] can isolate the misfits who would propel them into penetrating the ceiling of this bind [he and his] assistants have established in this country" (117).

Thus, all of the characters as unified, humanist subjects have limitations, and *Mumbo Jumbo* recognizes their constraints. But Reed, in undermining totalized, centered notions of historical events and of unified subjects among the Atonists and the followers of Jes Grew and in showing their diversity, heterogeneity, and plurality, represents history as characterized by a kind of dispersion in which groups and individuals have constructed, totalized histories. Describing the repression that accompanies unified notions of history, Michel Foucault in *The Archaeology of Knowledge* writes: "Take the notion of tradition: it is intended to give a special temporal status to a group of phenomena that are both successive and identical [. . .]; it makes it possible to rethink the dispersion of history into the form of the same; it allows a reduction of the difference proper to every beginning, in order to pursue within discontinuity the endless search for the origin. [. . .] We must question those ready-made syntheses, those groupings that we normally accept before any examination [. . .] we must accept [. . .] that [. . .] they concern only a population of dispersed events" (21–22). *Mumbo Jumbo* eschews tradition and a unified notion of history in order to redefine history as consisting of dispersions, ruptures, and discontinuities. Reed offers a notion of history that, to use Foucault's terms, "has broken up the long series formed by the progress of consciousness, or the teleology of reason, or the evolution of human thought" (8). It is a notion of history that presents "itself in the form of dispersed events— decisions, accidents, initiatives, discoveries; the materials, which through analysis, had to be rearranged, reduced, effaced in order to reveal the continuity of events" (8).

But Jes Grew, which is at the core of *Mumbo Jumbo,* unlike the characters in the text, does not possess this humanist constraint. It has "no end and no beginning (origin)." It has no class, race, or consciousness. It has no referent. It is what Jean-François Lyotard calls the postmodern: "that which, in the modern, puts forward the unpresentable in presentation itself; that which denies itself the solace of good forms, the consensus of a taste which would make it possible to share collectively the nostalgia for the unattainable; that which searches for new presentation, not in order to enjoy them but in order to impart a stronger sense of the unpresentable" (81). In a remarkable kind of way, *Mumbo Jumbo* gives us Jes Grew as the "unpresentable in presentation itself" because Jes Grew has no "good form." It has no "nostalgia for the unattainable," except as it is imputed by its followers. In *Mumbo Jumbo* Reed has found a "new presentation" to "impart a stronger sense of the unpresentable."

According to *Mumbo Jumbo,* Voodoo adapts: Muslim Nationalists, urban writers, Christian preachers, and Marxists are all part of the African American experience. To the extent that they remain flexible and nondogmatic, making use of various traditions or texts, the characters are "doing the right thing." But if, conversely, as does Woodrow Wilson Jefferson, the reverend's son, they allow themselves to be true believers in a single system or idea and thus become agents of a particular totalized ideology, attempting to enforce conformity on others, or force their views on others, those figures ultimately are as off-base as Hamid is.

Thus Reed, like Hutcheon and unlike Jameson, defines history in nonhumanistic terms. There is no movement toward utopia; history is a pendulum. It is a construct, and any attempt to totalize it is to repress the play of differences, to colonize and appropriate history, the variegated past, within a singular rhetorical embrace, enfolding and subduing its frustrating diversity and its motion.

Notes

1. Discussing Reed's concept of Voodoo, Reginald Martin writes: "Voodoo [. . .] thrives because of its syncretic flexibility; its ability to take anything, even ostensibly negative influences, and transfigure them into that which helps the horse. It is bound by certain dogma or rites, but such rules are easily changed when they become oppressive, myopic, or no longer useful to current situation" (71).

7

Troping the Renaissance: Postmodern Historiography and Early Modern History

Paul Budra

There are parallels between the early modern period and the emergent postmodern period, specifically cultural liminalities centered on the reconstruction of the subject and the fragmentation or subversion of established discourses, that lead to tempting analogues between the periods. This in part explains the interesting reevaluations of early modernity, especially early modern literary history, that scholarship has been witness to over the past thirty or so years.[1] Those reevaluations that have coalesced into theoretical stances firm enough to attract labels—new historicism, cultural materialism— have tellingly had at the center of their concerns the questions of historical narrative or, at the very least, have stressed, as Louis Montrose states, "a reciprocal concern with the historicity of texts and the textuality of histories" (5).

But, while these postmodern critical positions have been convenient sites from which to recognize both the cultural practices of the early modern period and its canonical historical representations (both early modern and scholarly), they have been less successful at recognizing the tropic nature of recent historical representations. I will argue that the conjunction of postmodern historiography and early modern literary history has resulted in the paradoxical entrenchment, or reentrenchment, of at least one teleology-driven historical narrative that merely substitutes, but does not deconstruct, postmodern paranoia for early modern providence. Further, this reassertion of narrative has blurred the lines between popular and scholarly representations of the Renaissance.

As is well known, postmodernity has not been kind to historical representation. And the postmodern distrust of master narratives has paralleled, or perhaps precipitated, a fragmentation of discourse which is itself an assault on the authority of all discourse: "the narrative function is losing its functors, its great hero, its great dangers, its great voyages, its great goal. It is being dispersed in clouds of narrative language elements—narrative, but also denotative, prescriptive, descriptive, and so on" (Lyotard xxiv). For historians and historiographers this dispersal is doubly problematic. For if all patterns of meaning, all teleologies, are suspect, then whenever one appears to emerge from the historical record two possibilities present themselves: either, and more likely, the pattern is a projection of the discoverer; or, second and more dramatic, if an undeniable pattern exists, it must be manmade, the manifestation of some historically located controlling facility. The historiographical implications of the former have been articulated in the theories of, among others, Hayden White who, calling on the earlier work of Claude Lévi-Strauss and Roland Barthes, recognizes the inescapably tropic nature of narrative discourse along with the cultural predetermination of those narrative tropes and the resultant inevitable encoding of the historical record (*Tropics* 51–80).

The result for historical narrative? Linda Hutcheon argues that "in both fiction and history writing today, our confidence in empiricist and positivist epistemologies has been shaken—shaken, but perhaps not yet destroyed" (*Poetics* 106). This has resulted, in Hutcheon's theory, in the emergence of historiographic metafiction, which "keeps distinct its formal auto-representation and its historical context, and in so doing problematizes the very possibility of historical knowledge, because there is no reconciliation, no dialectic here—just unresolved contradiction" (106). In this formulation, postmodern historical representations (including fiction and film) retain their parodic impulse and are, therefore, capable of performing an implicated social critique, but they are relentlessly self-conscious and, therefore, must position themselves ironically to their historical subject matter. And so the practice of postmodern historical fiction is to carefully eschew closure and to draw attention to the constructedness of the emergent teleology, its arbitrariness or its cultural specificity. John Fowles's *The French Lieutenant's Woman* (1969), for example, uses contradictory source materials and a double ending, one typical of nineteenth-century fiction and the other of twentieth-century fiction, to constantly remind its reader of the epistemological constraints inherent in historical narrative. As Hutcheon neatly summarizes, "to think historically these days is to think critically and contextually" (88).

But what about the second possibility? That is, what if an examination of the historic record reveals an undeniable pattern, the manifestation of that historically located controlling facility? This second possibility has informed popular culture of the postmodern period from Elvis sightings to *The X-Files;* indeed, it seems to have formed an essential part of the American psyche since the assassination of John Kennedy, so much so that Don DeLillo has declared this "the age of conspiracy" (qtd. in Pinsker 624). Popular literary discourse provides a form that specifically deals with the uncovering of such manmade teleologies, the recognition of master narrative constructs, the exposing of conspiracy. This is the mystery novel, or the thriller—a narrative in which a protagonist uncovers an elaborate crime, or a threat, a *real* master narrative, and, during a series of adventures, engages with it. It is not surprising then that DeLillo himself and other late-twentieth-century writers have adopted the conventions of this genre to dramatize the problems of coherence that the postmodern condition has imposed on representation, especially historical representation. The novels of Thomas Pynchon, such as *The Crying of Lot 49* (1967), or Umberto Eco's *Foucault's Pendulum* (1989), depict protagonists that stumble upon massive conspiracies—or do they? Perhaps they, like their readers, are imposing order where none exists.

Fredric Jameson has suggested that postmodern cultural texts have succumbed to nostalgia in their relation to history:

> Cultural production is thereby driven back inside a mental space which is no longer that of the old monadic subject but rather that of some degraded collective "objective spirit": it can no longer gaze directly on some putative real world, at some reconstruction of a past history which was once itself a present; rather, as in Plato's cave, it must trace out mental images of that past upon its confining walls. If there is any realism left here, therefore, it is a "realism" which is meant to derive from the shock of grasping that confinement and of slowly becoming aware of a new and original historical situation in which we are condemned to seek History by way of our own pop images and simulacra of that history, which itself remains forever out of reach. (*Postmodernism* 25)

This confinement in the collective has led, in historical narrative, to pastiche, the emotionally flat appropriation of previously articulated styles, often the styles of popular forms. For Jameson this slippage into "pop history" is a denuding of historic reality, a "loss of the radical past," a further indictment of postmodernity as the cultural logic of late capitalism.

But whether we view the historiographic metafiction generated by a paranoia about teleology as capable of implicated, if self-conscious, social critique (Hutcheon's argument), or lament the reduction of historical narrative to a pastiche of popular styles and images (Jameson's argument), what is interesting here is where the historical representations of early modernity, both fiction *and* nonfiction representations, have slipped. They have, in recent years, appropriated (or succumbed to) the narrative tropes of the thriller in order to trace in nascent modernity a substitute providence—a providence that is political and covert enough to satisfy a generation of scholars who cut their historical teeth on the writings of Michel Foucault and that serves as an analogue to their own postmodern interpretive act: as the thriller protagonist uncovers budding plots for world domination, so the scholar and writer uncovers the budding structures of political modernity in Renaissance history. This is a reworking, then, of the idea of the "scholarly adventurer" put forward in the middle of the Cold War by Richard D. Altick: "He must solve knotty mysteries by cryptography, scientific analysis of ink and paper, and the cunning use of, say, old railroad timetables and army muster rolls. [. . .] At the end of his trail may lie the imposing criminal record of the man who wrote the *Morte Darthur* [or] the truth about the last days of Christopher Marlowe" (3). But written larger, for now the scholar adventure is not merely uncovering obscured information, he is exposing the forces that would coalesce into the structures of capitalism, nationalism, and rationalism, the modern *Weltgeist* itself.

This would help explain why, of late, some historians of the Renaissance period have fetishized the spy state. These postmodern scholarly minds have been busy tracing the birth of modern surveillance and intelligence gathering to give us a picture of Tudor England peopled by shadowy figures, governed through secret plots, and ordered by covert agency. For example, Alan Haynes's *Invisible Power: The Elizabethan Secret Service 1570–1603* is an overview of Elizabethan espionage told through a series of specific cases that occurred during Elizabeth's reign. In this book Sir Francis Walsingham emerges as a central figure in the understanding of Elizabethan culture as a whole. For Haynes, he and his crew of cryptographers are largely finders of hidden meanings. Espionage, then, provides an emblem of the literary critic and historian, those who discover meaning where it is hidden or made obscure by the fragmentation of record.

Taking a broader view of espionage culture, John Archer in *Sovereignty and Intelligence* starts with the Foucauldian principle that "there is no power relation without the correlative constitution of a field of knowledge" (Archer 27) and examines a series of texts, from Michel de Montaigne's *Essais* to Francis Bacon's *New Atlantis,* for acknowledgment of the relation between the Elizabethan monarchy and a burgeoning surveillance bureaucracy.

While scholarly representations of the early modern literary period may be calling on the narratives of popular fiction to rewrite the period as conspiracy-laden, popular representations of the period either articulate it in narratives that blur the line between scholarly and popular representation, or reject conspiracy narrative for a more fractured, iconoclastic and, ironically, postmodern discourse. For examples of the former tendency I will look at recent representations, both biographies and novels, of the life of Christopher Marlowe, for the latter, I will look at fictions of the life of William Shakespeare.

In Charles Nicholl's 1992 history, *The Reckoning: The Murder of Christopher Marlowe,* Nicholl sets out to solve the riddle of Marlowe's death. He works backward and out from the coroner's inquest into the death of Marlowe by Ingram Frizer in a tavern on 30 May 1593. He begins with the setting, the official story, and the witnesses to the killing. Chapter 2 takes us into the reactions to Marlowe's death, and the subsequent chapters piece together the "scraps of paper, pieces of a jigsaw, the nagging sense of unfinished business" (329) that is the plot behind that death. Nicholl works primarily by tracing the histories of the three other men in the room with Marlowe when he died: Frizer, Nicholas Skeres, and Robert Poley. The latter two prove the most interesting; Nicholl places them both in the sting operation that exposed the Babington plot and, therefore, in the same circles of Tudor espionage as Marlowe. Once that connection is made a host of others emerges, ultimately leading us to the fierce rivalry between Sir Walter Raleigh and the Earl of Essex for the favor of the queen. Marlowe was, notoriously, of Raleigh's "School of the Night"; Skeres worked for Essex. Nicholl theorizes that Marlowe was killed during the machinations of the Essex faction to discredit Raleigh: "Until now, the biographers have seen the Dutch Church libel as the *chance* cause of Marlowe's troubles in 1593" (288). Nicholl, as his pointed italics suggest, isn't buying that. Rather, the libel was an attempt to smear Raleigh through association, but after Marlowe was sprung by the influence of Sir Robert Cecil, he became a liability. Thomas Phelippes, a former code breaker for Walsingham who moved into Essex's employ with the death of the spymaster in 1590, becomes the William Casey of this Tudor Watergate. "Little pockmarked Phelippes, peering out through his dusty spectacles" (301), dispatched Skeres to hire Frizer, the story's G. Gordon Liddy, and have Marlowe assassinated.

Now, in theory, that is, in *postmodern* theory, Nicholl should be able to allow the historical fragments surrounding Marlowe's death that he and other investigators have uncovered to remain: the "scraps of paper, pieces of a jigsaw, the nagging sense of unfinished business"

(329). This is exactly what Jean-François Lyotard is describing in his "clouds of narrative language elements." But Nicholl cannot let them stand in all their ambiguity. He ends the main part of the book like this: "Putting these fragments together, I conclude that the cause of Marlowe's death was a perception [. . .] of political necessity. He died in the hands of political agents: a victim, though not an innocent victim, of the court intrigues that flourished in his 'queasy time' of change and succession" (329). But the form of the book predetermined this conclusion. And, I would argue, that form is signalled by the book's title, a tip-off to the popular discourse it has engaged. *The Reckoning* has a Robert Ludlumesque gravity to it, the macho resonance of a crime pot-boiler or *film noir.* The book's subtitle, "The Murder of Christopher Marlowe," elaborates on these connotations: Marlowe's death was not accidental, was not death by misadventure or even manslaughter—it was murder, and murders need solutions. Further, political murders mean conspiracies, and conspiracies must be exposed. The book is prefaced by two epigraphs: the first is from Lord Burghley and is dated 1593: "I find the matter as in a labyrinth: easier to enter into than to go out." The second runs as follows: "Espionage is the secret theatre of our society." That is from 1989, and the writer is John le Carré. The early modern quote, ironically, summarizes the postmodern epistemology: reality is a labyrinth from which there is no exit, for to exit would be to allow for linear progress and absolute truth (the truth of the labyrinth's solution), both of which are denied by postmodern scepticism. The second quote, from le Carré, is, of course, the one that dominates Nicholl's book. For le Carré, as for Nicholl, it is espionage, a political practice that constructs teleologies all around us, waiting to be uncovered by the secret agent (or the Renaissance scholar), that shapes history. And while the historians of the Renaissance had God as the author of providence, Nicholl has Sir Francis Walsingham, Elizabeth's spymaster, exposer of the Babington Plot, a convenient figure who has emerged in recent scholarly and popular reconstructions of the Renaissance as a fixed center and generator of meaning, a playwright of the secret theater.

The Reckoning, like *Invisible Power* and *Sovereignty and Intelligence,* is a history book, but the line between it and historical fiction is often unclear. It was marketed to a popular as well as a scholarly audience, and many of the descriptive details of the text serve the function of heightening suspense rather than transmitting historical information. History or thriller? Metafiction or pastiche? The division is not clear in other recent "fictions" of the age of Marlowe. In

1993 two novels that deal with the death of Christopher Marlowe appeared. The first is a novel by Robin Chapman entitled *Christoferus, or Tom Kyd's Revenge.* Told in the first person by Thomas Kyd, who is recovering at the home of a mysterious great lady from the physical and emotional trauma of his interrogation in which he slandered Marlowe, the story traces Kyd's attempts to uncover the circumstances surrounding Marlowe's death and to revenge himself on those responsible. Amid assassination attempts, sexual encounters with the mighty and the low, and various double crosses, Kyd uncovers a complicated plot that brings him face to face, finally, with the three men who were in the room when Marlowe died, and points him back to Walsingham himself. The second novel is Anthony Burgess's *A Dead Man in Deptford,* which covers more or less the same material, although this time the story is that of a boy actor who knows and loves Marlowe. Again Marlowe is in the middle of intrigue, caught up in the Babington and other plots. Again his life and death unfold in the midst of conspiracy and the thrills and chills of political intrigue, most of them driven by Walsingham.

I have to mention another novel here. Although it does not deal with the death of Marlowe, it follows the form that I have been discussing (and is by far the best novel). Patricia Finney's *Firedrake's Eye* (1992) is set in London ten years before the death of Marlowe. It details an attempted assassination of Queen Elizabeth, during her Ascension Day celebrations, by a fanatical Catholic. The story brings together three lives, carefully chosen to give a broad overview of the Elizabethan experience: David Becket is a down-at-the-heels mercenary and Provost of Defence; Simon Ames is a Portuguese Jew and cryptographer to Sir Francis Walsingham; and Tom O'Bedlam is a madman, and sometimes poet, who narrates the story. Of all the novels it perhaps best fits Hutcheon's definition of historiographic metafiction, foregrounding, as it does, the arbitrariness of the narrative construct and the tenuous nature of the historical text on which it rests by having the narrator a madman who transcends the boundaries of naturalistic narrator presence. Again, in this novel, Walsingham is the man who controls the action: the generator of meaning in early modern political England.

So the Renaissance, the beginning of modernity, is being envisioned by these historians and novelists alike as an age of surveillance and conspiracy. The teleologies that dominated modernity are given their nascence in the court of Elizabeth and their agents in the beginnings of political paranoia. Walsingham, Elizabeth's spymaster, is emerging as the great generator of cultural meaning; like

Cancer Man in *The X-Files,* he is at the center of all plots, the back-rooms of all bureaucracies.

But representations of Shakespeare are different. While the Tudor age is being imagined as a setting for Jack Ryan-style heroics, Shakespeare himself is not imagined as a thriller protagonist. The recent novels that deal directly with his life go out of their way to normalize his experience, to explain it not as part of the culture of conspiracy that caught Marlowe, but in human, even mundane terms. So, in Leon Rooke's *Shakespeare's Dog,* Shakespeare's genius is treated with bathetic comic effect. The novel, told by the dog Hooker, depicts a Shakespeare at odds with his talent, his wife, and the up-heavals of Stratford life. Hooker steers Shakespeare through various crises, saving his life from drowning and offering advice and solace. When Shakespeare leaves for London, it is with Hooker, as a team. Philip Burton's *You, My Brother* presents a Shakespeare driven by a desire to avenge the disgraces heaped on his father. Shakespeare is tormented by a loveless marriage and an impetuous younger brother. Anthony Burgess, in *Nothing Like the Sun,* presents a Shakespeare cuckolded by his own brother and riddled with venereal disease he contracted from the Dark Lady, a prostitute. In Robert Nye's *Mrs Shakespeare: The Complete Works,* Anne Hathaway writes a memoir of Shakespeare seven years after his death. Shakespeare is presented as driven by sex and a lust for sugar. He prostituted himself with the Earl of Southampton for a thousand pounds, and he dresses as a woman when making love to his wife. In the film *Shakespeare in Love* (1998) Shakespeare is depicted as a charming but adulterous, writing-blocked financial schemer. Clearly, the fictional Shakespeare is an antidote to Bardolatry.

Why is the fictional representation of Shakespeare so different from the historical representation? I can think of two reasons, one tied to the writing of historical narrative, the other to conspiracy theory. First, Shakespeare was himself a great generator of historical narrative. However much his history plays were historically suspect, it is those plays that have, for centuries, impinged on the British historical consciousness. Combine this fact with Shakespeare's ap-parent disinterest in himself (that is, the putative lack of a narrative of his life) and you get, in Shakespeare, a model of the historical control-ling facility: a largely faceless entity generating popular historical meaning. Unlike Marlowe, Shakespeare is not a subject of the con-spiracies of his age; rather, he is the active agent of political meaning. We do not need to construct a narrative of the Tudor age to define Shakespeare; we need to work through Shakespeare's narratives to find the Tudor age.

Second, while historians and fiction writers representing the Renaissance have projected narrative cohesion back into the period by reifying conspiracy, Shakespeare is unique among Renaissance writers in having his own identity made the subject of long-standing conspiracy-theory attention. Unable to imagine a Shakespeare capable of massive narrative production without a concomitant stirring personal narrative, theorists have manufactured elaborate fictions of Shakespeare's life. Now, while doubts about Shakespeare's authorship were raised as early as the eighteenth century, it is only in the past thirty-odd years that an industry has arisen, with an alternate literature, to promote the idea on an international scale. And it is only in the past thirty or so years that this movement has begun to exhibit the signs of the paranoid imagination, itself so indicative of postmodern unease. But instead of just projecting that postmodern paranoid tendency back into representations of the Tudor age, the Oxfordians, the Shakespeare conspiracy theorists du jour, offer a sustained master narrative that runs from the original cover-up of Edward DeVere's alleged authorship of the Shakespeare canon to today, when this "hoax" is still being perpetuated by wilfully ignorant "Stratfordians," that is, the vast majority of Shakespeare scholars and enthusiasts worldwide.

That there is a conspiracy to be uncovered, and that the Oxfordians see themselves as the heroes fighting an international scholarly conspiracy, is made clear from their own descriptions of their pursuit. As Peter Sammartino, in *The Man Who Was William Shakespeare,* puts it: "The question of authorship is the greatest detective story of all times" (12). Richard F. Whalen, in *Shakespeare—Who Was He?* calls the investigation into Shakespeare's authorship "a fascinating literary detective story" (xviii).

The form of this heroic pursuit of truth is also marked by the signs of the paranoid imagination that accompany any conspiracy projection. As Richard Hofstadter pointed out in the 1960s, "A fundamental paradox of the paranoid style is the imitation of the enemy. The enemy, for example, may be the cosmopolitan intellectual, but the paranoid will outdo him in the apparatus of scholarship, even of pedantry" (32). The Oxfordian conspiracy theorists have not only fulfilled Hofstadter's dictum in the production of cumbersome monographs, but have begun to produce both newsletters and journals in an attempt to undermine the oppressive orthodoxy of Shakespeare scholars. The techniques they apply to the "evidence" also ape conventional scholarship. For example, close textual analysis is mimicked in the truly bizarre work of Ralph L. Tweedale who, in his *Wasn't Shakespeare Someone Else?* finds evidence of DeVere's authorship of the Shakespeare canon by tracing acrostics through the printed versions of Shakespeare's sonnets and plays. The convoluted patterns that he has to draw across the pages to find variations on the word "Vere" are a striking visual emblem of the labyrinthine propensities of the paranoid imagination. Charlton Ogburn, in *The Mysterious William Shakespeare: The Myth and the Reality,* includes chronological charts in his survey of the mysteries surrounding Shakespeare's life that are patterned like the charts in works such as Braunmuller and Hattaway's *The Cambridge Companion to English Renaissance Drama,* but Ogburn's charts contain damning columns marked for DeVere, "William Shakespeare," and William Shakspere. These apparatus all support an elaborate, meticulously detailed story of a historical conspiracy that "explains" virtually all the mysteries of Shakespeare's life and ambiguities of his works. In Hofstadter's words, "the paranoid mentality is far more coherent than the real world, since it leaves no room for mistakes, failures, or ambiguities" (36). It therefore produces closed narratives much like those of popular genre fiction, in this case the thriller.

The novelists who have attempted representations of Shakespeare's life, then, have had to work *against* the thriller format, against an inherited narrative, because it has been employed, with paranoid gravity, by the Oxfordian and other conspiracy theorists, writers purporting to be historians. Indeed, fiction writers have written accounts that carefully avoid the generic formulas of *all* popular literature. Because of this, it may be in novels of Shakespeare's life that we come closest to a clear imagining of the man. The novelists, consciously fighting the narratives that both historians and conspiracy theorists have adopted and imposed, have produced versions of Shakespeare's life which, though they may not be accurate, and may in fact be extreme in their interpretations of his character and motives, are at least free from the interpretative prejudice of inherited, culturally saturated literary forms. The novelists have imagined Shakespeare anew—without paranoia, without pastiche—and that, at least, is a start.

Notes

1. This reevaluation can be traced in the works of Stephen Greenblatt, Louis Montrose, Peter Stallybrass, Constance Jordan, Annabel Patterson, Jean Howard, Stephen Orgel, Paul Yachnin, and Lawrence Manley, to name a very few.

*Postmodernism,
Architecture, History*

8

Los Angeles, 2019: Two Tales of a City

Kevin R. McNamara

Architecture is frequently singled out as *the* postmodern art form. As "the one art form in which the label seems to refer, uncontested, to a generally agreed upon corpus of works," Linda Hutcheon writes (*Poetics* 22), it promises the best model for the poetics of a "postmodernism of complicity and critique, [. . .] that at once inscribes and subverts the conventions and ideologies of the dominant cultural and social forces of the twentieth-century western world" (*Politics* 11). For Fredric Jameson, however, architecture "has a virtually unmediated relationship" to the transnational flow of capital and the representation of power (*Postmodernism* 5). His belief that "the extraordinary flowering of the new postmodern architecture grounded in the patronage of multinational business, whose expansion and development is strictly contemporaneous with it" (5) no doubt motivates Jameson's otherwise very dubious choice of the Bonaventure Hotel for his one example of "a full-blown postmodern building" in his seminal essay on late capitalism's cultural logic (38). John Portman, he notes, is "a businessman as well as an architect and a millionaire developer" (44).

The consequences of these assumptions for interpreting an urban landscape are my subject. The cityscape in question is the Los Angeles of Ridley Scott's *Blade Runner* (1981). Curious as this choice might seem, to the extent that the displacement of the object by the image is a distinguishing characteristic of postmodernism, and that postmodernist representation problematizes the construction of Jameson's ideal of " 'History' as 'uninterrupted narrative' " (qtd. in Hutcheon, *Politics* 65), or as "the unity of a single great collective story" (Jameson, *Political* 19), a film about a future city whose design deliberately recalls and rewrites historic (predominantly modernist) fantasies of the future city would seem to be an ideal subject with which to test these theories of postmodernism. If it is allowed that postmodern art forms are meaning-*producing,* critical engagements of the "social past" and present, as well as the history of art or literature (Hutcheon, *Politics* 101), then the *Blade Runner* cityscape, especially its ironic treatment of elements that once expressed architecture's utopian aspirations to be "the instrument of [. . .] 'the larger

hope' and 'the greater good' " and to let "empirical facts [. . .] dictate
the solution" to spatial and social problems (Rowe and Koetter 3),
will be recognized as a commentary on the failure of modernist architecture and planning's utopian aspirations. If, on the other hand, we
expect from the film's mise-en-scène no more than a pastiche of historic styles, shorn of satire or other critical content (Jameson, *Postmodernism* 17), then the only possibility for critical interpretation of
the film's built landscape must be assumed to function on the order of
a symptomatic reading that cuts across the intentions of the film *qua*
object of consumption.

The language of this distinction is deliberate. Whereas
Hutcheon sees postmodern art as a practice that retains a critical
edge, even if it no longer claims to offer authoritative knowledge,
Jameson regards the preoccupation with the surfaces that he finds to
be the extent of postmodern cultural production to have everything to
do with the diagnosis of postmodern culture as "schizophrenic." Its
characteristic products are "pure material signifiers, or, in other
words, a series of pure and unrelated presents" (Jameson, *Postmodernism* 27). Andy Warhol's "Diamond Dust Shoes" becomes for
Jameson the supreme icon of this "new kind of superficiality in its
most literal sense" (9) that also includes the LANGUAGE poetry of Bob
Perelman, which shows how schizophrenia, "when it becomes generalized as a cultural style," loses its necessary relationship to "morbid
content we associate with schizophrenia and becomes available for
more joyous intensities" (29); Nam June Paik's "stacked or scattered
television screens," which are unwatchable either individually or as
an ensemble (31); and the unnavigable interior space of Portman's
Bonaventure Hotel (39–45). In all of Jameson's cases, the
"break[ing]down of the signifying chain" into "a rubble of distinct
and unrelated signifiers" (26) is not far removed from the repression
of a more fundamental narrative: the "effacement of the traces of
production" (314) from consumer goods that is the "precondition on
which all the rest [of consumerism] can be construed" (315).

That these two readings are significantly at odds with each other
over the politics of postmodernism is obvious. What I want to show
by bringing them to bear on the historical content of *Blade Runner's*
architectural spaces is not simply that a symptomatological interpretation of the film as an expression of "the cultural logic of late capitalism," although possible and even illuminating in many ways, is pur-
chased at the cost of a fuller appreciation of the film's urban-
architectural sign system. I want also to argue that when the now
seemingly ancient debate about the postmoderns moves beyond an

argument over the complicity of postmodern art to the work of producing readings, that the characteristic concerns of these critical practices can be significantly complementary as well.

Blade Runner seems in any number of ways to be an exemplary text for Jameson's theory of our present cultural dominant and its lost relation to history. The film's urban tableaux inarguably and vividly depict what both he and David Harvey were soon separately to describe as the cognitive, social, and architectural space of postmodernism. At least as much as *Body Heat, Something Wild,* or *Blue Velvet, Blade Runner* "mobiliz[es] [. . .] a vision of the past, or of a certain moment of the past" (*Postmodernism* 287) in order to tell its story. Because this film is putatively about the future, it uses a mode of metonymic nostalgia that "does not reinvent a picture of the past in its lived totality; rather, by reinventing the feel and shape of characteristic art objects of an older period [. . .], it seeks to reawaken a sense of the past associated with those objects" (Jameson, "Postmodernism and Consumer Society" 116). As a result, *Blade Runner,* more so than the other three films, offers an allegory of "a collective unconscious in the process of trying to identify its own present" and failing to do so (*Postmodernism* 296).

Several visual indicators of this blockage contribute significantly to the experience of watching *Blade Runner,* but in paradoxical fashion. The consequence of this blockage—the loss, with the sense of history, of the ability to imagine a future better than the past and present—is suffused throughout the film's dystopic imagination of Los Angeles, 2019. Yet viewers' first reactions to the film's cityscape are less likely to be despair at its evident decrepitude than, as Jameson predicts, a hallucinatory exhilaration. From the opening, aerial sequence of oil refineries sending their plumes of flame into the night, we consume the mise-en-scène of postmodernity as a series of entrancing tableaux: office towers that have literally become flat screens, doing Jameson's example of the Wells Fargo building's architectural trompe-l'oeil (*Postmodernism* 12–13) one better; faux-Mayan pyramids; art-deco interiors at the Tyrell Corporation's office; the exoticism of a street-level life whose stylized punk aesthetic infuses it with the energy of the oppositional and the funkiness of marginality; the interior of Taffy Lewis's club, which suggests some filmic Istanbul, or the Yoshiwara district of Fritz Lang's *Metropolis* (Thea von Harbou's own orientalist fantasy). Thus, the true content of the film's "visual splendor," Jameson avers in one of his few comments on the film, is a celebration of technology that has "little to do

with futures fantasized or not, but everything to do with late capitalism and some of its favorite marketplaces" (*Postmodernism* 384). Syd
Mead, an industrial designer retained by Scott as his "visual futurist," once characterized the ambiance he sought as " 'sort of an exotic,
technological interpretation of a Third World kind of country' " (qtd.
in Deutelbaum 66).

The surplus of surface historicism in the *Blade Runner*
cityscape must in this reading betoken its opposite: the disappearance of genuine historical thought from the discipline of architecture after the period of heroic modernism that Jameson, in *Postmodernism,* associates with Le Corbusier's "gesture [that] radically
separates the new Utopian space of the modern from the degraded
and fallen city fabric which it thereby explicitly repudiates" (41).
Jameson finds in that desire the pathos of heroic modern architecture,
even if the cost of such "utopianism" is exactly the repudiation of
history that Jameson once characterized as "the demiurgic hubris of
high modernism" ("Architecture" 51). Throughout the interwar
years, Le Corbusier had aspired to nothing less than a redefinition of
the city in his own terms; "the absolute of the planned unit" was the
goal toward which his efforts at "delimiting, classifying, differentiating, and standardizing" the spatial dimension of human activity were
directed (Tafuri, *"Machine"* 208). Early on, he balanced the language
of rationalization and efficiency with a promise of individual freedom that the standardization of whole areas of life was to create; yet
that freedom could only be private because "the great questions
[. . .] are never put to a vote. They are prescribed in the plan, which
has been promulgated by 'objective' experts" (Fishman 238). The
subsequent disregard of his own plans and his sense that France was
adrift led Le Corbusier in the 1930s to rethink his commitment to
liberty. As he proclaimed his belief that "France needs a Father"
(Fishman 237), he embraced a profoundly antidemocratic French
syndicalism and courted the patronage of Joseph Stalin, Benito Mus-
solini, and Marshal Pétain in his "desperate search for the absolute
authority that would say Yes to his plans" (Fishman 236). In the
middle of the decade, he dedicated *The Radiant City* "To Authority."

This excursus is intended not to censure Le Corbusier, but to
recall the context of modernist planning and the extremes to which it
was carried by a desire to plan "a future into which the entire present
is projected, [. . .] a 'rational' dominion of the future" (Tafuri, *Architecture* 52). Lacking this perspective on the rise and fall of modernism's "new Utopian space," it is too easy to dismiss *Blade Runner*'s
built landscape as exemplifying architecture that is "content to 'let

the fallen city fabric continue to be in its being' (to parody Heidegger)" (Jameson, *Postmodernism* 41) and to celebrate the vernacular as it has been, Jameson says, "emblematically 'learned from Las Vegas'" (*Postmodernism* 39).[1] However, the postwar Marseilles *Unity* singled out for praise by Jameson (*Postmodernism* 41; see also 63) is far more modest than the *Ville radieuse;* its pathos is quite other than the heroic schemes for spatial and social transformation. Manfredo Tafuri describes the *Unity* as "a fragment of a totality that was destined to remain only thinkable" ("*Machine*" 212); Robert Fishman concurs, describing the *Unity* as both a "crowning achievement" and a "crowning iron[y]" of Le Corbusier's urbanism (254).

To credit the critical power of the film's city of the future, we must begin by noting the relations of production that define *Blade Runner*'s Los Angeles: disparities in income, conditions, and life chances between a white elite and a predominantly darker-skinned labor force as a product of modernist planning methods, the failure of which might have been predicted from the situation of planners driven by a distrust of politics into an unreasoned dependence on the kindness of bankers and industrialists. This understanding of the social production of Los Angeles, 2019, must then be articulated to an interpretation of *Blade Runner*'s urban form as a critique of modernist urban form. One may even do so in terms suggested by Jameson, who once proposed that postmodern aesthetics replaces the high modernist will "to resolve contradiction by stylistic fiat" with "a new kind of perception for which tension, contradiction, and the registering of the incompatible and the clashing, is in and of itself a strong mode of relating two incommensurable elements, poles, or realities"—even if, in the next breath, he dismisses postmodern aesthetics for "simply ratif[ying] the contradictions and fragmented chaos all around it by way of an intensified perception of, a mesmerized and well-nigh hallucinogenic fascination with, those very contradictions themselves" ("Architecture" 59–60).

Unlike the "blockage" exhibited in nostalgia deco, which resolves itself via a retreat to an imaginary past, *Blade Runner* ought to be read as an attempt to think our relation to the present and a possible future. Harvey, a geographer whose account of postmodernity is strongly influenced by Jameson, has remarked that *Blade Runner* is prescient in its portrayal of the city's increasingly neocolonial relations, and the division of remaining production between multinational corporations and their poorly remunerated subcontractors. The market-stall manufacturing concerns in the film "indicat[e] intricate relations of subcontracting between highly disaggregated firms as well as with the Tyrell Corporation itself," Harvey suggests (311). If we follow Harvey's lead and study the city of 2019 alongside Edward Soja's and Mike Davis's histories of postwar Los Angeles, the film's city becomes recognizable as the product of a two-fold process at work over those decades. First, the "selective abandonment of the inner urban core" of Los Angeles and other of the United States's largest cities left behind less-competitive industries, the government and finance sectors, and an "irregular workforce composed primarily of minorities and the poorest segments of the metropolitan population" (Soja 181). Subsequently, selective redevelopment established isolated citadels of international finance amid these zones of immiseration. Davis argues that the groundwork for intensive development in Los Angeles was laid in 1957 with repeal of the city's earthquake height limitations. In the ensuing decades, the city's own Community Redevelopment Agency sold land at discounts to developers, whose projects were significantly funded by off-shore capital, especially during the Reagan years (Davis, "Chinatown" 71–72); it has been estimated that by the mid-1980s 75 percent of the office towers and multiblock developments in that area were foreign owned (Davis, "Urban" 109). Other sources put the figure for foreign construction funding at "as much as 90 percent" (Soja 215). At the other end of the economic spectrum, hundreds of thousands of recent immigrants were living in illegally converted garages (Davis, "Chinatown" 77), sleeping in shifts or living on the streets, and swelling the ranks of the marginally employed. Taking advantage of workers' anxiety, which was heightened by the loss of 75,000 manufacturing jobs to shutdowns and indefinite layoffs in the late 1970s (Soja 201), employers who remained in Los Angeles drove the regional average wage for nonskilled manufacturing jobs from 2 percent above the national average to 12 percent below it (Davis, "Chinatown" 76).

This history of urban restructuring, in no way exclusive to Los Angeles, is certainly within an audience's horizon of experience. Given the exponential increase in part-time or contract employment routinely offered without health care or other benefits, audiences are ever likelier to recognize that the replicants, who are humanized as the film progresses, represent "the ultimate form of short-term highly skilled and flexible labor power" (Harvey 309). That is, viewers are ever more likely to see the replicants as their own future, despite corporate apologists' disingenuous insistence that the new relations of production represent gains in choice and freedom for workers, and in spite of the neoconservative effort to define history as both a natural force *and* a moral tale (the obvious contradiction notwithstanding) and thereby to ascribe an aura of necessity to the new world economic order.

The film's built landscape has more to offer the attentive viewer than this general allusion to the urban condition in the late-capitalist United States. Historical references give depth and specificity to the film's use of architecture as a mode of critique. One scene in the film neatly allegorizes the discipline of viewing that the film demands. As Deckard submits to a computerized enlargement and analysis of a photograph taken by one of the replicants, it reveals unseen significances that open into a new "reality": not only does the scanning uncover information from spaces that should bear none because they must be smaller than the grain of the film (a nice visual metaphor for the transfer of memory to the media of recording), the photograph becomes a three-dimensional space as the analyzer tracks and pans through it. This scene reminds us that our knowledge of the past is always mediated through technologies of representation. (One only need recall the worldwide mourning for Diana, "The People's Princess," to understand that even our memories are profoundly mediated.) A visual pun within the scene further undermines the humanist faith in history as a mirror in which we see ourselves more clearly. Deckard does find his(tory's) object, the human subject, but only at two removes: The replicant Zhora is, more than most of us, a product of the technologies of the body and memory. She is not simply within the picture; she is discovered in a convex (distorting) mirror inside the visual field of a photograph that is itself a conscious quotation of the interiors of Flemish-school paintings (Deutelbaum 68–71).

As a metahistoriographic allegory, this scene exemplifies Hutcheon's axiom about the postmodern relation to history, that "what we 'know' of the past derives from the discourses of that past" (*Poetics* 136), a contention that is the ground zero of the Jameson-Hutcheon controversy. To the notion that historical activity is a rereading of the past through its signs and traces by subjects whose consciousness is significantly determined by constructions of the very past they interrogate, Jameson objects that to transform "the past into visual mirages, stereotypes, or texts, effectively abolishes any practical sense of the future and of the collective project" (*Postmodernism* 46). As much as he will insist on the necessity "to think [postmodernism] positively *and* negatively at once" (47), Jameson's own analysis leans strongly toward the negative conclusion that, immersed as we are in postmodern spatiality, we have lost the firm ground from which to undertake "the project of totalization" (332) that is the first step to the writing of what he unironically calls "partisan history" (369).[2] Yet it does not follow that postmodern historiography must result in an impoverished sense of history.

To say that signs change meaning over time is not to say that they *lose* meaning. The effect is often quite the opposite, an *enrichment* of the sign, whose accrual of multiple, often contradictory meanings over time ought rather to incite historical inquiry than to dampen it. Two buildings in the *Blade Runner* urban landscape activate this problematic—but also productive—relation of the present to the past: George H. Wyman's Bradbury Building of 1893, where J. F. Sebastian lives and Deckard pursues the last of the escaped replicants, and Frank Lloyd Wright's 1924 house for Charles Ennis, which serves as Deckard's ninety-seventh-floor apartment. The appearance of these buildings in *Blade Runner* effects an ironic reinscription of the utopian futures that informed their designs. As they map the present moment and its relation to the ideology of modernism, the recontextualized structures testify to the limits of the "activist utopia, utopia as 'a blueprint for the future,'" whose project, we have noted, was "to 'replace the government of man by the administration of things'" (Rowe and Koetter 20).

Wyman was among a phalanx of American and European acolytes of Edward Bellamy's vision of an administered, corporatist future. Disillusioned by politics as practiced in the Gilded Age, and believing that rationalization of production and distribution was the ready route to social equality, Bellamy reconceived society on the model of an "industrial army." To illustrate his belief that technology would become a moral agent when labor produced common wealth and material security guaranteed the freedom to cultivate spiritual pursuits, a theory later elaborated by Simon Nelson Patten as *The New Basis of Civilization,* Bellamy used the new cultural form of the department store; its array of commodities represents the cornucopia of spiritual riches that was to be achieved through scientific administration in an enlightened Boston at the turn-of-the-millennium. Esther McCoy (21) has traced the inspiration of Wyman's 1893 office-building design for Louis Bradbury to a Boston department store of the year 2000, as Bellamy had described it five years earlier in *Looking Backward:* "a vast hall full of light, received not alone from the windows on all sides, but from the dome, the point of which was a hundred feet above. [. . .] The walls and ceiling were frescoed in mellow tints, calculated to soften without absorbing the light which flooded the interior" (Bellamy 80).

Through its reimagining of the Bradbury Building, *Blade Runner* transforms Bellamy's brilliant Bostonian utopia. The dank, drizzly Los Angeles vividly portrays the dystopic possibilities inherent in *Looking Backward*'s social arrangements, in which laborers lack political rights and are subjected to constant surveillance. Bellamy intentionally disfranchised workers in order to prevent the corruption he regarded as a certain consequence of candidates and workers who would "intrigue for support." Only demobilized members of the "industrial army" may vote for "lieutenant generals" (guild leaders) while the "general-in-chief" (president) is even further removed from the soldier-citizens whom he commands; he is selected from among retired "lieutenant generals" by the professional class, who are exempt from the industrial army. To allow workers a voice, observes Bellamy's spokesman, Doctor Leete, would "be perilous to [the] discipline" maintained by the "inspectorate," an administrative bureau whose mission is "not [to] wait for complaints," but actively to pursue, "to catch and sift every rumor of a fault [. . . and] by systematic and constant oversight and inspection of every branch of the [industrial] army, to find out what is going wrong before anybody else does" (Bellamy 132–34).

The dehumanization of laborers denied political expression and differentiated primarily by the tasks they perform is expressed in the condition of replicants, producers who are more literally than the rest of us products of the system they serve. In *Blade Runner*'s reinterpretation of Wyman's rendering of Bellamy's department store, where "legends on the walls about the hall indicated to what classes of commodities the counters below were devoted" (Bellamy 80), the commodities for which Deckard hunts appear fully human; they are, however, members of an "industrial army" (each of the escaped replicants performs some military function related to the construction and protection of "off-world" cities) who are as powerless against the powers they serve as are the laborers of *Looking Backward*. The replicants' only possible political action is revolt, the prospect that motivated Bellamy to publish his vision in the first place.

While the Bradbury Building facilitates an ironic critique of the corporatist utopia, the Ennis House is turned against another modernist ideology, the extreme individualism that Wright espoused and embodied. Although Wright understood the modern city, which he hated, to be a product of the industrial revolution, and although he longed for a return to an America of farmers and artisans, he had no less confidence than Bellamy or Le Corbusier in technology's ameliorative powers. Believing that technological advances had made decentralization possible once again, he cobbled the arguments of C. H. Douglas and Silvio Gessel on Social Credit economics, Henry George on the right to land, and Bellamy on the public ownership of inventions and scientific discoveries into the basis for a new society that would "revive the democratic hopes of the eighteenth century: Edison and Ford would resurrect Jefferson" (Fishman 123). In 1935, Wright unveiled his plan for "Broadacre City," the fullest expression of his belief that "a planned physical structure of decentralization must be the basis of all other reforms" (Fishman 132). Designed as a decentralized (a)utopia in which the (one-car to five-car) family homestead was the norm, its population would never rise above 30,000.

Like Bellamy and Le Corbusier, Wright, too, distrusted politics as an arena in which the triumph of his truth was not assured, and so he thought it wise to replace politics with administration, guided by "'Spirit, [which] is a science mobocracy does not know'" (qtd. in Ciucci 363). Unlike Bellamy and Le Corbusier, who figured authority in variations on the engineer, Wright chose the artist as his ideal of authority; in that respect, he was faithful to the transcendentalism of his *"lieber meister,"* Louis Sullivan. Wright was, however, no less insistent than Le Corbusier that "his clients must submit to his vision of life" (Ciucci 370). Thus, even as he designed what he referred to as an "Architecture of Democracy," Wright imagined the individualism of others within a narrow compass, defined more by ownership and relative isolation than by a variety of interests, beliefs, desires, and practices, an ideal of individualism that is best supported in large cities, where "all the secret ambitions and all the suppressed desires find somewhere expression" (Park 18).

Defining the spirit of his age, Wright early proclaimed, "'My God is machinery'" and, further, "'The art of the future will be the expression of the individual artist through the thousand powers of the machine, doing all the things the individual worker cannot do, and the creative artist is the man who controls all this and understands it'" (qtd. in Fishman 108). That man is not Deckard, despite his mastery of technology that his job requires. Occupying an Ennis House transformed into a ninety-seventh-floor apartment, Deckard measures the distance of postmodern subjectivity from Wright's romance of autonomy. Set amid the crop of vaguely Mayan, pyramidal skyscrapers, Ennis House's allusively Mayan brickwork loses its cachet as the artist's signature; it is just another element of a city that is a collective memory of the 1930s turn-of-the-millennium city, something perhaps out of Francisco Mujica's *History of the Skyscraper.* Thus redefined, this house by a prophet of an "extreme individualism" (Fishman 132) becomes ironically appropriate for someone who, like the replicants, constructs a self through quotations from mass-cultural styles and photographic "memories" that have no certain referents. The film's other possible Wrightean heroes both subvert the spirit of his vision. Roy Baty, the escaped replicants' leader, may be allowed as a figure of the artist by the film's "Blakean Dialectics" (Rachela Morrison), but his autonomy is not innate. Eldon Tyrell, the genetic engineer whom Baty calls—not without severe irony—"the God of biomechanics," combines the power of Wright's "Artist" and Bellamy's "General-in-Chief." Yet he is an utterly colorless figure.

Far from being rendered meaningless, historical structures in the *Blade Runner* landscape produce complex meanings because they are signs whose meaning has changed in ways that register historical change and provide perspective on the past and present. As we recover the discourses that informed the hopes and the practice of modernist urbanism, the suggestion that "this voyeuristic film, which shows all, [. . . has not] shown us anything of politics" (Chevrier 56) becomes ever less convincing—at least as evidence of some postmodern superficiality. The film's political void remarks the expendability of politics in the postnational world of global capitalism, in which the hope for a well-managed (or even a manageable) future "into which the entire present is projected," in Tafuri's phrase, is likewise abandoned. "The state *is* withering," as Ron Silliman cautions, "in the precise sense that its scope no longer defines the outer limit of power" (31); over the past three decades and more, governments on all levels have hastened this denouement by abdicating their social and economic responsibilities through programmatic deregulation, devolution, privatization, and dismantling. If Marx and his students seem "not to have foreseen" the prospect that "in some utterly critical sense, the state might wither *prior to the abolition of capital*" and power revert "back into a civil society that has itself been technologically internationalized" (Silliman 31), the disposition of power in the film imagines just this possibility: a dystopian realization of the modernist faith in administration wherein "the harmony between the needs and hopes of individuals or groups and the functions guaranteed by the system is now only a secondary component of its functioning" because "the true goal of the system [. . .] is the optimization of the global relationship between input and output—in other words, performativity" (Lyotard 11).

This insight into the modality of power's dissemination throughout postmodern society can explain the film's departure from *Do Androids Dream of Electric Sheep?,* the novel by Philip K. Dick on which the film is based. Nostalgia for autonomy led Dick to concentrate power in his genetic designer, Eldon Rosen, who is a figure of identifiable evil: he runs a shadow police force and operates his company beyond the control of the two superpowers. One senses, therefore, that Rosen's death is unthinkable because it would resolve the conflict that structures the novel's world. Tyrell, dispassionate rather than evil, is murdered by Baty, without the act producing any perturbations of the circuits of power. The *lack* of consequence more faithfully represents the world mapped by systems theory, which achieves the modernist desire for the disappearance of politics as an arena of human contention, but installs in its place flows of economic and social power that circulate through systems so internationalized, so technical, as to exist beyond the possibility of punctual management.[3] Jean-François Lyotard's rhetorically dehumanized social cartography registers the life-world of an urban core whose deteriorating, "retrofitted" structures embody the intersection of the imperative of perpetual modernity with the political abdication of the public sphere that has rendered most forms of infrastructural spending dispensable. The sovereignty of economic institutions and mass subjectivity is registered on those public screens that do the work of ideological programming; the messages hawk the products of multinational conglomerates.

Jameson is right, then, in asserting that *Blade Runner* has much "to do with late capitalism and some of its favorite marketplaces." However, it has at least as much to do with undoing, or unsettling, the production of subjectivity and the consumption of history. While the recognizable, retro-future may promise transport to a childhood future with its identifiable heroes and villains, the mode of the metonymic nostalgia film is turned on itself. Viewers' identification with Deckard enables the film's utopian deconstruction of the human as a node of media and mediation, thereby denaturalizing the individualist hero and the structures of difference and privilege that subtend the novel's resolution. Elsewhere I have traced the film's dismantling of privileged subjectivity ("Blade" 425–27, 439–43), but it can here be remarked that the extent to which Deckard is plugged into a collective mindspace of images from which he constructs a self—the photographs and film-noir mannerisms that both predate him—reveals that memory has become alienable and mental space colonized by various technologies of recording and reproduction.[4] Deckard and his city equally participate in the logic of a culture that constructs itself from images.

It must further be noted that the disarticulation of viewers' identification with Deckard as yet another "last real man in America" disrupts the cultural logic of the nostalgia mode that has become the ideological dominant of another "favorite marketplace" of capitalism, one that is especially relevant to a consideration of the film's architecture: the festival marketplace that has become a staple of contemporary urban redevelopment. *Blade Runner*'s remembered futures and its own bazaar are in no way comparable to the festival marketplace in such venues as New York's South Street/Fulton Fish Market, Boston's Quincy Market, or Baltimore's Harborplace. If anything, Los Angeles, 2019, recalls what most, if not all, of these markets replaced. The festival marketplaces are theaters of nostalgia "laden with historical allusions to the traditional vision of the city" in its eighteenth- or early-nineteenth-century scale (Boyer 184); they offer a city less heterogeneous, more easily thinkable as a whole, and delivered from the conflicts and suffering that inform these cities' actual histories, as well as their presents. The festival marketplace is much more than the setting for acts of consumption; the contradictory visual spectacle of the "simpler" past and present luxury invokes an ideal of national destiny whose implicit promise of cultural stability and individual economic mobility is itself distractedly, yet reassuringly, consumed.

Blade Runner produces an opposite effect because its uses of nostalgia, its allusions to past futures, are double coded and contextualized in ways that create meaning-producing tensions. The film's urban aesthetic works in a manner that, I have already noted, Jameson himself once theorized as the production neither of homogeneity nor "differences randomly coexisting," but "a new kind of perception for which tension, contradiction, the registering of the incompatible and the clashing, is in and of itself a strong mode of relating" ("Architecture" 59). If Jameson's own trajectory has been predominantly a retreat from this possibility into a nostalgia for the Utopian, despite the dangers of such totalizing constructs, nevertheless, his characteristic concern for comprehending aesthetic production within the greater matrix of material-social practices is a necessary supplement to Hutcheon's concern for the epistemological and formal concerns of postmodern aesthetics. Together they lead us to what William Fisher has called the film's "peculiar utopian strategy," a productive destruction of the ideology of modernism that turns design against design and imagination against imagination "until the whole complex gives way at its roots" (198) and clears a space—so much more effectively in the Director's Cut, without the tacked-on, tacky escape to "the North"—for rethinking the metanarratives that locate us in the life-world of late capitalism.

Notes

1. Jameson's casual dismissal of Robert Venturi and Denise Scott Brown likewise fails to register their uses of irony and the historical texture of their architectural projects (see McNamara, *Urban* 221–46).

2. To Hutcheon's definition of *totalization* as unification "with an eye to power and control" (*Poetics* xi), Jameson responds, "*totality*" names no "privileged bird's-eye view of the whole, [. . .] which is also the Truth" (*Postmodernism* 332) but the work of "securing the fragile control or survival of an even more fragile subject within a world otherwise utterly independent and subject to no one's whims or desires" (*Postmodernism* 333). If he thus rejects any possible "Hegelian 'essential cross section' of the present," he maintains that "the various levels [of cultural production. . .] yet conspire to produce a totality" (*Postmodernism* xx) that is also the Truth.

3. After the October 1987 stock market plunge, we learned that most trading is run by computer programs. It would appear, too, that one effect of global capitalism is to render the now customary election year cries for economic nationalism a eulogy for politics.

4. What I have described is for Anne Friedberg precisely the articulation of "Cinema and the Postmodern Condition," wherein "the VCR has become a privatized museum of past moments—of different genres, times, commodities—all reduced to interchangeable, equally accessible units." Thus, "the cinema spectator and the armchair equivalent—the home video viewer, who commands fast forward, fast reverse, and many speeds of slow motion; who can easily switch between channels and tape; who is always able to repeat, replay, and return—is a spectator *lost in* but also *in control of* time" (427–28).

9

Postmodern Casinos

Shelton Waldrep

Gaming, as the gambling industry prefers to call gambling, is rapidly becoming a popular cultural phenomenon that not only increasingly influences trends in family leisure, but also represents one strand of postmodern cultural production that has thus far remained under-theorized. This situation is especially odd when one considers that our understanding of postmodernist architecture took a major step forward in the work of Robert Venturi, Denise Scott Brown, and Steven Izenour when they first began to theorize the landscape of Las Vegas as an American vernacular style that existed outside of Europeanized modernist systems of architecture. Though they tended to focus more on Vegas's noncasino buildings and features than on the casinos themselves, they were able to make a convincing argument that Vegas was structured as a system based specifically on the sign— both literally and in a structuralist sense—that announced the function and meaning of buildings from the vantage point of the road— specifically, the multilane roads of Vegas's famed Strip. That this conception of Vegas architecture has expanded to form a major tenet of what we call postmodern architecture is now a given. Postmodernist architects genuflect to this concept of architecture as a counterpoint not only to a modernist high art approach to architecture, but also to a subtle reading of the way in which mass-produced vernacular architecture has already changed the way that U.S. cities look and feel via the use of theming. That Vegas is already, then, a postmodern playground for architecture need not be disputed. That we need a theoretical approach to understand how to explain the changes in the morphologies of this postmodernism is another problem altogether. The current challenge posed by Las Vegas is twofold: on the one hand, it may well have morphed into an island of new postmodern architectural experimentation that has, at least for the moment, outstripped the prevailing theories that we have for analyzing postmodern architecture; it has also, in its post-seventies emphasis on family theming, posed an alternative to the Disney paradigm that is, finally, simply another kind of architectural form completely. The actual existence of the newer postmodern casinos, in other words, resists both the theories of "contradiction," on which postmodern architec-

tural theory is largely based, and the analysis of themed environments coming out of cultural studies. Perhaps Vegas architecture has,
to some extent, always been its own model. Certainly, its latest incar-
nation is, like the casino owners' designs in general, a disorienting
experience.

Constructing a Postmodern Architecture

With their competing theories of "parody" and "pastiche," respec-
tively, Linda Hutcheon and Fredric Jameson have provided the primary concepts for making sense of the postmodern strain of architectural production. In *A Poetics of Postmodernism,* Hutcheon reacts to
Jameson's famous formulation of the postmodern effect in his
detailed analysis of the Bonaventure Hotel in Los Angeles. Hutcheon
points out, accurately, that the building that Jameson refers to as
postmodernist is, more properly, late modernist. More to her point,
Hutcheon wants to counter Jameson's negative critique of postmodern architecture generally by making claims for the movement as a
whole—mainly, by pointing to the wide range in the use of tone that
is employed by various postmodernist architects, especially when
referencing history. Where Jameson sees a deracination of the past in
contemporary postmodern architecture, Hutcheon claims an ironic
play that attempts to connect the past to the present via references
that self-consciously recontextualize history for the present.

Early on in his discussion of postmodern architecture, Jameson
dismisses parody—a key term for Hutcheon—in favor of pastiche:

> In this situation [late capitalism] parody finds itself without a
> vocation; it has lived, and that strange new thing pastiche
> slowly comes to take its place. Pastiche is, like parody, the im-
> itation of a peculiar or unique, idiosyncratic style, the wearing
> of a linguistic mask, speech in a dead language. But it is a neu-
> tral practice of such mimicry, without any of parody's ulterior
> motives, amputated of the satiric impulse, devoid of laughter
> and of any conviction. [. . .]. Pastiche is thus blank parody, a
> statue with blind eyeballs. [. . .]. (*Postmodernism* 17)

It is to this concept of parody that Hutcheon takes exception—
especially the idea that parody might lack agency, in the hands of the
architect or artist, to reflect, among other things, political conviction.
Hutcheon claims that this effect can be best seen in a "study of the

actual aesthetic *practice* of postmodernism" as opposed to a "reaction against its implication in the mass culture of late capitalism" (*Poetics* 25). In other words, Hutcheon feels that postmodern architecture is being used as a metaphor for a (now dated) debate about the ideology of postmodern aesthetics without an inductive analysis of the actual artifacts of postmodernism. Further, she stakes a claim for an approach to postmodern cultural production that always posits a close reading of the products over a theorizing about postmodernism generally. Though she makes an effort to be sensitive to the variety of modernist architecture, she does downplay the ideological goals expressed in much modernist architecture; namely, the desire to better the lives of everyone through design. Indeed, in the desire of modernist architects to reject history—or the immediate past—can be seen a desire to break with the past horrors of history, to forge a new consciousness that is not so much an erasure of the memory of history as an attempt to avoid the social and cultural disparities that the weight of history placed on the European context. Of course, this idea might now seem naive, but it is still an important distinction to keep in mind as one ponders the irony of the reduction of modernism to a corporate style that has no utopian impulse whatsoever. Hutcheon prefers to view modernist architecture as essentially elitist and to posit postmodernist architecture as sharing characteristics that make it distinct—differences that she lauds, and which are now quite familiar: a "return to [. . .] the vernacular (that is, to local needs and local architectural traditions), to decoration and a certain individualism in design, and, most importantly, to the past, to history" (26). History, as she later explains, is the equivalent of parody, a concept that she thinks Jameson misunderstands, or simply reduces, to "the ridiculing imitation of the standard theories and definitions that are rooted in eighteenth-century theories of wit" (26). Hutcheon's claim that Jameson misdiagnoses the use of parody by postmodernist architects becomes the primary basis for her own claim to the productive use to which postmodernism is put in the hands of some of its most famous architectural practitioners.

Citing Paolo Portoghesi in response to Kenneth Frampton, Terry Eagleton, and Jameson, Hutcheon sees the postmodern use of parody as a playful use of irony that does not refuse modernism so much as rearrange the viewer's approach to architecture—one that puts the user on the inside of the conceit or the joke, rather than on the outside, as she claims the modernist architects did (*Poetics* 30). Indeed, what she terms the "double coding" of postmodern architecture is also supposed to allow the creator—especially marginalized ones of the Commonwealth countries or of Western society in general—to speak from within the dominate structure while simultaneously critiquing it. That is, parody implies a humorous, almost camplike awareness of not only contradiction, but also of the slipperiness of one's own subject position. Postmodern architecture should, according to Hutcheon's formulation, allow for a return of history in a form that is also self-conscious about its difference—how it plays within the radically different context of the present. Irony is what saves the architect from merely seeming to dredge up the past as superior to the present—to invoke nostalgia—as irony "critically confronts the past with the present, and vice versa" (39).

The problem with this claim is that the very principle on which Hutcheon bases her defense—the actual postmodernist structures themselves—have not survived the passage of time in much better shape than their modernist predecessors. Her detailed critique of Charles Moore's Piazza d'Italia in New Orleans, for example, fits uneasily with the abandoned site that that architectural space has become. The ironic use of references to classical architecture and Sicilian culture has become lost under the decrepitude of this monument to ethnic assimilation. Hutcheon's claims that postmodern architecture has—in the hands of Moore, Michael Graves, and Robert A. M. Stern—taken on a sophisticated sense of narrative deconstruction assumes not only that this story is there for the masses (in a form that they can and do interpret) but is recognized by them as a countermeasure to the suffering they have experienced at the hands of corporate modernism and its wholesale destruction of public space. The real story, however, is more complicated, and Hutcheon seems to replace a wholesale defense of modernism—or at least its purported goals—with a blanket defense of postmodernism's ability to bring back the past as an ideological critique of the anemic vocabulary of forms that modernism seems to represent. While Hutcheon is certainly correct that the discourse of postmodernism as it existed in its original form in the 1980s and early 1990s often underestimated postmodernism's ability to create interesting works, she is also too optimistic about both the political work that is being done by the architecture she champions, and the way in which her analysis actually displaces these very buildings from the flow of history to make them seem like hermetically sealed texts created by auteuristic architects for the purposes of countering modernism. For all that one might say in criticism of Jameson, his discussion of postmodernism does attempt to place the phenomenon within a larger field of historical forces for which it might be a symptom. Hutcheon ties postmodernist production too closely to a reaction to modernism and ignores its effects on the present as well as its relationship to the distinct ethos of the period in which it was first conceived: the time of Reagan, Thatcher, and Mulroney.

In *Postmodernism, or, The Cultural Logic of Late Capitalism,* Jameson's other close reading of a particular work of postmodernist architecture is of Frank Gehry's house in Los Angeles. As Jameson acknowledges, Gehry's house is an unusual example of postmodern architecture for the simple reason that it does not, pace Moore and Graves, attempt to tell a story (108). The postmodernism that Hutcheon enjoys is that which constructs narratives—stories that the buildings tell to anyone who can "read" them. Yet, one might argue that what is essential to an understanding of postmodernist architectural production is whether or not one likes the stories that are being put forth—and, quite possibly, whether one is comfortable with a style of architecture that attempts to privilege the temporal and verbal over the spatial and visual aspects of modernism. If the narratives that a postmodern architect tells are not themselves "blank parody," then they must mean something. "Who authors these stories?" and "toward what ends?" become important questions to ask. If Graves or Stern are creating works for the Disney corporation in Orlando or Paris—or for a corporate giant in another location—the story may well be authored by the client, even if it appears in an ironic form. Likewise, the narrative-as-building that Hutcheon praises can appear to even an informed viewer like a mere Barthian exercise in metanarrative: fictions about fictions that ultimately comment only on themselves, and not on the stories from history that have been occluded by modernist architects and writers.

As Jameson notes, the importance of irony to postmodern architecture is already in the formula presented by Venturi in *Learning from Las Vegas,* which "proposes that the new, architect-designed building stand out ever so slightly from the vernacular surrounding it by way of a barely perceptible ironic distance" (*Seeds* 143). The problem with this idea, as Jameson concludes, is that "it does not quite seem to work, particularly since irony itself was traditionally a sign fully as much as a weapon of just those condescending upper classes from which we were supposed to escape." Whether or not Jameson is furthering the idea of irony or parody in what Hutcheon terms its "eighteenth-century" definition, the mistrust of irony that he evidences clearly reads for him as a failed project whose very play with tone makes it suspect politically. Jameson does analyze the actual buildings of postmodernism—his analysis of Graves's work, for example, is accurate. As he says, in the newer incarnations of Venturi's idea, "The question of the part [. . .] seems dominant, well beyond the merely 'superficial' matter of 'ornamentation' as such, insofar as [. . .] it is somehow the empty or paradoxical relationship of the various parts to each other that often seems to constitute the building as such" (*Seeds* 185). In other words, not all postmodern architecture functions equally, and Graves's buildings, rather than fitting to the schema of postmodern ideology, seem to function like so many collections of systems of signs that do not even hold together as a narrative or ironic critique. Because a Graves building fetishizes the part and the detail, the fetish overwhelms any one aspect of the building's announced theme. Irony alone, apparently, does not a postmodern building make. One has to look at the specific types of postmodern building to distinguish the differing effects.

Though Jameson is incorrect in calling the Bonaventure a postmodernist hotel, he does identify some aspects of it that could now be said to apply to a new class of hotel-casinos in Vegas. Jameson says that the John Portman-designed hotels that dot the U.S. landscape "seek to speak . . . [the] lexicon and syntax as that has been emblematically 'learned from Las Vegas'" (*Postmodernism* 39). Portman's buildings, however, do not speak this way. The newer versions of Vegas mega-hotels do. Just as Jameson laments the loss of the old-fashioned hotel, including "the monumental porte cochere with which the sumptuous buildings of yesteryear were wont to stage your passage from city street to the interior" (*Postmodernism* 39), the Vegas hotel brings this theatrical concept back with a vengeance. Indeed, the hotels try so hard to make an immediate impression that they often succeed in displacing the viewer in much the same way as described by Jameson's definition of "postmodern hyperspace," which "has finally succeeded in transcending the capacities of the individual human body to locate itself, to organize its immediate surroundings perceptually, and cognitively to map its position in a mappable external world" (*Postmodernism* 44). Casino architecture, in general, is a perfect fit for postmodern effects, and could be said, as Venturi and company realized, to constitute postmodernism *avant la lettre*. When Jameson notes that "postmodern buildings [. . .] seem to have been designed for photography, where alone they flash into brilliant existence (*Postmodernism* 99), he is not only explaining Disney World, but what it means to take in a themed Vegas casino: a monumental stage-set whose visual coding is best understood when studied in a photographed or video-recorded form. As a mere human, standing before the MGM lion or the Luxor pyramid and sphinx, one is overwhelmed by the immense size and monumental scale of an architecture designed to stun as many senses as possible—not just at one time, but as one moves through it, or from one huge building to the next. Postmodern casinos challenge our notions of what architecture is or might be while they also reinforce both Hutcheon's and Jameson's sense that the advent of postmodernist architecture meant a paradigm shift in the use of building as signification.

Theming the Family

It is fair to say that gambling as entertainment or leisure activity is on the rise and will, in the next century, emerge as a major player in vacation and architecture design. As the theming of adult utopian desires, gambling has transformed itself from a shady activity into a ubiquitous pop cultural phenomenon that will ultimately shape not only the imaginations of the middle-class vacationer, but also the lives of many into a new middle class itself. The casinos that line the Strip in Las Vegas have come to represent a fantastic utopia in the form of Disneylike built environments. Holding the same relationship to gambling that Walt Disney World in Orlando does to theme parks, Vegas—with the help of new complexes like the MGM Grand—represents the cutting edge of technological entertainment. With volcanoes erupting every half hour and pirate frigates dueling on cue, Vegas is in a position to challenge the Disney empire's lock on advanced uses of the themed environment. Vegas is beginning to fashion itself as an alternative to the theme park vacation. The existence of theming at Vegas is supposed to bring more people there—especially the families that the corporate owners of the casinos (hotel chains, mainly) seem to want to court—as Martin Scorsese's film *Casino* (1995) suggests. The problem, if there is one, is that Vegas as a cultural phenomenon hasn't actually changed. Theming is simply what the Rat Pack or Elvis were before them: another lure, another attempt to get you to put one more quarter into the slot machine. At the World Gaming Congress and Expo held in Vegas in 1991, Paul Rubeli asked of theming, "What business are we in?" If the answer is "theming," then what does that mean—particularly for Vegas? As Mark C. Taylor notes, "None of the nostalgia that pervades Disney World haunts Las Vegas. In the simulated environment of Vegas, the real becomes blatantly hyperreal. The primary motivation for thematizing Las Vegas is economic. As we have seen, to attract people who never considered gambling, illegitimate vice had to be turned into legitimate entertainment" (259). For Taylor, there is no mystery to the use of theming in Vegas because the casinos proudly display every aspect of their theming as an obvious attempt to make money. Taylor also argues, however, that the mega-hotels of the new Strip have created a "mallscape" of "facades, which dissolved the boundary between inside and outside. Most of the casinos that are still set back from the street are framed by simulated movie sets depicting everything from erupting volcanoes [. . .] to Italian lakes" (261). Although Taylor is mainly interested in the idea that the Strip functions as much as a pedestrian space as the space for automobiles (of Venturi's 60s era), his argument suggests that the themes at Vegas are moving in the direction of increased attention to the idea of theming as narrative as opposed to theming simply as general opulence or privilege. We can see this movement at work in the changes that have occurred in theming from the 1950s to the 1990s. The Sands, for example, which was demolished in the summer of 1996, at one time represented the hangout for the Rat Pack (see fig. 9.1). The general air of Orientalism and quasi-tropical adventure (desert sands) helped to mask the bastion of male privilege that the Vegas "show" seemed to represent. Postsixties theming has followed two paradigms: the Mirage (tropical elegance, perhaps an update of the older theme; see figs. 9.2–3), and Circus Circus, which was built in 1968, and which began the vogue of pirate ships (Treasure Island) and medieval castles (Excalibur) that obviously draw on the Disneyfication of the North American suburban landscape (see figs. 9.4–7).

Many of these resorts do create a Disneylike feel: the midway theme of the casino at Circus Circus undercuts the usual associations with gambling to present a child's-eye-view of what is going on there. (Likewise, the heightened security and cleanliness of Vegas certainly parallel Disney standards—especially interesting since the Vegas casinos are, of course, not all owned by the same company.) Yet the attempts at Disney-level theming in Vegas are probably often misunderstood or even overlooked. The creation of Excalibur, for instance, involved a great deal of research into actual Medieval castles—even if the resulting structure seems much more fanciful and over-the-top than anything that Disney might build. The point is that though theming has always been a part of Vegas, it is only since the 1980s that Vegas designers have lavished so much care on the themes they choose and the elaborateness with which they carry them out. One case in point is the elaborate story told by the Luxor Hotel—a theme that goes way beyond the high-concept themes of most Strip hotels (the Wizard of Oz for the MGM Grand, King Arthur for Excalibur, and

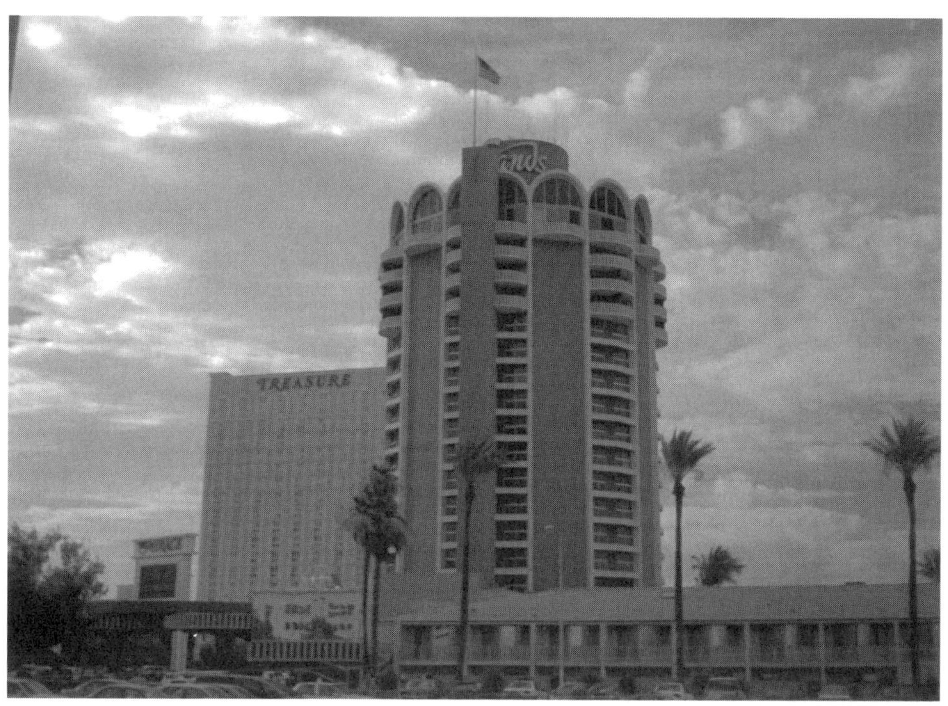

Figure 9.1 Exterior of the Sands Hotel.

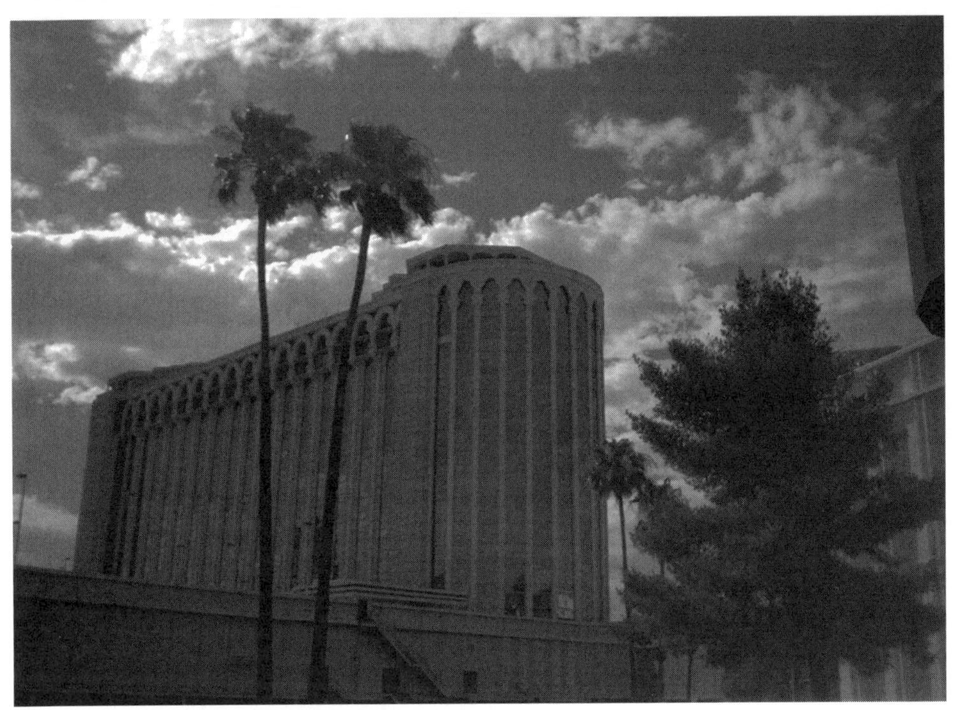

Figures 9.2 and 9.3 Exteriors of tropical-themed hotels.

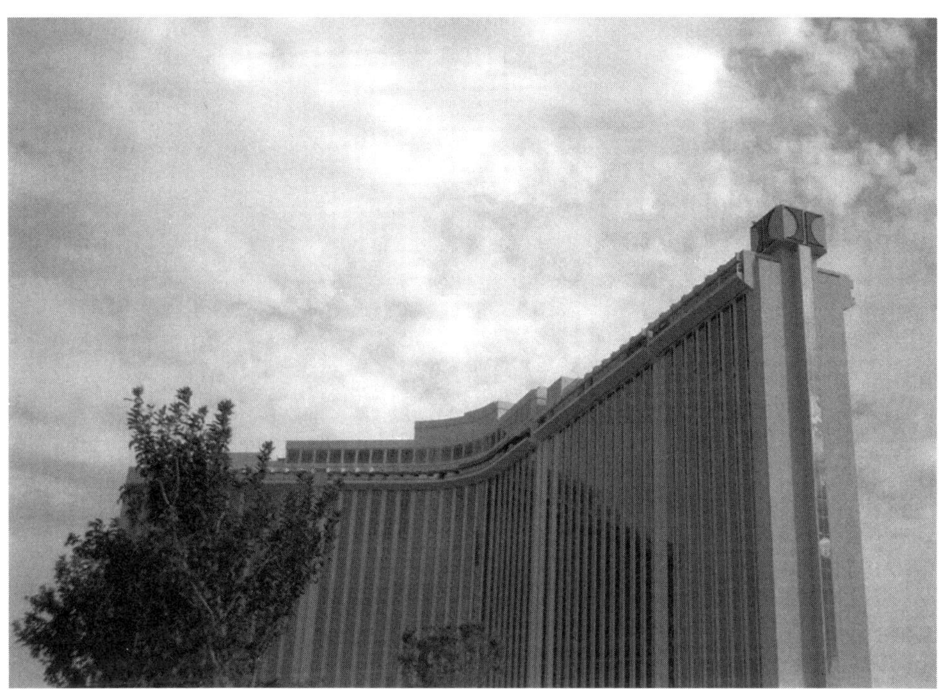

Figure 9.3

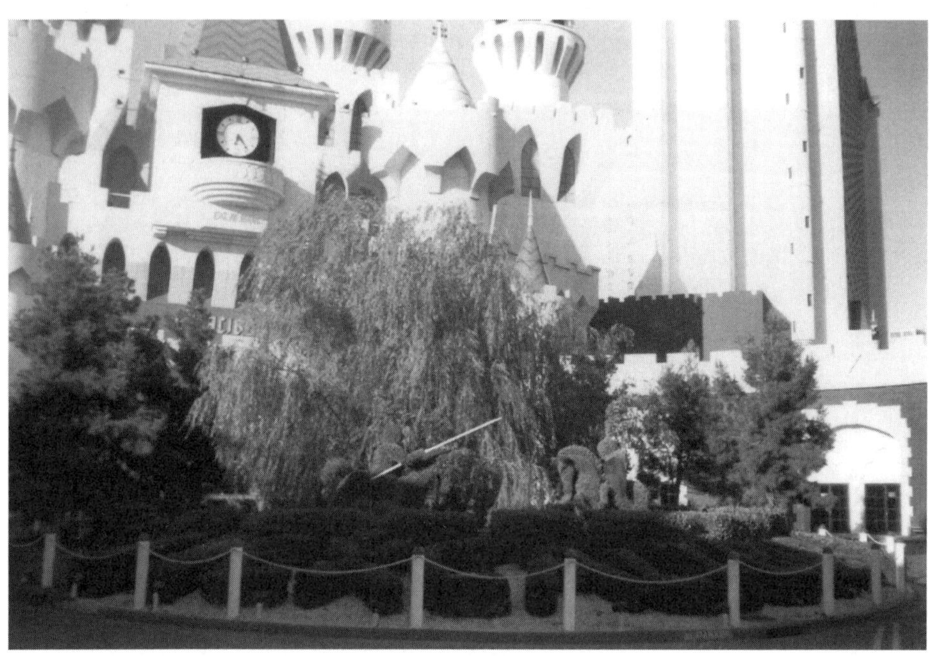

Figures 9.4–9.7 Exterior and interior of the Excalibur Hotel.

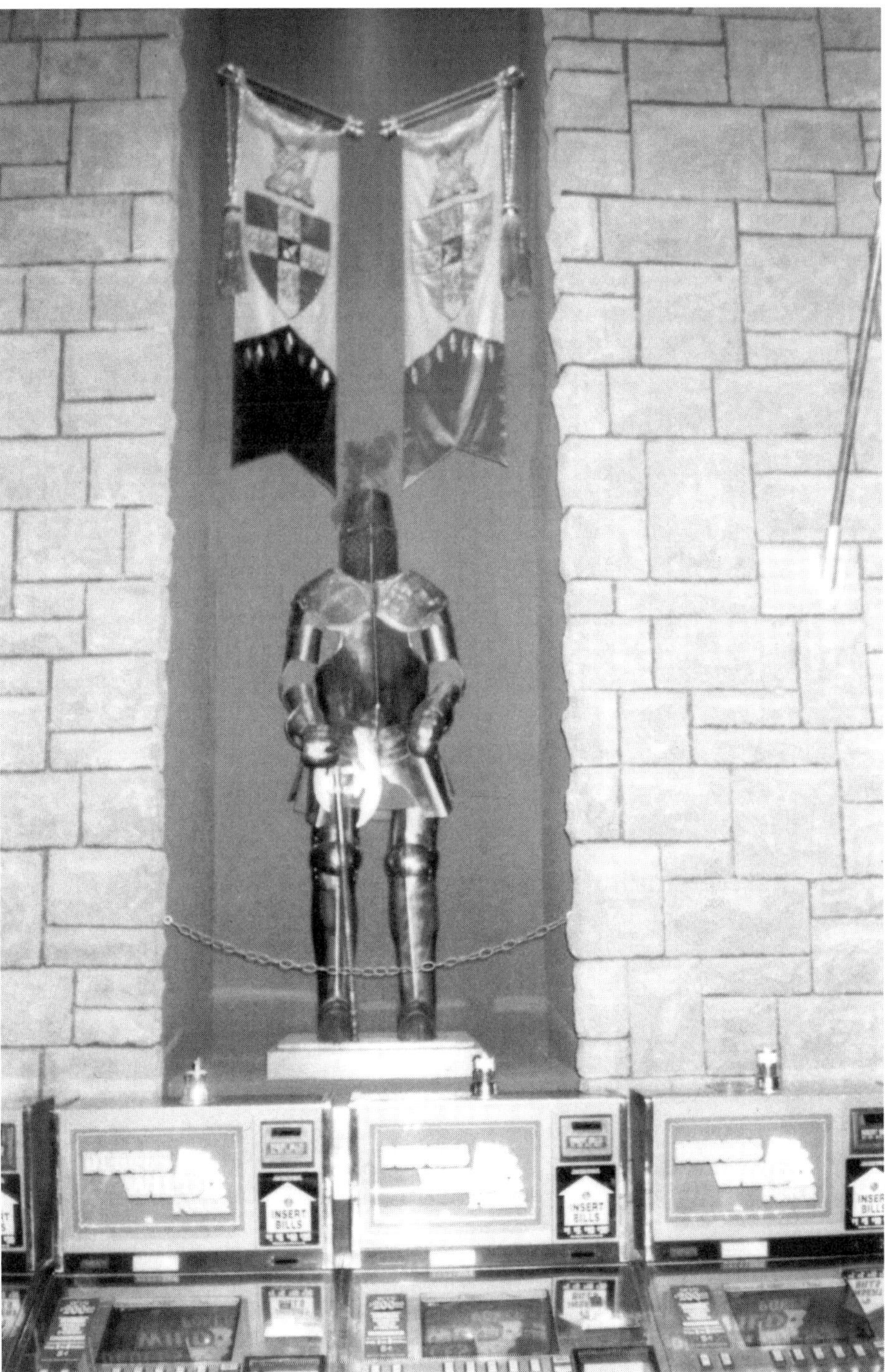

Figure 9.5

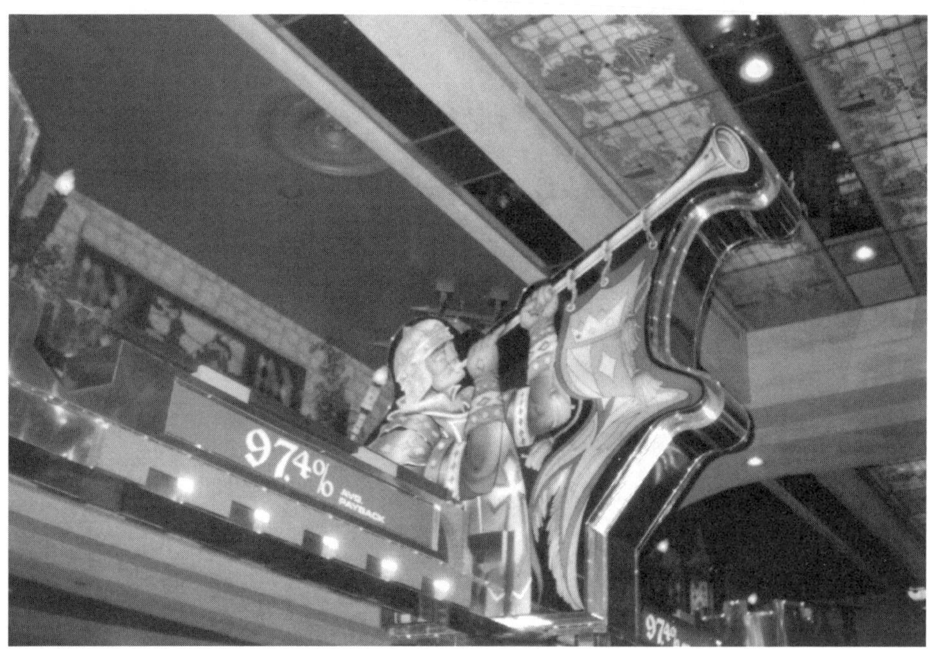

Figure 9.6

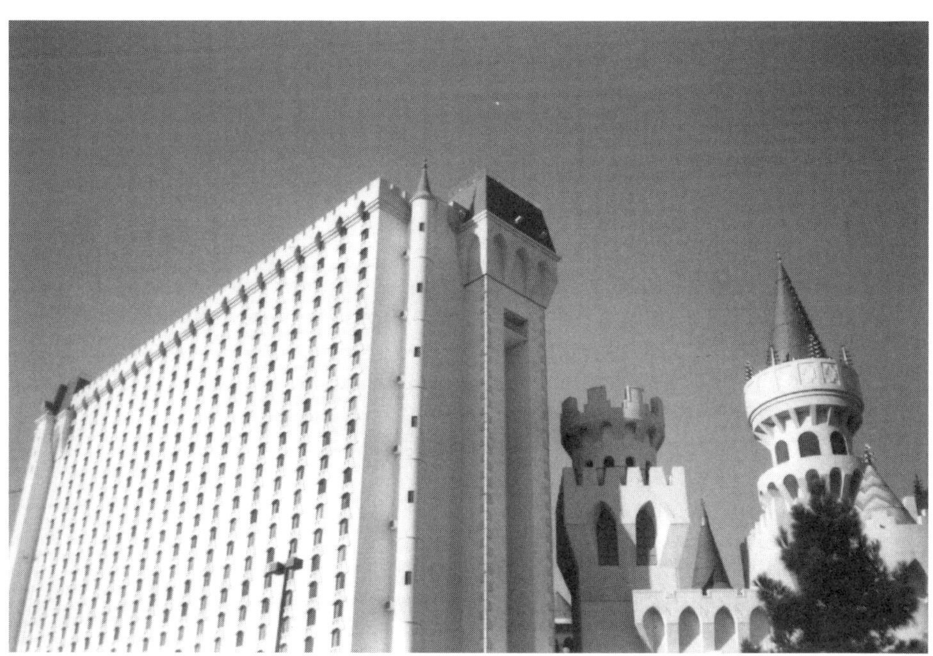

Figure 9.7

so on) to present a "crypto-Egypto" narrative about a pre-Egyptian civilization that has conquered gravity (*Making*). With everything from thirty football fields of carpeting to a model of the sphinx that is 50 percent larger than the original, the designers of Luxor downplayed gaming and focused instead on architecture and high-tech special effects to create a complicated theme that begs to be read as a story.

"The strange mystery beneath the Las Vegas desert" is how Luxor is described in one of three films that visitors can pay to see (see fig. 9.8). Though most guests probably associate Luxor with an attempt at theming ancient Egypt, the design for the resort was developed by Douglas Trumbull, a special effects expert who cut his teeth on Stanley Kubrick's *2001* (1968) and later oversaw special effects in such films as *Star Trek: The Motion Picture* (1979) (see fig. 9.9). His idea for the theme of Luxor—surely the most elaborate in Vegas—is a strange amalgam of postcolonialism and sci-fi, based on a plot much like the film (now television series) *Stargate.* As the first of three films informs us, the Luxor pyramid is supposed to be built on top of a 100,000-year-old temple. "It was discovered in a vision during an eclipse," a young female archaeologist tells us and then goes on to explain that she was suddenly able to decipher hieroglyphics (as in Mormon beliefs), which then allowed her to read a map that led her to someone's back yard, to a shaft, and finally to the temple. Once at the temple site, the archaeologist and her fellow adventurers find a "monoled": a "magnetically levitating flying vehicle." If one is interested, one can experience the rest of their "adventure" as it unfolds in the other two films. The overall plot involves a military type who is trying to take control of the discovery from the archaeologist who is trying to save it for the future. The "hero" of the tale, not surprisingly, is the developer: he has the legal rights to the land the shaft was found on, so he is able to control the future of the new discovery.

Of course, it would not be unusual for the average visitor to Luxor to miss the point of the resort's strange design. With its odd mixture of the fantastic and the historical, Luxor is simply the latest—and perhaps most conceptual—installment in Vegas's strange pastiche approach to architecture and theming. Like the other large hotels that anchor the corner of Tropicana and Las Vegas Boulevard, Luxor presents an immensely imposing facade (see fig. 9.10). After the appearance of Luxor, perhaps grandness was necessary just as a way to keep up. Indeed, it's not an exaggeration to say that the mega-hotels have their own skylines—something made literal after the opening of New York, New York, located on the strip next to

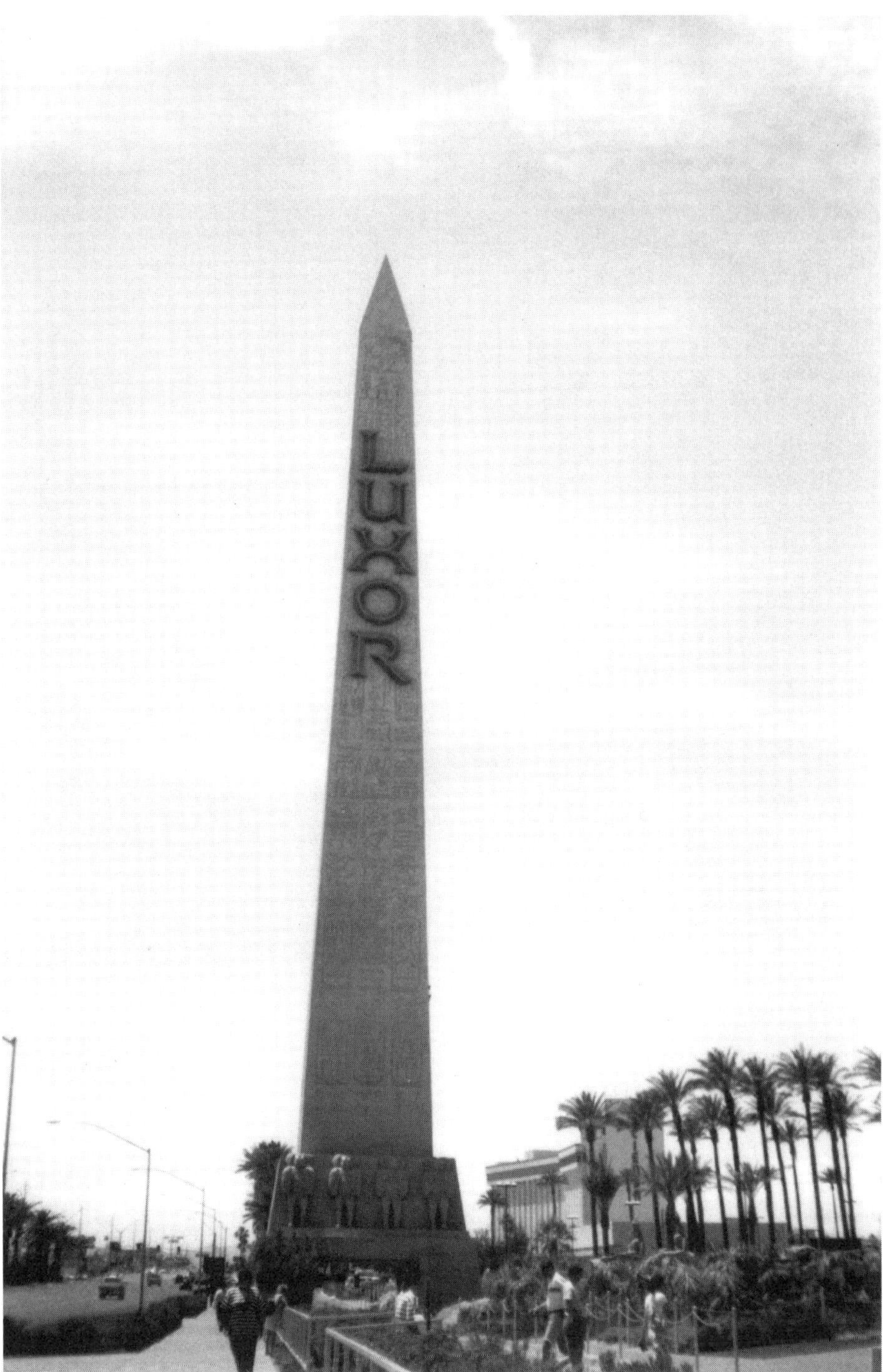

Figure 9.8 Luxor sign.

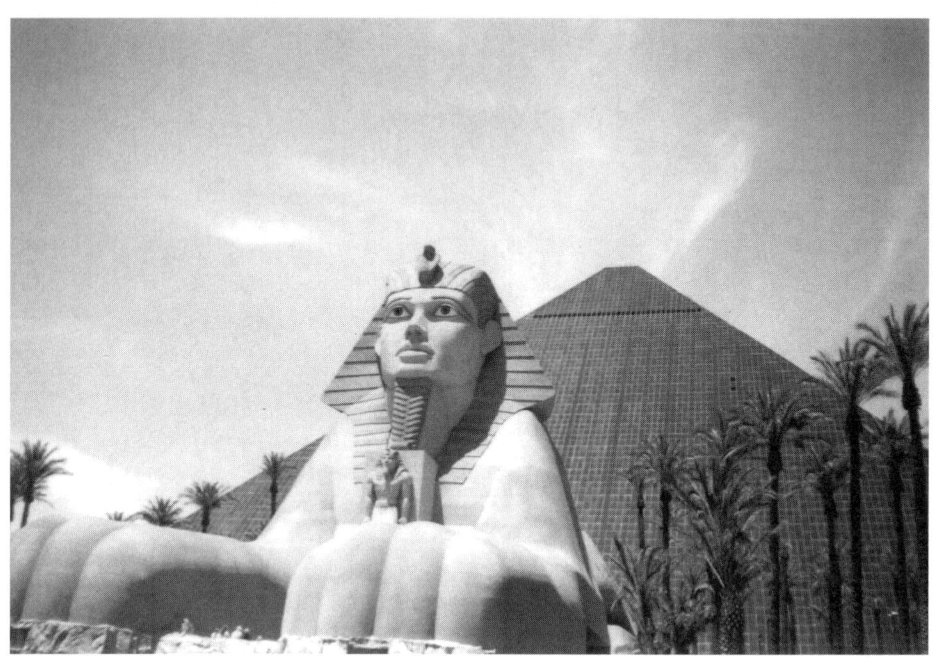

Figure 9.9 Exterior of the Luxor Hotel.

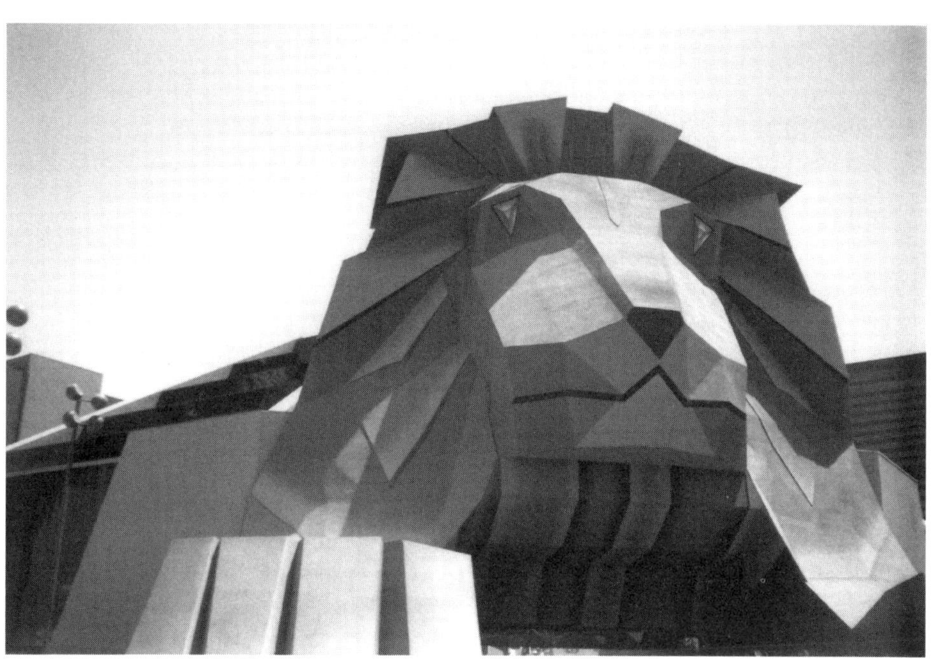

Figure 9.10 Exterior of the MGM Grand Hotel.

Excalibur (see fig. 9.11). Even with these elaborate external dressings, however, in the main, all the casinos feel the same: each has a lavish pool area; a huge casino or two; a hotel tower (towers being important to pack in as many guests as possible); a buffet area; a couple of theaters; and, finally, some theming in order to distinguish the products. Yet, despite the hype that each new Vegas hotel generates—the Stratosphere; New York, New York; Monte Carlo; Belagio; Paris—the fact is that Vegas is about gambling, not about the interactive cultural synergy that Walt Disney created in the 1950s when he unveiled a new concept for a theme park and linked it to a television show based on the same idea. This was a conceptual breakthrough that forever changed the landscape of popular culture—and how we think about space and the built environment. Vegas may be attempting to learn from Disney, as we've all learned from Las Vegas, but for the purposes of sucking in more guests to gamble and not for them to enjoy theme parks.

Luxor was later topped by the new MGM Grand Hotel, a rebuilt casino that more than dwarfs the original MGM Grand that was destroyed by fire. The new MGM even has its own theme park. That is, though the resort is themed for the Wizard of Oz, there is also on the premises a separate theme park—a mini Six Flags or Busch Gardens (see figs. 9.12–14). Interestingly, it doesn't appear that many people go there. In fact, the theme park seems in every possible way like an afterthought—or certainly not the primary reason that anyone would want to visit MGM. Once again, the question gets begged: in the end, what is the product that the casinos are selling? And, of course, what are we to make of a theme park that doesn't theme very well? Would one go into MGM's theme park if it were less derivative and functioned in either of the two ways that most theme parks function: either as themed environments (Disneyland), or as a place with increasingly larger or rougher roller coasters (the Six Flags chain of amusement parks)? Or is MGM's theme park just the equivalent of the rather mediocre three-dollar prime rib dinner? What do you expect; after all, it's more or less free?

Unlike Disney World, in Vegas one is handed pornography as one walks along the Strip. Though there is elaborate security, there is also the feeling that—as one sees in the tragic death of rapper Tupac Shakur—there is the possibility of violence. There is also the tawdriness of much of the downtown, and the obvious knowledge that Vegas plays on the ideas of sophistication and insiderness, rather than fantasy and/or nostalgia such as at a Disney park. Indeed, Vegas is about getting ripped off, enjoying the grift. The disorientation of

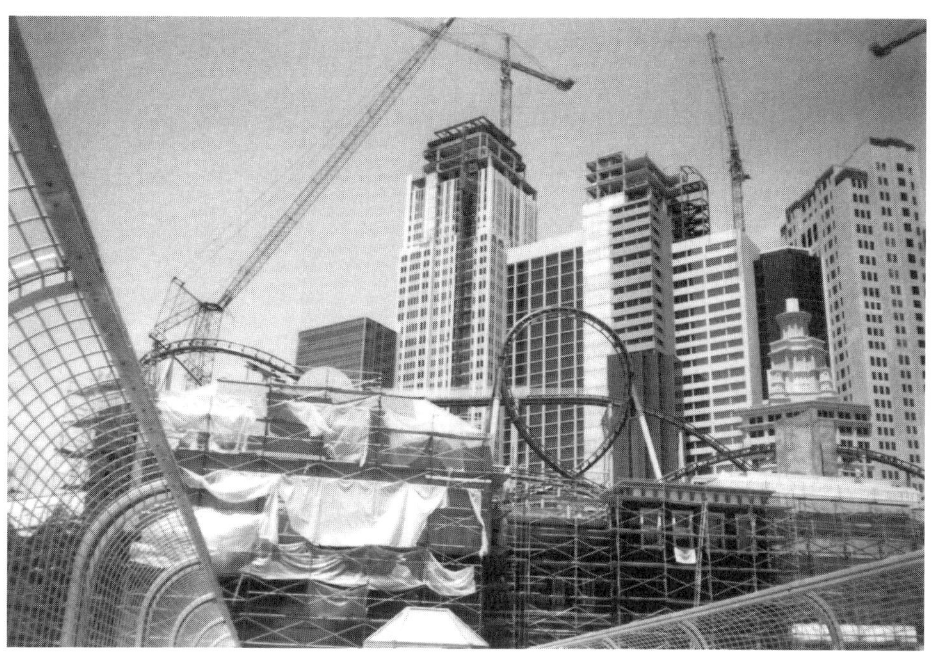

Figure 9.11 New York, New York Hotel under construction.

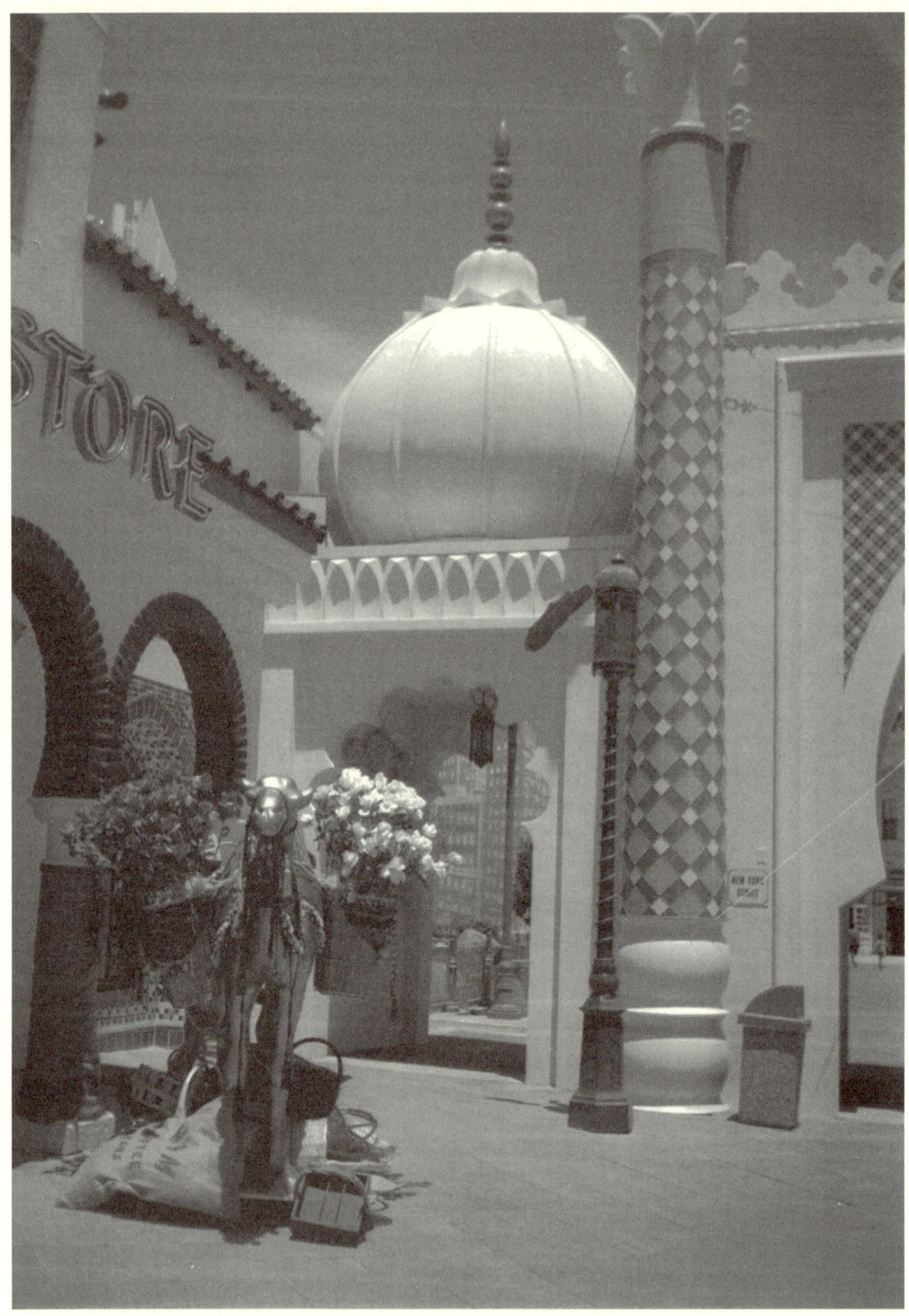

Figure 9.12–9.14 The theme park at the MGM Grand Hotel.

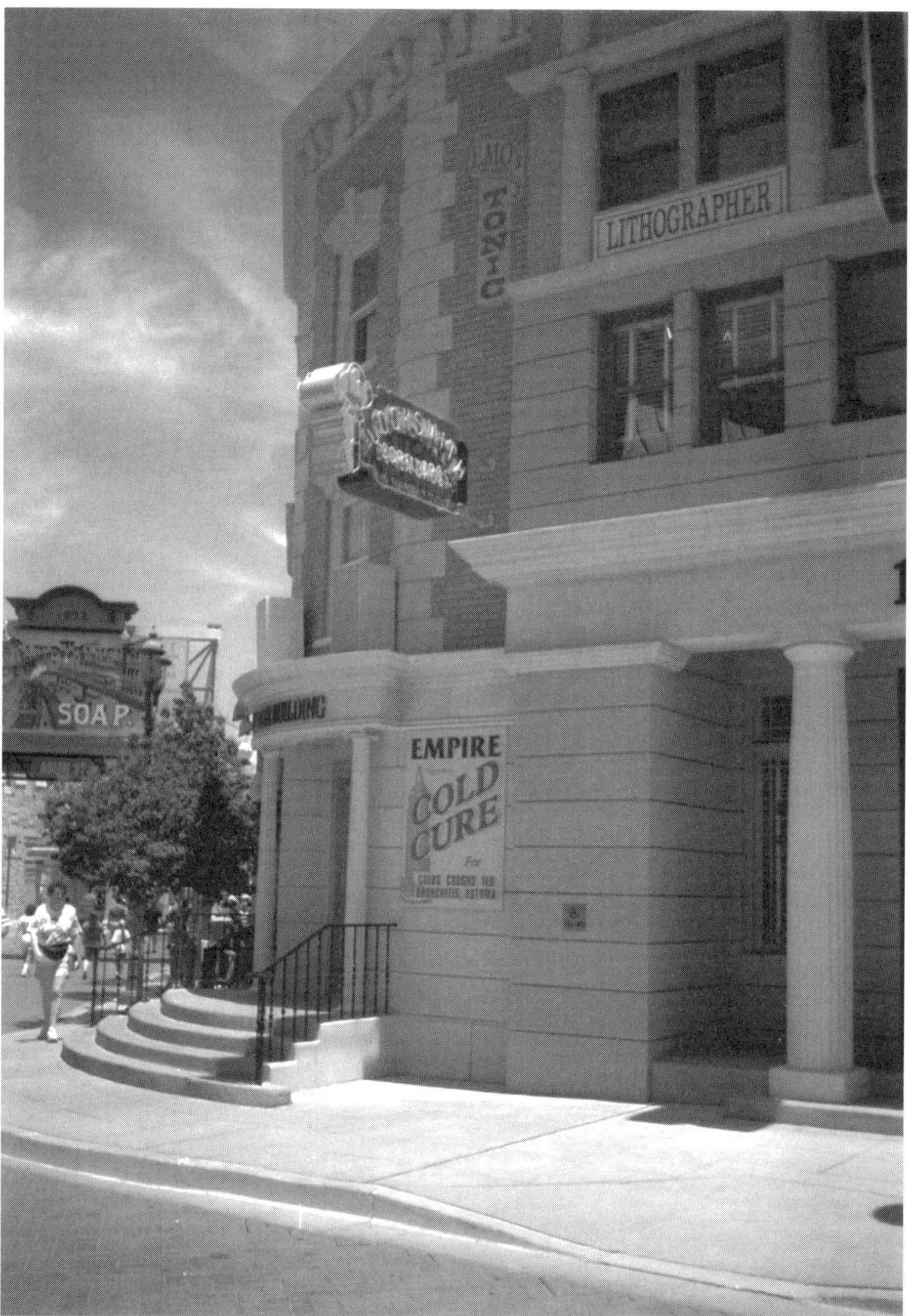

Figure 9.13

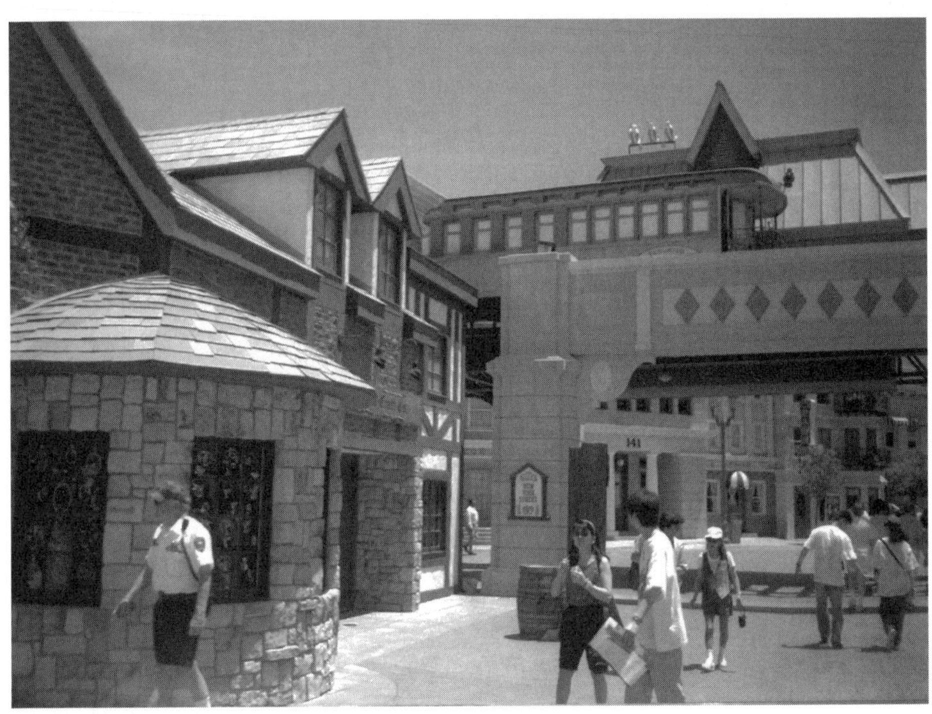

Figure 9.14

light and sound that occurs at Vegas twenty-four hours a day is not planned to amuse, but to distract—or attract—for the reasons of getting you to spend more money. The carny atmosphere of the state fair—the very thing Walt Disney so wanted to erase or suppress in his parks—is very much alive at Vegas. This atmosphere permeates the place at all levels, sitting very much at odds with the idea of "family" or even of "children." Vegas isn't for those who disdain overkill, but likewise, it isn't for those who don't understand the enjoyment of gambling—and the often related pleasures of scopophilia, drinking, and feeling that you are getting a lot of food and a lot of high-class entertainment at rock-bottom prices. There are costs in Vegas, but only indirect ones: you feed the slots rather than pay the waiters.

Though the Vegas resort hotels attempt to create the same kind of all-encompassing isolation from the world that Disney does, unlike Disney, Vegas corporate designers don't make their amusements accessible. If Disney creates "lands" or "worlds" that you are asked to explore and to get lost in, Vegas is a semiotic system of signs that function in such a way as to tell you only enough to catch your attention, but not necessarily as much information as you might like to have. To access the narrative of Luxor you have to pay to see three separate movies. As Taylor observes, the meaning behind Luxor is, finally, like the space-age hieroglyphs, "indecipherable" and "irreducibly cryptic" (248). Themes must normally work as stories that involve the viewer or participant in a narrative. Vegas tells you nothing about itself other than what you see—what was once transmitted via the signs and that is now implicit in the architectural theming. Disney attempts to "educate" its public by offering mountains of information about how a particular lake was dredged, or what the historical referent for a particular ride's architecture is, but Vegas, like "the Mob" that created it, wants you to know as little as possible. You aren't allowed to take photographs of the slot machines at Caesar's Palace. To enter into Vegas is to enter into an entire city of muted communication. There is no one to talk to; random interpersonal communication between guests is extremely unlikely; there are no information packets about the casinos. Vegas is a sign that consists of such a jumble of referents (extreme pastiche), that they don't relate to anything real, but then they don't relate to anything simulated (or representational) at all. To do either thing would be to communicate something to the viewer. Vegas prefers to remain silent.

Vegas doesn't try to offer the experience of theming that Disney does. What Vegas provides for most visitors instead is a strange mix of the elite—the myth of the underground world of the high roller—and the chance to wallow in one's own middle-classness: finding the cheapest buffet in town, for instance. These two "cultures" manage to exist in a very comfortable relation to each other, but this relationship also partly explains the schizoid aspects of Vegas's theming. Does "Las Vegas World" really know what it wants to be? Doesn't there have to be a meta-theme at work for the other themes to function (for example, EPCOT as the future, and the future as spatial)? Doesn't there also have to be a sense of trust between the person experiencing the place and the corporation, rather than one built upon suspicion? If environment, as opposed to spectacle or show, are what people want, then Vegas isn't a threat to Disney, even with the mammoth hotels like Luxor and MGM Grand. Lounge acts are still what Vegas does well. Originally a combination of comedy, strip tease, and singing, the latest formulation seems to be an unobjectionable performer such as a magician paired with a comic who performs "adult" humor. The lounge act stresses the way in which Vegas is a couple's place, rather than a family place. Or, one might say, Vegas is the destination for young, as yet childless couples: those who are not quite ready for the family paradigm. These young people constitute one of many waves of visitors: busses of West Coasters on the weekends; foreign tourists; older visitors on respirators, seemingly here on, or for, their last breath.

At the OZ Buffet in MGM, people try to sit on the white picket fence because there is no place to wait for the buffet to open. If one just wants to watch people gamble, then one has to sit at a slot machine—with one's back turned toward it. Basic human needs are not acknowledged in Vegas, even though the traditions of Vegas are to encourage human waste. One overeats, overgambles, overdrinks, in the middle of a desert, in a postmodern environment that is literally a manmade oasis that one flies into at night, so that one will forget about time, forget that one is, indeed, any longer on the planet at all. The socialist idea that everyone should eat well cheaply is used to serve a conservative capitalist ethos. Everyone can enjoy Vegas, though there is a distinction between the big spender and the three-night guest. No auteuristic spirit need abide here. The casinos avoid innovation because they can just borrow it. Disney does this, too, but it Disnifies its sources. Vegas never tries to make something that is borrowed into something new—tackier, bigger, maybe—but that's not the same thing.

What really works best in Vegas are structures or environments that are themed in a restrained way—or perhaps inadvertently as nostalgia for Vegas's traditional glitz (The Mirage, for example).

Theming in Vegas is interactive and full-scaled, while the sort of fantasy world of Disney's Magic Kingdom section is not in evidence. Vegas is about monotony: each casino replicates the same thing over and over again. All the casinos are the same, separated only by their themes, which are clearly secondary. Disney, in contrast, has one of everything (one camp ground, one merry-go-round ride, one haunted house, etc.), but each is part of the integrated system of Disney thematics. Vegas is a repeating island, or oasis, or mirage, but the repetition is serial. The desert may be, finally, the ultimate paradigm here. The ancient paleographies that encrust the rocks outside the city are also hieroglyphs, parts of a sign system that stand out from the beauty of the natural surroundings (see fig. 9.15). The desert reflects not back onto Vegas, but echoes or structures its inability to seem inevitable, ancient, or overwhelming, even as it presents the spectacle of its own always recurring discovery.

Gambling on the Future

Vegas as it exists on the Strip is gambling as a postmodern phenomenon: family entertainment that completely avoids any acknowledgment that pleasure and leisure consumption should come about in any form other than via the glitz of Vegas-style simulacra. The total reliance on capitalist markers of excess sit in odd contrast to the simultaneous reification of one's position outside the hierarchy of show business, say, as well as within the middle-class tourist paradigm. One is an insider to one's own stratification. The future that is bet on by laying the odds on gambling as both financial bonanza as well as a new paradigm for mass entertainment is one in which the nascent optimism of much consumer leisure production is exchanged for a vision of the future that is controlled by the odds set by the house. One becomes, in a casino, a betting machine: an anonymous part in an infinitely replicating orgy of self-denial. Casinos go beyond the Disney paradigm to create worlds that are devoid not only of spontaneity and play, but even of limited choice or everyday freedom. Casinos and gaming generally offer a glimpse of the next wave of postmodernist themed culture. Though the iconography of gambling is that of the frontier and the nineteenth-century landscape of the United States, the goals of casino designers and the corporate avatars of gaming are ones firmly set on the continued growth of popular culture. One need only look at the seventy-million-dollar themed environment, Star Trek: The Experience, in the Vegas Hilton

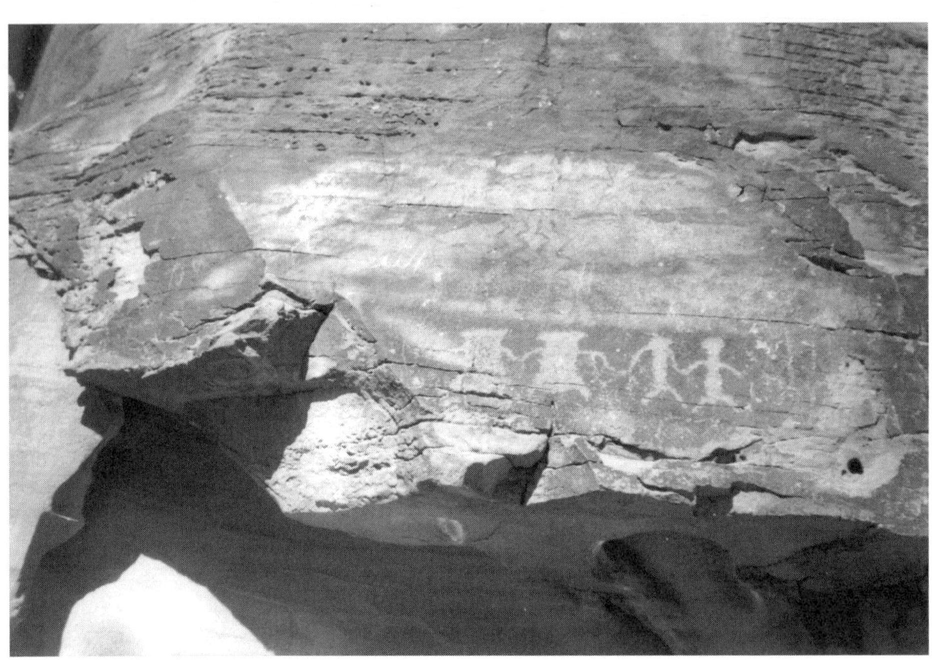

Figure 9.15 Petroglyphs

to understand the synergy perceived to be at work between an entertainment conglomerate like Viacom, the owner of the Star Trek franchise, and an international hotel chain like Hilton. Vegas may become the place to go to for pop cultural experiences that cannot be had anywhere else. What Vegas may eventually evolve into is as yet unknown, but that it is be a major player in postmodern cultural production now seems inevitable.

Taylor sees the new architecture of the Strip as existing beyond the categories of modernism and postmodernism: "If modernism has lessons to learn from Las Vegas, it is because Las Vegas has always understood modernism better than modernists themselves. Like the desires circulating through it, ornament never disappears even when it is denied. The Strip strips bare the pretenses of modernism by exposing structure as ornament and form as figure rather than ground. If ground is figure and figure ground, foundations collapse" (250). But if implosion does occur, as Taylor suggests, then Vegas isn't the "ground zero" of a war between Le Corbusier and Gehry but an evolution in the themed environment that either freezes at the flashpoint because of the inevitable allegiance that theming has to gambling, or suggests a form of themed architecture that takes the lessons of Disney but applies them to corporate competitiveness to create a new form of theming as spectacle—as a nonnarrative hyperspace that questions or extends the definition of architecture as a mere physical entity rather than as the simulacrum of an event.

In the 7 June 1958 issue of *The Nation,* Julian Halevy speculates on the relation between Disneyland, then only three years old, and Las Vegas to conclude "that both of these institutions exist for the relief of tension and boredom, as tranquilizers for social anxiety, and they both provide fantasy experiences in which not-so-secret longings are pseudo-satisfied. Their huge profits and mushrooming growth suggest that as conformity and adjustment become more rigidly imposed on the American scene, the drift to fantasy release will become a flight" (513). He was, of course, correct in this prediction and in the idea that Vegas is not about gambling so much as the illusion of gambling as the house always has the advantage and gamblers play the house, not each other. Likewise, the atmosphere of Vegas is distinct from Disney, though it is related in that one travels to Vegas to enter—or reenter—a specific kind of place: "You live in a luxury world where the fact of money seems beneath notice; a world of Olympic swimming pools, hanging gardens, waitresses beautiful as movie stars, marble baths and bars a block long [. . .] royal buffets and obsequious waiters offering free drinks. The illusion is created that we are all rich, that money means nothing" (Halevy 511). The difference between Disney and Vegas is that for the latter money is fantasy and illusion, either disappearing or seeming to magnify in its power to buy. In either case, you feel tacky for holding on to it as though you thought it had value. Money, in Vegas, becomes what you learn to forget. The fantasy, if you buy it, is that money has no meaning in life—that it is either something we can live without, or something that we can give up for the feeling that the distraction is value enough. If Disney World offers escape as fantasy—as themed stories we can enter via nostalgia or the preprogrammed sense of following the prescription of the family vacation—Vegas offers the thrill of forming a habit, deciding that giving your money away for free is fun to you. Constituting the excitement of the illusion of chance, it is a choice you make.

10

Postmodernism and Holocaust Memory: Productive Tensions in the U.S. Holocaust Memorial Museum

Nancy J. Peterson

In *Twilight Memories: Marking Time in a Culture of Amnesia* (1995), Andreas Huyssen contemplates the fate of memory in postmodern culture, a culture he describes as "terminally ill with amnesia" (1). In a world capable of being connected instantaneously via the Internet and various mass media, Huyssen argues, "active remembrance," in the traditional forms of personal and collective memory, has almost become obsolete (249). This contemporary crisis of memory and remembering has become particularly urgent in reference to the Holocaust. The survivors of the camps are becoming aged, and their memories—which are critical to a contemporary understanding of the trauma—may die along with them. To alleviate the potential fragility of Holocaust memory, videotape archives of survivors' testimonies have been established in various locations throughout the United States (the Fortunoff Video Archive for Holocaust Testimonies at Yale University being perhaps the best known). In this respect, postmodern culture offers a high-tech solution to a potential loss; saving these testimonies on tape for posterity enables the survivors' memories to become "rememories," in Toni Morrison's sense, for those who have not experienced the trauma firsthand.[1]

Simply making these tapes or having them on hand is not sufficient for the cultural work of Holocaust remembrance, however. Huyssen emphasizes the need for memory to be active, not "frozen"; to be collective and public, not just individual and private. The museum, for Huyssen, offers one kind of postmodern public space where the cultural work of remembering can be actively and collectively engaged. In fact, noting the proliferation of museums in recent decades, Huyssen argues that "museummania" characterizes contemporary Western and American culture because it is one instantiation of a profound desire to memorialize history, "to articulate memory in stone or other permanent matter" (*Twilight* 253). The Holocaust is the focus of well-known museums in Jerusalem (Vad Yashem), Los

Angeles (the Beit HaShoah-Museum of Tolerance), and Washington, D.C. (the United States Holocaust Memorial Museum), as well as many memorials elsewhere.[2] The proliferation of such museums is not only a testament to the desire for remembrance in contemporary culture; it also indicates the degree to which Holocaust remembrance has acquired a certain kind of market or tourist value. Indeed, the United States Holocaust Memorial Museum is currently the most visited national museum in this country. As a national site, the U.S. Holocaust Memorial Museum embodies the complicated relations of Holocaust history and memory in postmodern culture. By closely examining the design and purpose of the museum, this chapter explores the difficulties attached to sustaining a vital collective remembrance of the Holocaust in contemporary America and at the same time locates unexpected ways by which the museum may assuage cultural and historical amnesia.

Americanizing the Holocaust

The U.S. Holocaust Memorial Museum has become such a popular tourist attraction that visitors to Washington, D.C., typically need to procure advance passes to ensure that they will be able to tour the permanent exhibit on a given date. It is no small irony, then, to note that the committees charged with planning the museum feared at the beginning of the project that perhaps no one would want to visit a museum commemorating such a tragedy. One of the issues they have faced from the start of the process is the marketing of the museum to an American public. In fact, the consideration of market value entered into the originating impulses for the museum: in 1979, needing to win over Jewish voters for his reelection campaign, President Jimmy Carter approved the recommendation of a commission he had appointed the previous year to build a "living memorial" to the Holocaust under federal auspices (qtd. in Linenthal 37).[3]

Those working on the development of the museum were aware that the establishment of a Holocaust museum on the national Mall would require a tailoring of the building, its contents, and its purposes for a predominately American audience. The original plans for the building were amended in response to concerns about whether the museum would be a good neighbor to the memorials on the surrounding Mall. Architect James Ingo Freed was asked to scale down the Hall of Witness so that it would not obtrude beyond the outlines of the adjoining buildings, and a couple of committee members urged him to provide transparent windows in the Hall of Remembrance so that visitors could glimpse the Washington monument and the Mall area more generally to remind them of American democratic ideals (see Linenthal 99–104).

The impetus to Americanize the story of the Holocaust is also clearly evident in the permanent exhibit space, which opens with a blown-up, wall-sized photograph from April 1945 showing American troops looking profoundly disturbed as they view charred corpses of Ohrdruf concentration camp inmates. This image bears the title "Americans Liberate the Camps." Text and image together evoke a nationalist narrative that frames the story of the Holocaust in the museum: the depiction of American soldiers as liberators of the camps is a necessary point of entry because it coincides with popular patriotic narratives of America as the "home of the free" and "the land of the brave." The museum, to its credit, does present episodes and evidence in the permanent exhibit that run counter to this rosy patriotism; this becomes particularly clear in the detailed narration of the fatal consequence of the United States' refusal to accept the refugees from the *S.S. St. Louis*,[4] as well as in the part of the exhibit that discusses the failure to bomb Auschwitz despite the availability of aerial photos that may have enabled a precise bombardment of the crematoria. But the narrative of Americans as liberators is never entirely displaced. Right after the monumental photograph of American soldiers at Ohrdruf, viewers encounter photographs of Eisenhower witnessing the camps and read his words condemning them: "The things I saw beggar description. [. . .] The visual evidence and the verbal testimony of starvation, cruelty and bestiality were [. . .] overpowering. [. . .] I made the visit deliberately in order to be in position to give firsthand evidence of these things if ever, in the future, there develops a tendency to charge these allegations merely to 'propaganda.'"[5] Eisenhower's words, alongside these images, suggest a particular relation between patriotism and witnessing: American museumgoers, they imply, should be like Eisenhower in bearing witness to the Holocaust to make the world safe from Nazism and for democracy.

As Carol Duncan's analysis of museums and citizenship suggests, museums are "monumental creations" designed not only to preserve and display objects, but also to "carr[y] out broad, sometimes less obvious political and ideological tasks" (90). Duncan goes on to observe that "every major state, monarchical or republican, understood the usefulness of having a public art museum. Such public institutions made (and still make) the state look good: progressive, concerned about the spiritual life of its citizens, a preserver of past achievements and a provider of the common good" (93). While the U.S. Holocaust Memorial Museum is not an art museum, as a monumental creation designed to fit into the Washington, D.C., Mall surroundings, it corresponds to Duncan's observations about the subtle ideological investments of museums as public, national spaces. The museum is designed in part to produce good American citizens, a purpose made manifest in the fundraising letter the museum sent out in 1997 to invite people to become members. The letter states unequivocally that "this is an American museum," for, as the letter goes on to specify, it is "*a museum of American values,*" "*a museum of American experiences,*" "*a museum of American history,*" and "*a museum of American people.*"[6]

One might argue that the carefully placed images and texts of Americans as liberators narratively frame and contain the disturbing evidence of American indifference presented elsewhere within the body of the exhibit.[7] Indeed, it is tempting to be suspicious of the ideological maneuvering overtly represented in the framing photographs and narrative of the Holocaust museum. The important work of Holocaust scholar James E. Young, however, demonstrates the degree to which Holocaust memorials may "take on lives of their own, often stubbornly resistant to the state's original intentions" (*Texture* 3). Following Young's observation, we might see these opening tactics as essential to the pedagogical potential of the museum. By the strategic use of such photographs, the exhibit planners have made it possible for visitors to enter this traumatic space gradually, to prepare themselves to face the moments in the museum when unmitigated despair and utter hollowness are the only appropriate responses. Clearly the pedagogic intentions of the museum would be in vain if some sort of transitional space did not enable visitors to enter and immerse themselves in this bleak historical narrative.

The building itself both Americanizes the museum and offers important resistance to a patriotic narrative. While the exterior of the building is a good neighbor to its surroundings, the building as a whole remarkably resists its placement in the symbolic geography of the Mall. Visitors entering the building first must pass through metal detectors, a moment that underscores the ways in which this museum provides a narrative that is potentially explosive.[8] The first public space, where visitors await their timed entry to the permanent exhibit, is the Hall of Witness: a hall that is designed not to represent mimetically but to suggest obliquely the world of the camps through the use of red brick and steel beams (see fig. 10.1).[9] The cold metallic

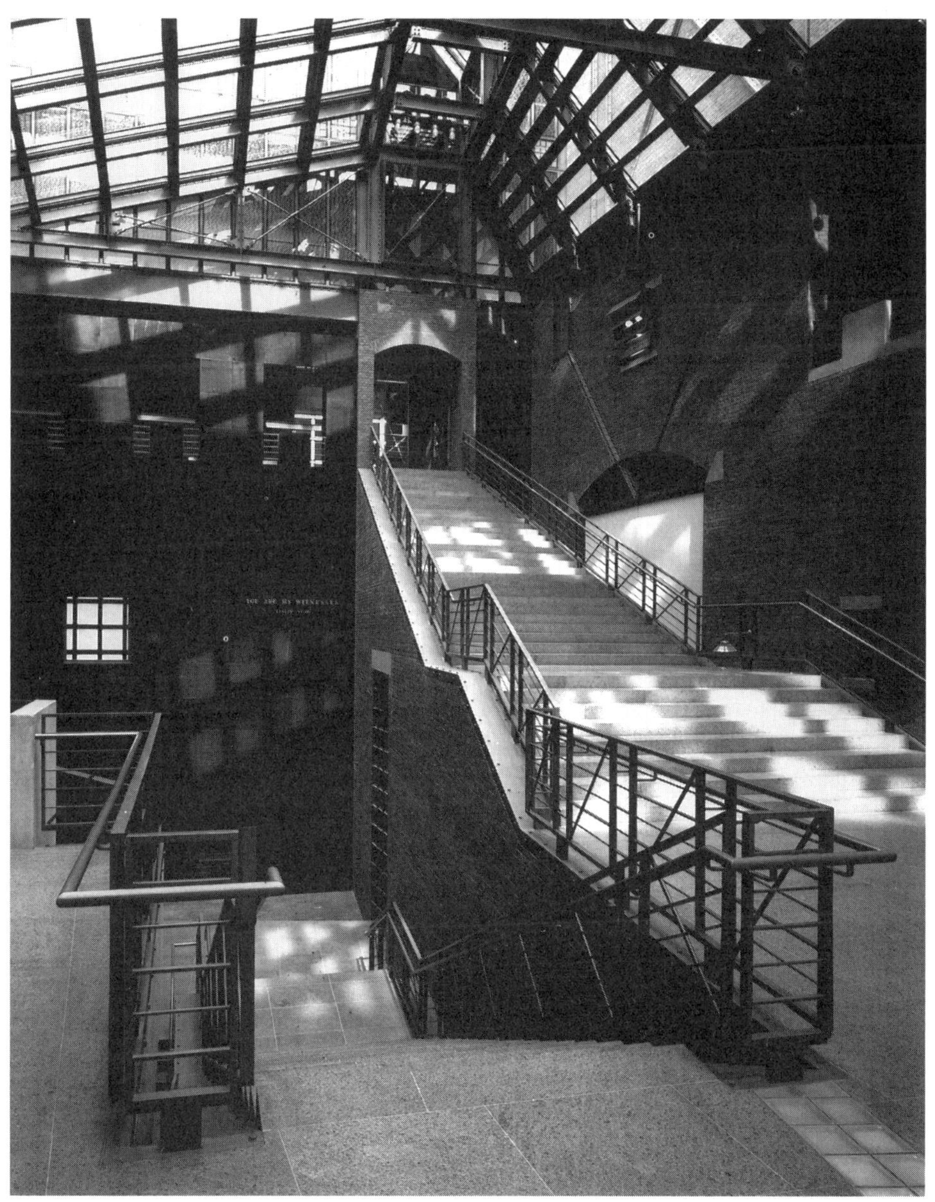

Figure 10.1 The Hall of Witness. Photograph © Norman McGrath.

elevators that carry visitors to the beginning of the permanent exhibit on the fourth floor evoke resonances of the efficient modern technologies that made the Final Solution possible. These details suggest, then, that as one enters the museum building, the interior creates an atmosphere that leaves the symbolic space of Washington, D.C., far behind.[10]

Even the Hall of Remembrance, the public commemorative space that visitors enter at the conclusion of the permanent exhibit, does not offer a clear, redemptive view of the Mall. I mentioned above that Freed was asked to provide windows that would provide such a view, but he refused. He did include narrow windows that run from floor to ceiling where the six walls that make up the hall intersect each other, but Freed carefully made most of the window panes opaque so the visitor's vision is dramatically fractured, thus calling into question glib symbolic or redemptive connections (see fig. 10.2). Thus, while market and political pressures influenced the redesigning of the exterior facade of the Holocaust Museum, the building experienced from the interior fits neither the logic of the history and art museums that are proximate to it, nor does it adhere to the patriotic symbolism of the Washington Monument and the Lincoln and Jefferson Memorials, which dominate the Mall surroundings in which the museum is located (see fig. 10.3). In fact, in 1987, when museum planners proposed tearing down a nearby building (Annex 3) to give the museum more space, the Fine Arts Commission in Washington rejected the proposal. By preserving Annex 3, the commission prevented the museum from coming directly into the lines of sight of the Washington Monument and Jefferson Memorial and perhaps overpowering them as a national symbol. The national monument closest in its sobering tone to the Holocaust Memorial Museum is the Vietnam Veterans Memorial, designed by Maya Lin, which was also the subject of heated disputes and contentions for its "failure" to "properly" commemorate the war and the nation. And in fact, the same black granite used for the Vietnam Memorial recurs in the Hall of Remembrance (Freed 456). As a monumental public space evoking a terrible historical wound, like the Vietnam Veterans Memorial, the U.S. Holocaust Memorial Museum ultimately resists its interpellation within the patriotic narratives and nationalist interests that would seek to contain its critical potential.

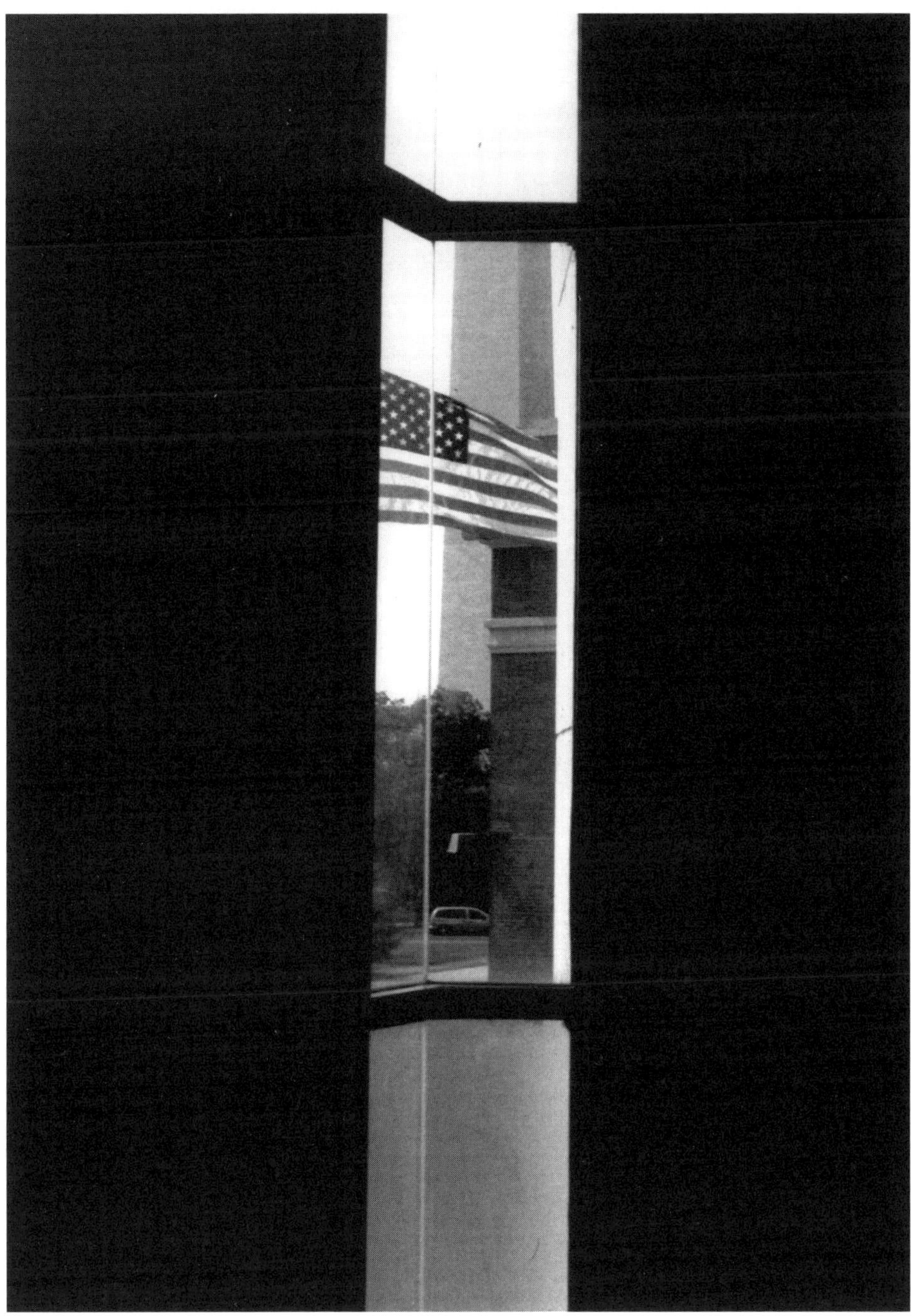

Figure 10.2 Opaque window panes in the Hall of Remembrance. Photograph by Nancy J. Peterson.

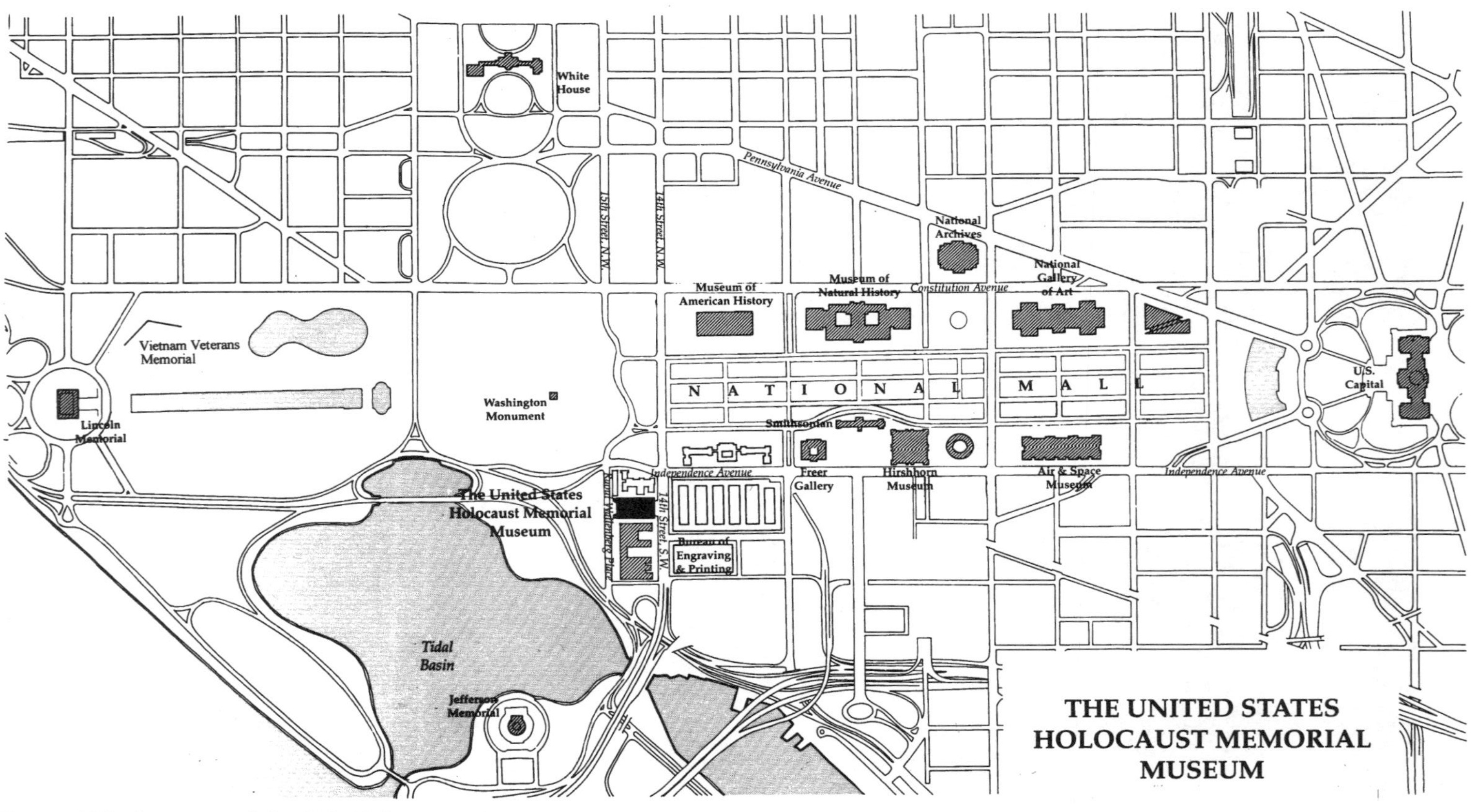

Figure 10.3 Courtesy of the U.S. Holocaust Museum

Exhibiting Holocaust History

It is not only the location of the museum, however, that is laden with productive tensions and contradictions; as an institution, it occupies sometimes harmonious, oftentimes conflicting roles as a museum and as a memorial. Most of the space on the second, third, and fourth floors is allocated to the permanent exhibit, whose major purpose is to preserve evidence, or traces, of the past. To function as a museum, this space must necessarily foreground archival and documentary projects—projects that have been radically called into question by many postmodern theorists.[11] As a memorial, however, the building must resonate as a "sacred space,"[12] as a place to reflect upon the Holocaust as a historical tragedy that cannot and will not ever be registered, known, or articulated fully. To put this another way, while the role of a Holocaust *museum* is to represent the past as real, the role of a Holocaust *memorial* is to call attention to the failure of all attempts at representation.

A close look at the principles of organization and selection of the permanent exhibit can help to explore the tension between these divergent purposes. The exhibit is divided into three parts: "Nazi Assault 1933–1939," " 'Final Solution' 1940–1945," and "Last Chapter" (a look at rescue and resistance, liberator and survivor testimonies). As this sequence suggests, the museum relies on an emphatically clear and coherent historical narrative—a point reinforced by the museum guide given to all visitors, which carefully maps each floor of the museum and the permanent exhibit. Enabling visitors to gain an overarching understanding of Holocaust history by touring the permanent exhibit is certainly an important part of the museum's educational mission, but such a guiding principle can also lead to instances where the complexities of history are oversimplified or denied. For Edward T. Linenthal, who has written a detailed book on the development and design of the U.S. Holocaust Memorial Museum titled *Preserving Memory: The Struggle to Create America's Holocaust Museum,* such oversimplification occurs in the exhibit about the failure to bomb Auschwitz. Citing several reliable authorities who disagree with the interpretation presented in the museum that bombing Auschwitz was possible and would have saved the lives of Jewish prisoners, Linenthal argues that this is one instance in the museum where interpretation has been "elevated" to "historical truth" (224).[13] Linenthal's discussion of this contentious issue suggests the degree to which the museum is invested in presenting an authoritative, unequivocal historical narrative. Like all the labels in the permanent exhibit, the labels and text accompanying the discussion of the failure to bomb Auschwitz adopt a professorial tone, and the labels and text are unsigned. This practice produces a facticity that masks the interpretive dimension of this part of the exhibit.[14]

The visual artifact that dominates this part of the exhibit is an aerial photograph of Auschwitz-Birkenau, which is carefully labeled to show the locations of the gas chambers, the rail lines and trains, SS headquarters, and so on. An attentive visitor to the museum, however, will notice a small detail in this display that unsettles some of the assumptions of the accompanying text. In the lower right corner of the aerial photograph is a label that reads "Enlarged from the original negative and captioned in 1978 by the CIA." I take this label to indicate that this particular section of the original image was not enlarged or labeled in September 1944 when the aerial photograph was taken to allow American planes to bomb with precision the Buna factory, which was located approximately five miles east of the camp. Knowing that the carefully labeled image on display was created in 1978 (and not in 1944) is essential to comprehending the complexities of this moment in Holocaust history: the failure to enlarge this part of the image in 1944 might indicate callous indifference to the possibility of bombing Auschwitz and saving the lives of Jews, or it might indicate the degree to which bombing industrial centers was paramount for the Allies in their intensive efforts to stop the Nazi war machine. My purpose is not to take one side or the other in this debate, but to call attention to the ways in which the insistence on chronology, legibility, and authority in the permanent exhibit of the museum can lead to a misleading erasure of ambiguity. It might have been more instructive for visitors to the museum at this point to experience contradictory pieces of evidence and interpretation than to have one particular view represented as unequivocal truth.

In the careful selection of objects for the museum, one can discern another important principle that helped to shape the museum's mission and philosophy. The developers and planners were adamant that all the artifacts on display be authentic or genuine. Their commitment to this principle resulted in the astonishing recovery of pieces of Holocaust history: archivists for the museum, for example, went to Warsaw to talk with survivors and were shown a section of the original wall of the Warsaw Ghetto that public and official histories had forgotten. A section of this wall was cast, and the reproduction is on display in the museum. (Perhaps more important, a plaque commemorating the wall and its significance in history was placed at the original site in Warsaw.) The definition of "authentic" becomes rather ambiguous at times, as the above example suggests. By "authentic," the museum designers mean either that the actual objects themselves are displayed *or* that a casting or reproduction of the actual object is on display. Because of their interest in providing as complete a chronological narrative of the Holocaust as possible, the designers had to resign themselves to this almost postmodern definition of authenticity. The result is that canisters of Zyklon B on display are accompanied by a sign reassuring museumgoers that the pellets of gas are "inactive,"[15] while the Polish Karlsruhe freight car on display is carefully described as being "one of several types used to transport Jews to the camps."[16] The question is whether these differing degrees of authenticity have distinctive effects on visitors to the museum.

Huyssen argues that one important reason fueling contemporary museummania is that museum objects have an "aura" of the real for observers, an effect that has become increasingly valued in a fast-paced, mass media world of various simulations and simulacra (*Twilight* 32–33).[17] There are certain objects in the Holocaust Museum that create such an aura. A mud-encrusted milk can on display, for instance, is one of three that Emanuel Ringelblum filled with documents concerning life in the ghetto and buried under the streets of Warsaw (see fig. 10.4). This humble object becomes more than just a milk can: as an auratic object, it testifies to the heroism and foresight of people like Ringelblum and the resistance fighters of the ghetto. It also gives us occasion to pause and reflect on the conditions that surround the production of historical knowledge: what would the quality of our knowledge be if these milk cans had not been utilized, had not remained intact or been uncovered?[18] (In fact, one of the three milk cans has never been found.)

Whether or not an "aura" of the real can be evoked by obvious reproductions, no matter how authentic the casting, is another matter. The reproduction of the infamous "Arbeit Macht Frei" entrance gate to Auschwitz in the museum, for instance, is so clean and obviously well preserved that it could almost be a movie prop. This entrance gate, in fact, is featured prominently on the first page of a brief but satirical article on the museum that sports the title "Welcome to the Holocaust Theme Park" (Appignanesi and Garratt 122). This article insists that what visitors encounter in the museum is not the real, but the hyperreal. While we might be inclined to dismiss this argument as excessively critical or predictably postmodern, it does allow us to understand the ways in which the careful display of objects and the

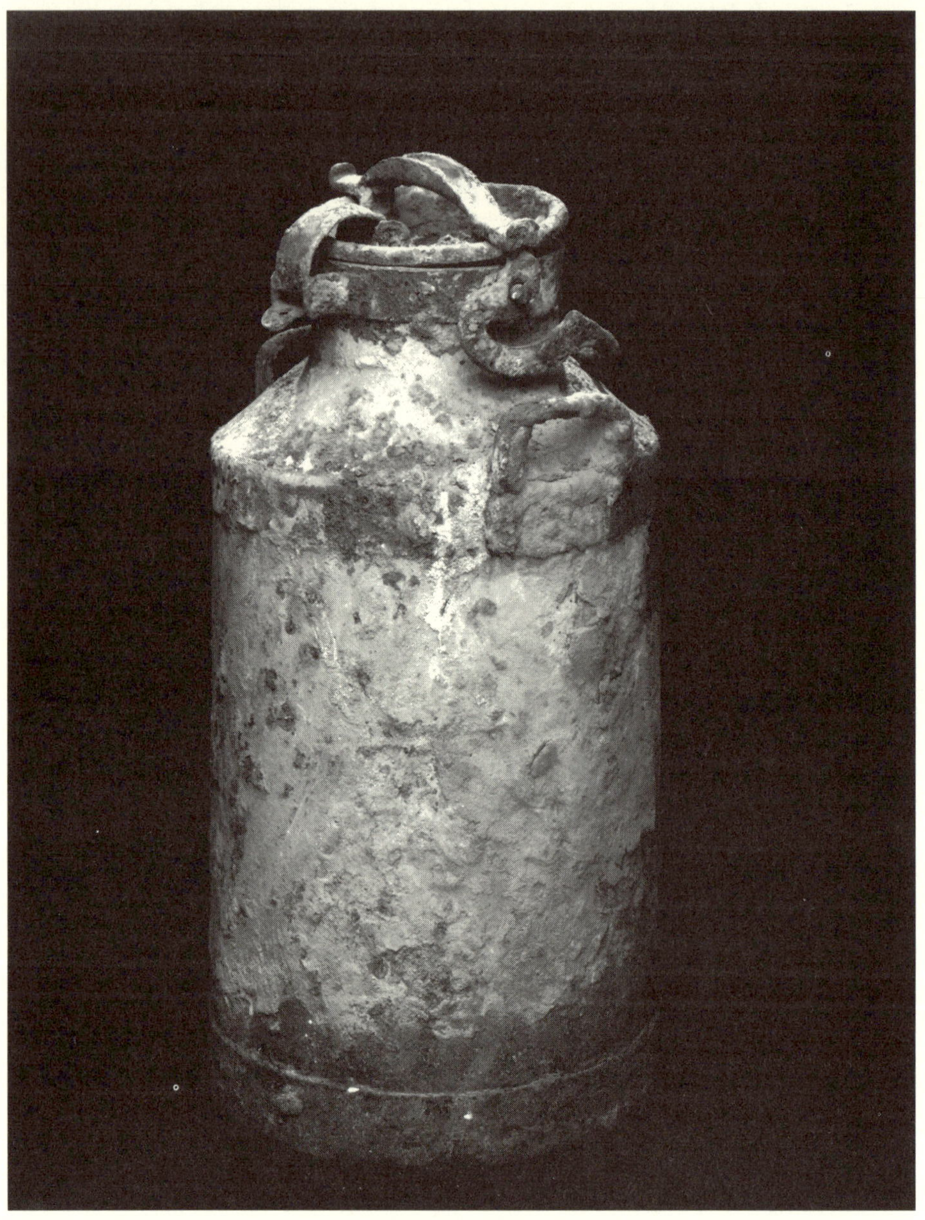

Figure 10.4 Ringelblum milk can. Zydowski Instytut Historyczny Instytut Naukowo-Badawczy, courtesy of the U.S. Holocaust Memorial Museum Photo Archives.

use of strategic spotlighting are exhibition techniques that the Holocaust museum shares with other museums. And because these exhibition techniques are the same, it is entirely possible that the carefully arranged and lit mound of shoes from Majdanek, for instance, or the cases of toothbrushes, scissors, and cutlery on display, may take on aesthetic qualities that empty these objects of their historical aura, thus preventing them from functioning as potent signifiers of enormous tragedy. Are such objects being enshrined through these techniques of display, or are they contextualized sufficiently to become metaphorically linked to unimaginable loss?

These objects, in fact, are accompanied by other texts designed to enable them to "speak" appropriately. The utensils on display are framed by photographs of camp workers sorting the possessions of recently arrived Jews. The shoes are supplemented by lines from a poem written by Moses Schulstein, a Yiddish poet who lived from 1911 until 1981. Reproduced on the wall in monumental type, these lines read:

> We are the shoes, we are the last witnesses.
> We are shoes from grandchildren and grandfathers,
> From Prague, Paris, and Amsterdam,
> And because we are only made of fabric and leather
> And not of blood and flesh, each one of us avoided the
>   hellfire.[19]

Schulstein's poem not only tells the visitor why the shoes are important, it suggests a method of reading: by contemplating the shoes that remain, visitors grasp what is absent—the lives of millions of victims. In making this appeal, the poem suggests that the shoes cannot signify adequately on their own, a point Fredric Jameson raises in his analysis of postmodernism when he contrasts the viewer's experience of Vincent Van Gogh's painting *A Pair of Boots* to Andy Warhol's photographic negative *Diamond Dust Shoes*. Jameson argues that, in contrast to Van Gogh's painting, which evokes "the whole object world of agricultural misery, of stark rural poverty, and the whole rudimentary human world of backbreaking peasant toil, a world reduced to its most brutal and menaced, primitive and marginalized state" (*Postmodernism* 7), Warhol's *Diamond Dust Shoes* functions as "a random collection of dead objects hanging together on the canvas like so many turnips, as shorn of their earlier life world as the pile of shoes left over from Auschwitz" (8). Clarifying this point, Jameson continues, "Andy Warhol's *Diamond Dust Shoes* evidently no longer speaks to us with any of the immediacy of Van Gogh's footgear; indeed, I am tempted to say that it does not really speak to us at all" (8). If the shoes from Majdanek displayed in the U.S. Holocaust Memorial Museum are akin to Warhol's shoes, as Jameson maintains, then the shoes do not speak by themselves, cannot signify in any kind of adequacy to the tremendous loss and devastation of human life. The designers of the museum, at some level perhaps recognizing this problem, have strategically placed Schulstein's poem above the shoes to guide the viewer's experience of them.

This analysis of the shoes rests on a specular economy, however. What is moving about the mound of shoes may not be the sight of them, but the smell. As Vivian M. Patraka observes in her reading of the museum, "despite constantly blowing fans, the shoes smell from their own disintegration" (103). The smell of leather disintegrating becomes an unexpected synecdoche for the devastation of the lives (no longer) attached to these shoes, and as Patraka asserts, the smell assists "our bodies in making memory" of this history (103). What happens to museumgoers in this encounter with the mound of shoes is a complex interaction with the evidence on display, an interaction that emphasizes simultaneously the inadequacy of the representation and the effectiveness of such inadequacy.

In an essay titled "Resonance and Wonder," Stephen Greenblatt draws a useful contrast between two principles for organizing museum exhibits. "Wonder," for Greenblatt, is the reaction evoked by a carefully managed display of unique works—it positions museumgoers as exalted *viewers.* By "resonance," Greenblatt indicates the power of a displayed object, often a "wounded artifact," to evoke a world beyond the boundaries of the exhibit and the museum, and to position museumgoers as engaged *readers.* "A resonant exhibition," Greenblatt elaborates,

> often pulls the viewer away from the celebration of isolated objects and toward a series of implied, only half-visible relationships and questions: How did the objects come to be displayed? What is at stake in categorizing them as "museum quality"? How were they originally used? What cultural and material conditions made possible their production? What were the feelings of those who originally held the objects, cherished them, collected them, possessed them? What is the meaning of the viewer's relationship to those same objects when they are displayed in a specific museum on a specific day? (45)

His example of a resonant exhibition is the State Jewish Museum in Prague, which includes artifacts from synagogues (silverwork, textiles, and Torah scrolls) as well as artwork from the Terezín concentration camp and a wall of names commemorating the Jews of Czechoslovakia who suffered at the hands of Nazis. The artifacts are not spectacular or monumental, they are not subjected to the kind of boutique lighting he sees as central to typical art museum exhibitions, and so the State Jewish Museum in Prague functions for Greenblatt not so much as a museum but as a memorial complex, a site that prompts visitors to recognize "barely acknowledged gaps, the caesurae, between words such as *state, Jewish,* and *museum*" (48).

The shoes from Majdanek in the U.S. museum are "wounded artifacts" in Greenblatt's sense: while they are "compelling not only as witnesses to the violence of history but as signs of use, marks of the human touch" (Greenblatt 44), they alone cannot make meaning; they require museumgoers to move beyond their role as viewers and to assume a role as readers. Such critical subjectivity is fostered as visitors continue their walk down this particular hallway in the U.S. Holocaust Memorial Museum. A few paces after the shoes, museumgoers encounter an entire wall given over to photographs of forearms bearing the tattooed numbers prisoners were assigned in the Nazi camps; and off to the left side of this display, separated from the main path by a wall to create its own sacred memorial space, visitors encounter a monumental photograph of piles of human hair collected at Auschwitz. The photographs of forearms are unsettling not only because of their number (Philip Gourevitch counts seventy-two photographs on this wall [61]) but because of their framing: while one large image does give us a view of some survivors' faces and upper bodies, most of the photographs do not—they are closely cropped to show just the forearms, and in this way they underscore the dehumanization that is suggested in the practice of assigning numbers to human beings. But this narrow and restrictive framing has other productive effects: viewers begin to long for a broader perspective, long to see the rest of the person beyond the frame, even while the display denies such a view. In similar ways, the photograph of the mounds of hair at Auschwitz denies the logic of representative artifact found in most of the permanent exhibit. What is on display is a photograph, not the hair itself,[20] yet being asked to view this obvious reproduction or representation of human hair is profoundly affecting. If the "Arbeit Macht Frei" gate from Auschwitz suggests the dangers of authentic, or transparent reproductions in the museum, the photograph of hair demonstrates the tremendous possibilities of self-conscious reproductions: this display in the museum suggests that the hair is too powerful an auratic object to be displayed in itself; viewing even the photograph of human hair requires visitors to enter a separate memorial space, a sacred space, in which to contemplate the (absent) object. In its ability to call into question—if only occasionally—its own guiding principles of representation and exhibition, the U.S. Holocaust Memorial Museum creates spaces in which museumgoers may become critically engaged readers.

Performing Holocaust Memory

In a recent essay revising the concept of authenticity for museums, Spencer R. Crew and James E. Sims argue that traditional ideas of authenticity centered in objects or artifacts limit the kind of exhibitions that can be developed. To stage exhibits on subjects for which authentic artifacts are difficult to find, they suggest a turn to narrative and to the event structure of the exhibit. In their view, visitors to a museum can have an authentic experience, even when the objects are obvious reproductions. Their emphasis on creating an authentic experience for museumgoers coincides with some of the features of the U.S. Holocaust Memorial Museum.

All visitors to the permanent exhibit are asked to select an identification card (also referred to as an identity passport) to take with them during their tour (see fig. 10.5). The cards are grouped according to gender so that women can read about women, men about men (unless individuals choose to cross gender lines). Each passport contains the story of a Holocaust victim or survivor, and to encourage visitors to identify with this story, the passport cues visitors to turn a page at certain points in the permanent exhibit to find out what is happening to their counterpart. Clearly designed to personalize and humanize the story of massive cruelty and murder, the passports also emphasize identification and performance as important elements of the experience of the museum. Whether this temporary and safe assumption of a Holocaust identity has lasting effects is still debatable, however: Gourevitch notes with dismay seeing discarded identity passports filling trash cans outside the museum (62). Turning these passports quickly into refuse may indicate a refusal to think about this subject outside the sober atmosphere of the museum.[21]

The use of video monitors throughout the museum might also be seen as contributing more to hyperreal tendencies in the museum

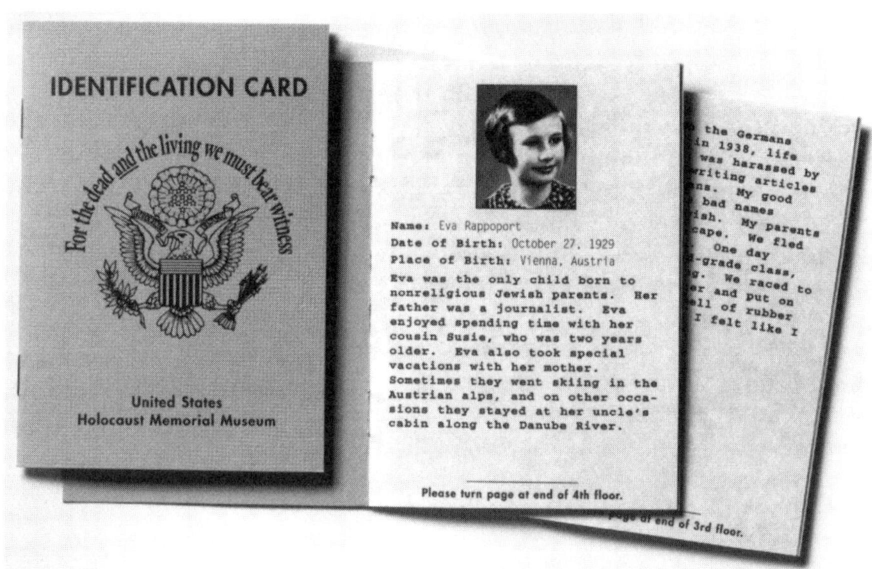

Figure 10.5 Identification Card. Courtesy of the U.S. Holocaust Memorial Museum Photo Archives.

than to its educational mission. Indeed, the developers and designers were aware of the potential problem for the museum to create a version of "Holokitsch." When museum director Jeshajahu Weinberg insisted on integrating audiovisual materials throughout the permanent exhibit, committee members became concerned that the exhibit would end up having a Disneylike atmosphere.[22] In response, Weinberg asserted that to fulfill its pedagogical purpose, the museum must use "modern audiovisual technology": "we must speak the language of 1990 and 2000," he emphasized (qtd. in Linenthal 142, 143).

True enough, but television monitors can lead to less appropriate responses from visitors: televisions are part of living rooms, not memorials typically, and so they may elicit behaviors that would ordinarily not be part of public performance. Visiting the permanent exhibit in June 1997, for instance, I saw a teenage boy self-consciously planting himself in front of one of the monitors with a protective, or privacy, wall that was showing footage of naked women being shot by Einsatzgruppen. He seemed titillated by the depiction of full female nudity—a reading surely at cross-purposes to the museum's interest in documenting atrocities. One might hope that this reaction is atypical, but Gourevitch also found the potentially sexualized representation of violence in this video footage disturbing as he toured the museum. In a diary entry he made during his visit to the museum, he writes: " 'Peepshow format. Snuff films. Naked women led to execution. People are being shot. Into the ditch, shot, spasms, collapse, dirt thrown in over. Crowds of naked people. Naked people standing about to be killed, naked people lying down dead. Close-up of a woman's face and throat as a knife is plunged into her breast—blood all over . ." (60). For Gourevitch, "the potential for *excitement,* for titillation, and even for seduction by the overwhelmingly powerful imagery" of the museum is a fundamental weakness, and he protests against visitors "repeatedly [being] forced into the role of a voyeur of the prurient" (61).

Patraka takes a much different view of this matter in her analysis of the museum. She argues that by using privacy walls to shield the monitors that display the most disturbing footage, the museum prompts us to reflect critically on our position as spectators. She writes, "when we crowd around the monitors, we become voyeurs (and not a community of witness). Our curiosity *to see* is itself thrown back at us and we are challenged, I think, to create a more self-conscious relationship to viewing materials about atrocity, to take more responsibility for what we've seen" (101). This may, indeed, be the case for some museumgoers, but it is not necessarily the case for everyone, as my visit to the museum in June 1997 demonstrated. My attention was drawn to a young father wearing a baseball cap accompanying two children, both boys—one appeared to be about 5 or 6, the other maybe 8 or 9—reassuring one of them that he would get his turn to see soon enough.[23] We were all standing beside the exhibit with the highest privacy wall in the museum; this wall surrounds the monitors that show footage of some of the medical experiments the Nazis inflicted on camp inmates. I could barely stand to look directly at these monitors, and so I couldn't help but wonder how—or even whether—the boys would understand these images. As I watched the scene unfold, I began to speculate about the motivations of this father. The museum was exceptionally crowded the day of our visit: by lifting his sons over the wall, the father was allowing them to be lifted out of the press of the crowd to gain a clear sight of the spectacle, and in the competition for space in the very crowded museum, one might say that he and his sons had "won." By insisting that his young sons look at these disturbing images of abused and violated human bodies, he was perhaps teaching them to become "men," and to be a man according to our cultural logic, one must be able to look at the grotesque without flinching, without becoming emotional.

For all the exhibit planners' emphasis on historical accuracy and thoroughness, despite all their efforts to create a narrative space that would compel visitors to always remember, it is clear that the responses and motivations of individual tourists is ultimately beyond such control. Nowhere was this demonstrated more clearly to me than in the theater on the fourth floor that shows a short film discussing the rise of the Nazis and Adolf Hitler to power. At the end of the film, two teenage boys standing next to me turned toward the screen and gave the "Heil Hitler" salute: their faces were dead serious, registering no suggestion that this might be an ill-conceived high-school prank. Their terrible gesture demonstrates that it is entirely possible to read the first part of the permanent exhibit as a primer in learning how to commit genocide and get away with it. This narrative, of course, runs counter to the intentions of the museum, but the museum exists within a postmodern culture, marked by proliferating and competing narrative possibilities, and so the careful documentation of the Nazi Party's rise to power and their terrorist tactics in the museum—intended to enable visitors to recognize and resist fascism in any form—can be read against the grain of these intentions as a training manual for neo-Nazis.

This particular counternarrative is ultimately not as alarming to me, however, as narratives that deny that the Holocaust ever happened. As we have seen oftentimes dramatically in recent years, certain individuals in contemporary culture may decide *not* to believe a certain narrative or explanation even when that narrative is supported by the existence of what would seem to be clear and unambiguous evidence. The planners of the Holocaust museum insisted on the principles of historical accuracy and authenticity to counter effectively and decisively the arguments of Holocaust deniers. I remain skeptical, however, that by playing according to those rules the museum can resist such arguments. The Holohoaxers have proven themselves very capable at seizing on any bit of knowledge or evidence—however slight—that has been revised by subsequent scholars and using that revision to insist on radical historical reinterpretation. (Recognizing that Dachau was a concentration camp, not a death camp, for instance, led to false revisionist claims that there were in fact no death camps.) As academic historians continue to uncover new information about the Holocaust, it is possible, even probable, that some of the carefully researched exhibits in the museum will also be called into question. The truth value—or authenticity—of the museum then, I would argue, cannot ultimately be the standpoint for its pedagogic potential. Rather, the museum's greatest influence will lie in its ability to compel the majority of its visitors to *believe* in the particular presentation of the Holocaust marketed in the exhibit space. And I do think the museum succeeds admirably in this respect. Though the permanent exhibit is organized along rather neat lines of chronology, the experience of physically walking through the exhibit is chaotic and disorienting spatially at times; it is a bit like finding oneself in a maze. This effect is suggestive of the ways in which Holocaust history is a complicated layering of evidence and interpretation, and so perhaps visitors in their postmuseum lives will be rightly suspicious of any attempts to oversimplify the complexities of this history, either by the media or by the deniers.

While the museum's emphasis on documentation and authenticity is problematic for the reasons I have outlined above, it nonetheless may prove useful in an unintentional way. The overwhelming amount of information provided in the permanent exhibit has a strong visceral effect: visitors to the museum physically and psychologically begin *to bear the weight* of Holocaust history—hence the need to provide respite via the daylit, white-walled "lounge" spaces between each floor of the permanent exhibit. Yet even while this weightiness increases as visitors proceed through the museum and encounter further information, a useful paradoxical reaction emerges: the realization that a single afternoon spent in this museum is not enough to master the subject—this tour is only a beginning.

The part of the permanent exhibit that best illustrates this effect is the Tower of Faces (see fig. 10.6). At the end of the fourth floor of the permanent exhibit, and again at the end of the third floor, visitors enter a tower that extends up into a skylight; all four walls of this tower are covered with photographs of Jewish residents of Ejszyszki, Lithuania, taken between 1890 and 1941. Patraka describes the effect of this space as "making the density of detail unmanageable for the spectator" (102); looking up at the overwhelming number of photographs, Patraka continues, "we rehearse with our bodies not only the immeasurability of the loss, but the imperfect structure of memory itself" (103). By allowing us to see what cannot be entirely seen, the Tower of Faces viscerally suggests for museumgoers the limits of our knowledge, our inability to take in all the detail.

It is also important to consider the careful placement of these photos in the narrative of the permanent exhibit. When viewers first encounter the photographs on the fourth floor, they seem almost out of place in the exhibit because they depict smiling faces, family groups, ordinary life—scenes that are jarring, considering the narrative of racism and increasing terror that predominates this part of the museum. The text accompanying the photographs when visitors first see them on the fourth floor gives some background information: we are told that the photographs were gathered by Dr. Yaffa Eliach; that the town Ejszyszki is called Eishishok in Yiddish and lies close to present-day Vilna in Lithuania; that Jews had lived in this town for 900 years; and that in 1939, 3,500 Jews lived there. On the fourth floor, these photographs might be said to be a poignant reminder of the rich history and culture of Jews in Eastern Europe that was also destroyed by the Holocaust. When visitors enter the tower room on the third floor to reencounter the photographs, however, it becomes clear why these photographs are in this part of the museum. Accompanied by a label that reads "The End of a Shtetl," the text talks about September 25 to 26, 1941, when Einsatzgruppen killed all the Jews in this town. While looking at photographs of life, visitors read: "Nine hundred years of Jewish life and culture in Eishishok came to an end in two days. Today, no Jews live in Eishishok." The gap between text and image looms large, and the devastating reencounter with these photographs perhaps impresses on visitors the need to remain vigilant and open to a renegotiated understanding of the Holocaust. The

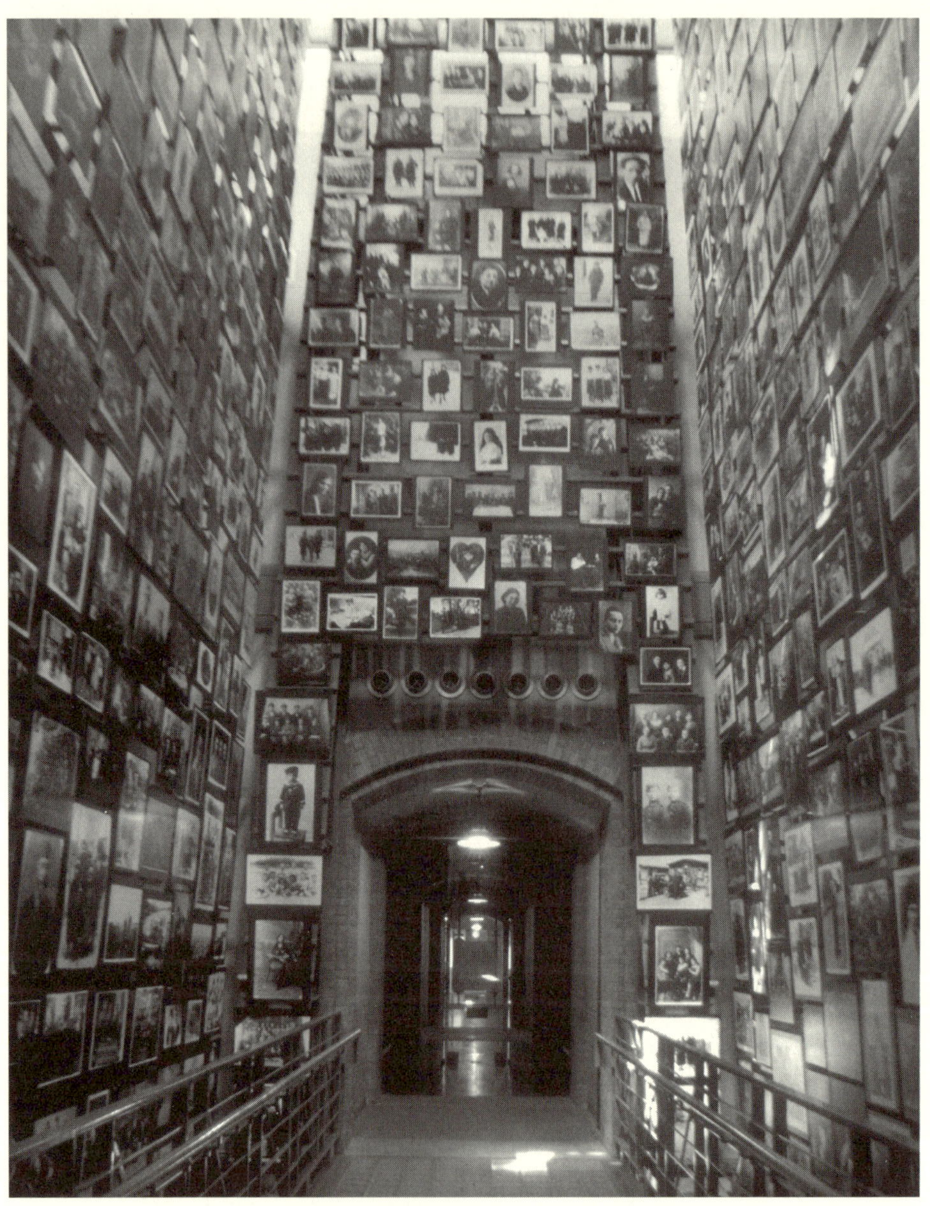

Figure 10.6 The Tower of Faces. Photograph by Edward Owen, courtesy of the U.S. Holocaust Memorial Museum Photo Archives.

re-presentation of these photographs in the museum, in other words, makes it clear that Holocaust history is not a finished product but an ongoing process.

This move to situate history as process is significant for the ultimate success of the museum. As Pierre Nora has eloquently argued, history and memory are typically in opposition in the contemporary world, with the result that history continually threatens to annihilate memory in order to remain a "universal authority" (9). Nora coins the term *lieux de mémoire* to describe a relationship of history and memory that he sees as crucial to the late twentieth century; Nora's *lieux de mémoire* are informed by critical, self-conscious history, but they ultimately "escape from history" to mobilize the will to remember (24). As visitors near the end of their tour of the permanent exhibit of the U.S. Holocaust Memorial Museum, the museum shifts from its emphasis on history to an invocation of memory. At the end of the permanent exhibit, visitors watch a film titled *Testimony,* which consists of short video segments in which twenty survivors recount their Holocaust experiences. Filmed in contemporary surroundings, the survivors and their stories remind visitors that the Holocaust is not in the past tense for them, it continues today to affect their lives in profound ways. As we become witnesses to these witnesses,[24] the obligation to remember takes on a pressing urgency.

After exiting the permanent exhibit, visitors then enter the hexagonally shaped Hall of Remembrance: a space occupied by absence (see fig. 10.7). The Hall of Remembrance is directly connected to the purpose of the building to function as a memorial, and to draw attention to the absence of six million, the architect deliberately designed the hall to have an unoccupied center. Visitors, overwhelmed by the data and images they have just absorbed in the permanent exhibit, enter this deliberately emptied space to complete the pedagogic narrative of the museum. It is a space onto which the visitor must project his or her own images and impressions, and in this way, the Hall of Remembrance underscores the crucial role that the performance of memory plays in making Holocaust history a vital, useful project. The Hall of Remembrance is also significantly a public space, a space for collective enactment of the will to remember.

Upon exiting the Hall of Remembrance, visitors may record their impressions and feelings in comment books, or they may visit the Wexner Learning Center, where they can use multimedia computers to explore their own lines of inquiry concerning the Holocaust. Both options emphasize the need for active engagement with the museum and the materials of the permanent exhibit. But the shape

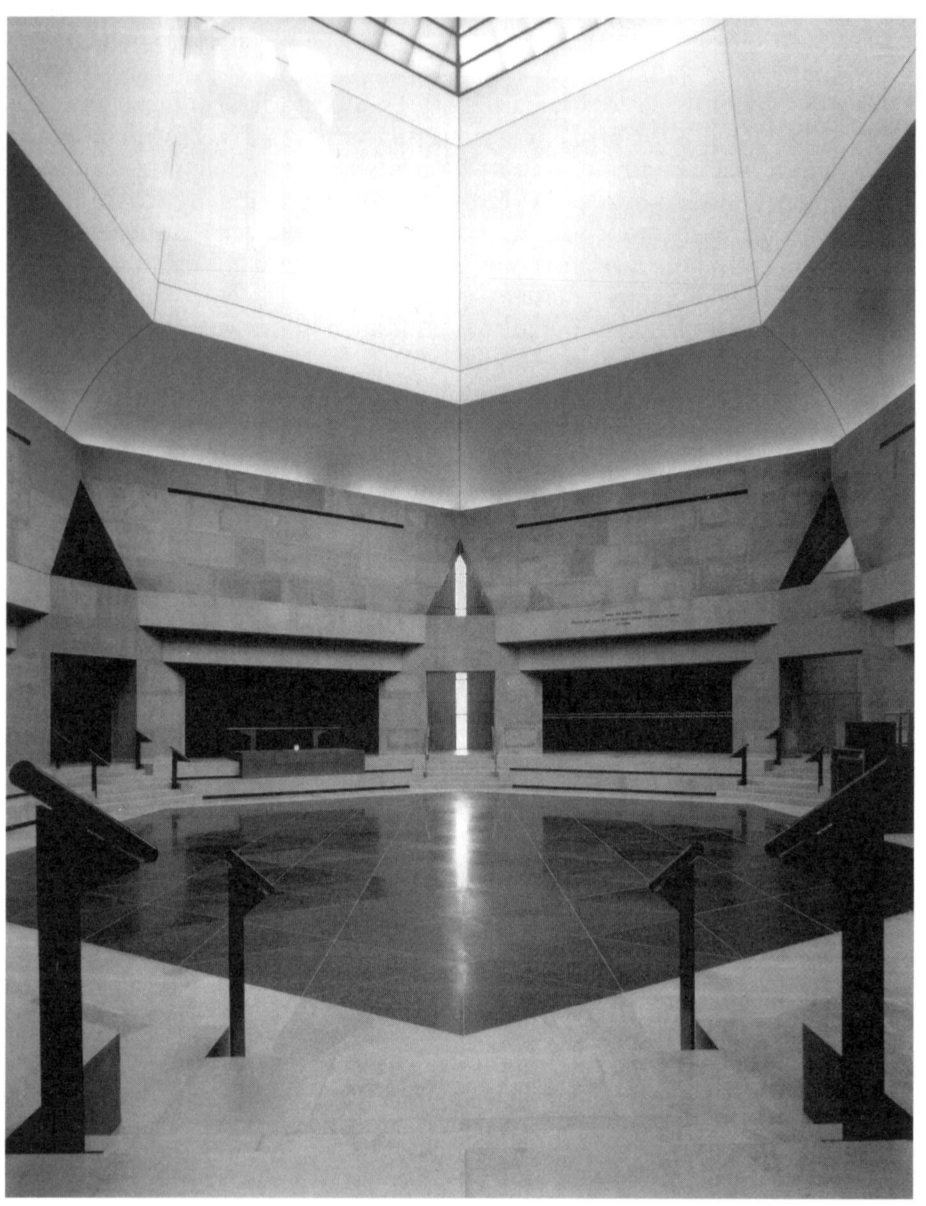

Figure 10.7 The Hall of Remembrance. Photograph © Normal McGrath.

and value of these forms of engagement remain open to question. The computers might just as easily provide the opportunity for multimedia entertainment or passive viewing as for amplifying someone's knowledge of the Holocaust. And as I read through the pages of one of the comment books in June 1997, I was struck by the number of enthusiastic responses from well-satisfied tourists. "I loved it. It was great!" wrote one visitor, while another commented, "I found this museum a very amusing and touching place." How could anyone "love" this museum or describe it as "amusing"? I wondered; perhaps the designers were too successful at making the museum appealing to American tourists. Another response from a visitor, however, made me pause to consider a slightly different method for reading the language of the comment books. "This is a wonderful museum," the person wrote. "I will never forget it." Never forgetting is perhaps the best lesson visitors can take away from the museum. In the wrenched language of the comment books—a tourist discourse that is strikingly incongruous with the subject of this sacred space—we may glimpse the effectiveness of the museum in the desire of individuals to make some comment, any comment, even while lacking an adequate language.

Acknowledging the difficulties of resisting amnesia in a postmodern culture, Huyssen pointedly asks, "How, after all, are we to guarantee the survival of memory if our culture does not provide memorial spaces that help construct and nurture the collective memory of the Shoah?" (*Twilight* 258). The U.S. Holocaust Memorial Museum cannot help being read as part of the museal, tourist economy that predominates the Mall in Washington, D.C. But in its ability to create a useful excess and to exploit the contradictory imperatives of its own proper name, the museum begins to function precisely as the sort of memorial space Huyssen calls for.

Notes

A substantial portion of this chapter is drawn from my book *Against Amnesia: Contemporary Women Writers and the Crises of Historical Memory* (Philadelphia: U of Pennsylvania P, 2001). I am grateful to Lindsay Harris of the United States Holocaust Memorial Museum for her assistance with obtaining several of the images used. An earlier version of this essay was presented at the American Studies Association meeting in Washington, D.C., on November 1, 1997: I am indebted to Miles Orvell, Priscilla Walton, my fellow panelists, and members of the audience who responded with invaluable questions and suggestions. I also appreciate the efforts of Marcia Stephenson and Aparajita Sagar, who read and commented on several drafts.

1. In a spirited reading of Morrison's *Beloved* and Holocaust narratives, Walter Benn Michaels incisively analyzes the desire for memory, history, and identity that is intricately connected in such works. He scathingly critiques an American obsession with gaining access to memories of experiences we have not had ourselves, and while I find his critique interesting, I do not ultimately find it persuasive since he does not take seriously the profound cultural work of such narratives in helping to trouble conventional narratives of American history and national identity.

2. For perceptive readings of a wide range of Holocaust museums and memorials, see the groundbreaking work by James E. Young, who has edited an important collection titled *The Art of Memory* and has developed his own full-length analysis of various memorials in *The Texture of Memory*. See also the essays by Edward Norden and Vivian Patraka, which compare in detail the Holocaust museums in Los Angeles and Washington, D.C.

3. In 1977, the Carter Administration outraged Israelis and many Americans Jews by deciding to recognize the Palestine Liberation Organization as a legitimate partner at the Geneva Peace talks. In 1978, the administration supported the sale of F-15 fighter planes to Saudi Arabia, exacerbating an already tense situation.

4. In 1939, the *S.S. St. Louis,* a German steamer with more than 900 Jewish refugees on board, set sail for Cuba. When the ship arrived, Cuba refused to accept the refugees. As it became clear that further negotiations with the Cuban government would be useless, appeals were made to the U.S. government to accept the refugees. The U.S. refused, and the *St. Louis* eventually returned to Europe, with the result that many of the Jews on board eventually were killed in Nazi camps.

5. These sentences are taken from a letter dated 15 April, 1945, that Eisenhower wrote to Chief of Staff George Marshall.

6. The main letter is accompanied by supporting texts that emphasize the museum's relevance to Americans. One of these texts is a (simulated) personalized letter from Curtis R. Whiteway, who identifies himself as "one of the American soldiers who liberated [. . .] Dachau"; the point of his letter is to lend credence to identifying the museum as an "American" institution and not just a "Jewish museum." The mailing also includes two small photographs that present images of Americans liberating the camps with (simulated)

handwritten explanations on the back. The ease with which a patriotic narrative can be conjoined to the significance of liberation and rescue is suggested by these lines from the back of one of these photographs: "Mühldorf inmates cheer 7th U.S. Army liberators. Many of these prisoners were going to be killed by the Nazis the *same week* we liberated them." I am grateful to Vincent Leitch for bringing these materials to my attention.

7. Patraka pays close attention to a moment from the film *Testimony* that concludes the permanent exhibit, in which a (female) Jewish survivor talks about marrying the (male) American soldier who liberated her camp. Patraka persuasively reads this moment of the film as symbolic of the nationalist impulses of the entire museum: "Indeed, this marriage emplotment seems to embody a crucial strategy of the whole museum, with Jews and Jewish history (the feminized victim) married to American democracy (the masculinized liberator)" (93).

8. When I visited the museum in October 1997, an elderly woman became terrified on being asked to walk through the metal detectors. She adamantly refused and was obviously anguished to learn that she would not be permitted access to the building unless she walked through them. Eventually the museum guards were able to assuage her fears by assuring her that the metal detectors were "just like those you see at airports."

9. The red brick chimneys of the Auschwitz crematoria, because of the intensity of the fire used to burn the bodies, would not hold together without steel braces for reinforcement.

10. From 14th Street, "what you see is a beautiful, classicizing, symmetrical limestone front that bows gracefully outward," art critic Ken Johnson writes. But, he notes, "when you step through the tall rectangular portals of the front you discover that it is in fact a false facade not actually integrated into the building proper—from behind it you can see straight up to the sky. What this pseudo-classical screen hides is a geometrically skewed architecture of brick and bolted steel beams reminiscent of the industrial tectonics of the Nazi death machine" (96).

11. Linda Hutcheon, for instance, does an especially fine job in *The Politics of Postmodernism* of demonstrating how postmodernism destabilizes concepts of authenticity, originality, and documentation.

12. I am borrowing this term from a collection of essays titled *American Sacred Space,* edited by David Chidester and Edward T. Linenthal.

13. A comparison of Michael Berenbaum's discussion of the failure to bomb Auschwitz (144–45) with Linenthal's (217–24) demonstrates that vastly different, yet equally tenable interpretations can be reached using the same evidence.

14. In an essay that incisively examines typical museum practices, Elaine H. Gurian observes, "Unsigned exhibitions reinforce the notion that there is a godlike voice of authority behind the selection of objects" (187).

15. The original arrival of these canisters at the museum caused such consternation that one of the staff members contacted the Environmental Protection Agency, while another considered suing the museum for exposing employees to a hazardous substance. Because the canisters had been exposed to air for forty years it was unlikely that they would cause anyone harm; nevertheless, Berenbaum, the project director for the museum, took them home one night after hours, put them in his garage, and had them tested to make sure there was no hazard (Linenthal 157).

16. This rail car was so important to the museum planners that construction of the building was altered to allow the freight car to be lifted into place while the structure was being built. The Washington, D.C., museum is not the only American memorial to fetishize such a rail car. At the Dallas Memorial Center for Holocaust Studies, visitors enter the museum by walking through an actual Belgian boxcar that once transported Jews eastward during the Holocaust. The boxcar had to be shortened to fit into the building; nonetheless, its authenticity was so potent for survivors at the dedication of the museum that they refused to walk into the car—"once had been enough," Young observes, describing their reaction (*Texture* 298). The museum now has a hidden entrance to be used by survivors who cannot bring themselves to enter via the boxcar.

17. Although he does not mention it directly, Huyssen's concept of auratic objects is clearly indebted to Walter Benjamin's work, particularly the essay "The Work of Art in an Age of Mechanical Reproduction."

18. The *Encyclopedia of the Holocaust* calls the Oneg Shabbat archive (Hebrew for "Sabbath delight") saved in these milk cans "the most important single source for the history of Polish Jewry during the war and the Holocaust" (Gutman 1087).

19. See Berenbaum 147 for the full text of Schulstein's poem.

20. Linenthal details the controversy that arose among content-committee members and museum staff over the planned display of human hair. The separate space was created in the museum to display

actual hair, but because of the controversy, the hair remains in a warehouse somewhere outside of Washington, D.C., while the photograph of hair on display at Auschwitz occupies the space. See Linenthal 210–16.

21. A couple of years ago, personnel at the museum painstakingly removed all the shoes from Majdanek on display to clean them properly. They needed to do so not only to remove the dust that had built up on the mounds of shoes, but also to remove the bits of paper, wadded up Kleenex, and gum or candy wrappers visitors had deposited among the shoes over the years.

22. In her essay examining exhibition styles, Gurian observes that most exhibitions deliberately avoid the sensual and the emotive, seeing them implicitly as opposed to respectable intellectual exhibits. She cites Gary Kulik's work on P. T. Barnum's and Moses Kimball's transformation of the first history museum in America from a serious endeavor to a carnivalesque (or circuslike) vehicle for entertainment, adding that this unfortunate precedent resonates in the contemporary success of Disney in similarly blurring the boundaries of the museum and the carnival to promote entertainment as education (182). She nevertheless goes on to argue that museums must develop ways to elicit active engagement from visitors.

23. The museum recommends that parents not bring children under age 11 into the permanent exhibit. A separate exhibit about the Holocaust designed for children, titled "Remember the Children: Daniel's Story," is on the first floor of the museum.

24. This phrase echoes an observation from Dori Laub, who writes in one of his chapters in *Testimony,* "I recognize three separate, distinct levels of witnessing in relation to the Holocaust experience: the level of being a witness to oneself within the experience; the level of being a witness to the testimonies of others; and the level of being a witness to the process of witnessing itself" (75).

Afterword

"Acting from the Midst of Identities": Questions from Linda Hutcheon

As the years have passed since postmodernism's first defining moment, a series of questions has continued to haunt me about the fate of the postmodern in cultural theory and practice: Has postmodernism become the generic counterdiscourse of the present? Is it now more (or less?) tied to modernism than it was perceived to be a decade ago? What, if anything, has succeeded it? (Electronic textuality? Celebrity fiction: *People* pomo?) Have its politics changed, especially in the face of its often contentious confrontation with, first, feminist, and then postcolonial challenges? Not surprisingly, therefore, my responses to this collection are in an interrogative vein, and are offered from a position that might be defined as being in "the midst of identities" (Bhabha 438)—some that I recognize and others that are utterly unfamiliar. These are the scholarly identities implicitly constructed by the authors of the preceding chapters, who have rethought and reconfigured ideas once very familiar to me and now distanced by time and further consideration. Therefore, I find Homi Bhabha's words about plurality that constitute the citation in my title both descriptive and comfortingly normalizing, as I offer these three questioning responses to the engaged and engaging chapters in this volume.

Can the Postmodern Be Both Textualized and Worldly?

Neither John Duvall's oppositional construction of the positions of Fredric Jameson and myself nor Tom Carmichael's complementary model is entirely recognizable to me. My sincere and continuing admiration for Jameson's important work dates from graduate school, when a visit by him set us all buzzing—and reading—for weeks. But neither critic's representation captures what it really felt like, later in the mid-1980s, to be reading Jameson's influential "Postmodernism, or, The Cultural Logic of Late Capitalism" in the *New Left Review* and at the same time reading and teaching what people were already calling postmodern literature. The lack of fit between the theory and the practice is what started me thinking and writing.[1] I have never felt comfortable moving from a predetermined theoretical stance to its application in the analysis of texts; in (perverse) reverse order, I've always tried to theorize from—and thus learn from—texts. Therefore my interest has been not in the producer, but in the text and its reception. The problem is that, when parody is involved—as it so often is in postmodern texts—we inevitably posit intentionality in our very designation of a text as parodic: at the very least, when we call something a parody, we *infer* that someone intended this to be a parody of something else.[2]

But this act of interpretive inference is not a retrograde act, even in a poststructuralist universe; it is simply the particular form that readerly/viewerly hermeneutic engagement takes when parodies are brought to bear upon parodied texts. And arguably it is through understanding what is at stake in such hermeneutic activities that postmodernism as a *textualized* phenomenon can be understood to have "worldly" consequences (to use Edward W. Said's well-known term).[3] When texts are placed together in a parodic relationship—Salman Rushdie's *Midnight's Children* (1981) and Laurence Sterne's *Tristram Shandy* (1759), for instance—it is not only their formal connections that are brought to our attention; instead, the similarities of form point to the ironized differences of both form and content. This is where the satiric power of ironic juxtaposition comes into play; this is how Rushdie can articulate both his (postmodern) ambivalence about his cultural debt to a British aesthetic tradition and his (postcolonial) contestation of British imperial domination—cultural, historical, and political.[4] As Roland Barthes once put it: "To parody a well-known saying, I shall say that a little formalism turns one away from History, but that a lot brings one back to it" (112).

Can the Postmodern Be Both Ironic and Nostalgic?

There is little doubt, as the chapters in this volume repeatedly point out, that postmodern theorists cannot agree on the political efficacy of irony as a discursive strategy. For some, the irony of postmodern historiographic texts is what has saved them from falling into the kind of sanitizing nostalgia to which some versions of antiquarian historicism certainly do fall prey. Where Jameson perceives irony as trivializing historical representation, I see it as offering a critical edge to ward off precisely the debilitating nostalgia Jameson perhaps rightly locates in certain "fashion-plate historicist films" (*Postmodernism* xvii). But as Anne Friedberg has pointed out, what Jameson is really protesting in these films when he laments the "enfeeblement of historicity" (*Signatures* 130) is not postmodernism at all but the distanced relation of every film from its historical referent. In other words, at least in this case, it is the medium and not the postmodern that gives the illusion of a "perpetual present interminably recycled" (Friedberg 427).

However, nostalgia commands a complex position in Jameson's theorizing: it is definitely used as a negative when describing certain theories, films, and novels. But his own rhetoric and self-positioning have themselves at times sounded strangely nostalgic, as he has repeatedly expressed a desire for a return to what he has always called "genuine historicity." Even on the Left, some have occasionally found this yearning for a "lost authenticity" in itself either regressive or defeatist.[5] But does the idealizing of an earlier, more stable, pre-late-capitalist (read: modernist) world necessarily imply an aesthetics (or politics) of nostalgia? If so, it would be one shared with his predecessor, Georg Lukács, for whom it was not modernism, of course, but realism that constituted that implied "moment of plenitude" (Jameson, *Marxism* 38) in the past around which literary historical nostalgia revolved.[6] Either way, it is the *present* that is deemed unacceptable, whenever that present is actually situated. Michael Bérubé has argued that the Left in America has at times seemed paralyzed "by dreams of days when things were better": "It was only the repeated interventions of women, ethnic minorities and variously queer theorists that finally shattered the pernicious sense of nostalgia to which so many men on the antipostmodern left fell victim" (14). If the present is indeed considered unsalvageable and irredeemable, we have no choice but to look either backward or forward, and the nostalgic and the utopian both, therefore, figure prominently in Jameson's interpretation of late-twentieth-century America.

Lacking, alas, even the semblance of a nostalgic bone in my body, I feel that, despite the temptation of comparison, the end of the twentieth century actually bore little relation to the end of the nineteenth. Yes, they had common doubts about progress, shared worries over political instability and social inequality, and comparable fears about disruptive change (Lowenthal 394–96), but so did many *mid*-centuries. In the 1890s, nostalgia was an obvious consequence of fin-de-siècle panic, as "manifest in idealizations of rural life, in vernacular-revival architecture, in arts-and-crafts movements, and in a surge of preservation activity" (Lowenthal 396). If the urge at that time was to turn nostalgically to the historical novels of Walter Scott and Gothic Revival architecture, the cultural tendency today seems to be to look back with irony—as in the historiographic metafictions of Timothy Findley or Angela Carter or in the provocative architecture of Bruce Kuwabara or Frank Gehry. Gone is the earlier sense of belatedness of the present vis-à-vis the past; now, the act of ironizing undermines modernist notions of originality, authenticity, and the burden of the past (all so central to Jameson's theorizing), even as it acknowledges their continuing (but not paralyzing) historical validity as both aesthetic and "worldly" concerns. Parody can historicize as it contextualizes and recontextualizes.

Can the Decentered Postmodern Be Political?

"Acting in the midst of identities"—both familiar and strange—I could not help noticing the emphasis on American materials in this volume. We read of Don DeLillo, Donald Barthelme, Ishmael Reed, Toni Morrison, Thomas Pynchon, Ridley Scott and of Los Angeles, Las Vegas casinos, the U.S. Holocaust Memorial Museum. (Paul Budra's chapter discusses European, British, and Canadian figures such as Umberto Eco, John Fowles, Robin Chapman, Anthony Burgess, Patricia Finney, Leon Rooke, Philip Burton, and Robert Nye, but my own sense of postmodern writing includes other non-American writers, such as Angela Carter, John Banville, Christa Wolf, Patrick Süsskind, Gabriel García Márquez, Manuel Puig, Thomas King, Robert Kroetsch, Michael Ondaatje, and Margaret Atwood, to mention only a few.) Generally speaking, neither the national nor the gender concentration in this volume is new in first-world theorizing of the postmodern, as many feminists and non-Americans have pointed out over the last fifteen years. Some of us, in fact, felt that it was the civil rights and women's movements in the 1960s that had really helped make possible the postmodern concern for both difference and the politics of representation. Both feminism and postmodernism had been part of the same general crisis of cultural authority, as Craig Owens pointed out as early as 1983 (57), although not quite in the same way. The political differences between the two were what feminist cultural commentators and art producers saw as differentiating their work from the postmodern: sitting on the fence, both complicitous with and contesting of the cultural dominants within and against which it operated, postmodernism differed significantly from feminism's distinct political agenda of resistance and change.[7]

Apart from feminist concerns, the issue of nationality and its politics crucially informs the particular and differing positions Jameson and I have taken on the postmodern. I am suspicious of what happens when a decentered phenomenon like postmodernism is theorized from the center. In his first important essay on the topic—and ever thereafter—Jameson has been firm in his national identification of postmodernism: "The whole global, yet American, postmodern culture is the internal and superstructural expression of a whole new wave of American military and economic domination throughout the world" ("Postmodernism" 57; *Postmodernism* 5). As a Canadian, I have had to become accustomed to having my country referred to (in culturally defined, Wallersteinian terms) as "the semi-periphery of the American core" (Jameson in Stephanson 64). Nevertheless, that peripheral—and, in national (economic and cultural) terms, complicitious—position has always seemed a good political vantage point from which to theorize a cultural enterprise like the postmodern that both participated in and yet still wanted to critique, among other things, the dominant capitalist culture of the United States.

All of the chapters in this volume raise political—or "worldly"—issues crucial to postmodernism, such as power, identity, and how we interpret as well as tell the stories of the past. More specifically, they deal with the thematization and enactment in fiction (and other cultural forms) of postmodern subjectivity (Zeitlin, Olster, McNamara), of historiographic theory (Olster, Budra, Davis), of the limitations of Western metaphysics (Hogue), of the multiple machinations of power (Waldrep, Peterson, and indeed all the others). Waldrep particularly addresses the major, deeply politicized debates that have engaged postmodernism in the last two decades. One—the 1980s debate with feminism—I have already alluded to. The other is the parallel 1990s "conversation" with the postcolonial.[8] As Kwame Anthony Appiah cogently put the question in the title of an article, "Is the Post- in Postmodernism the Post- in Postcolonial?" Given this concern, this collection too should not close without some brief thoughts on this important and usually conflictual relationship.

In a manner similar to many feminist texts, what we label as postcolonial cultural texts have carried out their contestation of imperial historical accounts through an adroit use of the discursive weapons of irony and parody. Again, we need only think of Rushdie's invocations of Sterne—not to mention dozens of other writers. Theorizing from texts, we should be able to account for the differences between this kind of parodic deployment and that of the postmodern (see Rush), and the difference might well be located, once again, in the interventionist political agendas of postcolonial cultural work, both imaginative and scholarly. While postimperialist histories like Said's *Orientalism* analyzed the potent construction of the "Oriental

Other" in the discourses of the West, postcolonial histories have looked instead to tell the stories of those subjugated by such discourses (as well as by the military and administrative structures that, Said argues, they legitimated and even made possible).[9]

Robert Young has called postmodernism "orientalism's dialectical reversal: a state of dis-orientation. Which would mean that history can no longer be a single story, even though Western history continues to conspire with its 'vast unfinished plot' of exploitation" (117). For Young, postmodernism's decentered and decentering politics is a sign of "European culture's awareness that it is no longer the unquestioned and dominant centre of the world" (19). Said has argued that the cause of this postmodern realization lies in the response to modernism. He points to the "disturbing appearance in Europe of various Others, whose provenance was the imperial domain. In the works of Eliot, Conrad, Mann, Proust, Woolf, Pound, Lawrence, Joyce, Forster, alterity and difference are systematically associated with strangers, who, whether women, natives, or sexual eccentrics, erupt into vision, there to challenge and resist settled metropolitan histories, forms, modes of thought" ("Representing" 222–23). The theorizing of that challenge and that resistance is what postmodernism has taken on as its particular decentering mission. Tackling Jean-François Lyotard's interpretation of the postmodern solely in terms of the failure of modernity's "grands récits" of emancipation and enlightenment, Said sets up the terms of the crisis somewhat differently: "The subaltern and the constitutively different suddenly achieved disruptive articulation exactly where in European culture silence and compliance could previously be depended on to quiet them down" (223).

Working these very contradictions and disruptions, the postmodern critique is a direct result of this modern crisis. To locate only in the postmodern present our inability to "map the great global multinational and decentered communicational network in which we find ourselves caught as individual subjects" (Jameson, *Postmodernism* 44) is to ignore what it might have felt like to be subjugated by empire—itself the great communicational and economic precursor to our current global multinational capitalism. Said has argued that it was the European empires' patterns of possessions that "laid the groundwork for what is in effect now a fully global world" (*Culture* 6). By 1914, he reminds us, European powers held roughly 85 percent of the earth as "colonies, protectorates, dependencies, dominions, and commonwealths" (8). Said argues further that "the great imperial experience of the past two hundred years is global and universal; it has implicated every corner of the globe, the colonizer and the colonized together" (259). In short, globalization is not new to late capitalism. European imperialism of earlier centuries had already created a "web of global commitments" (Hall 174; see too Appadurai 279) to rival anything electronic communications and transnational capitalism can produce today.

In these and other ways, the political debates with feminist and postcolonial theorists in recent years have honed postmodern theory's focus, as they have increased its reflexive awareness of its pragmatic limitations in actual interventionist arenas. But the issues raised also recall that postmodernism as an aesthetic or cultural category is not a synonym for the contemporary—where modernism, realism, and many other "isms" of the past (and future) still exist and indeed flourish. Let us not forget that these "isms" are merely heuristic labels that cultural historians create in their attempts to chart changes and continuities or to give names to perceived differences. For that reason, therefore, just as we are usually careful to define modernism in historically specific terms (since no one would claim that everything written in the early years of the twentieth century was modernist), so too should we be careful about what we label as postmodernist. The confusion with the larger philosophical category of postmodernity admittedly makes for certain difficulties, but these are not insurmountable: after all, literary modernism seems to be distinguishable in most people's minds from the more general category of Enlightenment modernity.

Yet, postmodernism has clearly been constructed by different theorists in different ways as they too act "from the midst of identities." Therefore, "Whose postmodernism?" is as important a question to ask today as it was in 1987 when Brian McHale first asked—and answered—it. But this is as it should be—at least in a decentered postmodern context. Bhabha's words cited in my title are used by him to describe what he calls the problematic and "agonistic" state of hybridity that many live today because of race. If we add creed, gender, sexual choice and, of course, class, we can see that postmodern theorists—like all others—are bound to theorize (and thus to theorize differently) from such a state of multiple identities. As Said has put it: "No one has ever devised a method for detaching the scholar from the circumstances of life, from the fact of his involvement (conscious or unconscious) with a class, a set of beliefs, a social position, or from the mere activity of being a member of society. These continue to bear on what he does professionally" (*Orientalism* 10). They continue to bear on what she does too.

Notes

1. My feelings then, as now, are not unlike those expressed by Aijaz Ahmad responding to Edward Said. Expressing both apologetic resistance and respectful difference, he too has concluded that "[s]uppression of criticism [. . .] is not the best way of expressing solidarity" (160).

2. See Hutcheon, *A Theory of Parody,* chapter 5, "Encoding and Decoding: The Shared Codes of Parody," 84–99; and Hutcheon, *Irony's Edge,* chapter 5, "Intention and Interpretation: Irony and the Eye of the Beholder," 116–40.

3. See *The World, The Text, and the Critic,* but also any of Said's other works, for the term reverberates through them all.

4. See Bush on *The Satanic Verses* as a similarly "postcolonial/ postmodern narrative."

5. See, for example, Frow 135 and During 32–35; Kadir refers to Jameson's "nostalgic reveries of the still wishful and utopian" (19).

6. Jameson's cited phrase is used by him to describe Theodor Adorno's critique of theories of history organized around the covert hypothesis of such a "moment of plenitude" in the past or future. That both Jameson and Lukács themselves create such a moment has been noted by many.

7. "While feminism would agree that the common ideological position of all these 'truths' ["Humanism, History, Religion, Progress, etc."] is that they are patriarchal, postmodern theory [. . .] would be reluctant to isolate a single major determining factor" (Creed 52).

8. A third politicized "conversation" has been with queer theory, but here the relationship has been less one of contestation than of coordination of efforts, in a sense. Queer theory and culture have been considered by many to be the postmodern form that gay and lesbian cultural work took when ironic resignification became its major discursive strategy. See Savoy.

9. On the distinction between postimperial and postcolonial, see Hutcheon, *"Orientialism."*

Works Cited

Adam, Ian, and Helen Tiffin, eds. *Past the Last Post: Theorizing Post-Colonialism and Post-Modernism.* Calgary: U of Calgary P, 1990.

Adorno, Theodor W. et al. *The Authoritarian Personality.* 1950. New York: Wiley, 1964.

———. "The Culture Industry Reconsidered." Bronner and MacKay 128–35.

Ahmad, Aijaz. *In Theory: Classes, Nations, Literatures.* London: Verso, 1992.

Altick, Richard D. *The Scholar Adventurers.* New York: Free Press, 1950.

Appadurai, Arjun. *Modernity at Large: Cultural Dimensions of Globalization.* Minneapolis: U of Minnesota P, 1996.

Appiah, Kwame Anthony. "Is the Post- in Postmodernism the Post- in Postcolonial?" *Critical Inquiry* 17 (1991): 336–57.

Appignanesi, Richard, and Chris Garratt. "Welcome to the Holocaust Theme Park." *Introducing Postmodernism.* New York: Totem, 1995. 122–25.

Archer, John Michael. *Sovereignty and Intelligence: Spying and Court Culture in the English Renaissance.* Stanford: Stanford UP, 1993.

Barthes, Roland. *Mythologies.* 1957. Trans. Annette Lavers. New York: Hill and Wang, 1994.

Barthelme, Donald. *Unspeakable Practices, Unnatural Acts.* 1968. New York: Pocket Books, 1976.

Baudrillard, Jean. "The Ecstasy of Communication." Trans. John Johnston. *The Anti-Aesthetic: Essays on Postmodern Culture.* Ed. Hal Foster. Port Townsend: Bay P, 1983. 126–34.

———. *Simulations.* Trans. Paul Foss, Paul Patton, and Philip Beitchman. New York: Semiotext[e], 1983.

Bellamy, Edward. *Looking Backward, 2000–1887.* 1888. New York: Signet, 1960.

Benjamin, Walter. "The Work of Art in the Age of Mechanical Reproduction." *Illuminations.* Ed. Hannah Arendt. Trans. Harry Zohn. New York: Schocken, 1968. 217–51.

Berenbaum, Michael. *The World Must Know: The History of the*

Holocaust as Told in the United States Holocaust Memorial Museum. Boston: Little, Brown, 1993.

Bérubé, Michael. "Just the Fax, Ma'am; or, Postmodernism's Journey to Decenter." *Village Voice* Oct. 1991: 13–17.

Best, Steven. "Jameson, Totality, and the Poststructuralist Critique." Kellner 333–68.

Bhabha, Homi. "Minority Maneuvers and Unsettled Negotiations." *Critical Inquiry* 23 (1997): 431–59.

Blade Runner. Dir. Ridley Scott. Warner Bros., 1982.

Blade Runner: The Director's Cut. Dir. Ridley Scott. Warner Bros., 1982. [First commercial release, 1992.]

Boyer, M. Christine. "Cities for Sale: Merchandising History at South Street Seaport." *Variations on a Theme Park: The New American City and the End of Public Space.* Ed. Michael Sorkin. New York: Hill and Wang, 1992. 181–204.

Braunmuller, A. R., and Michael Hattaway. *The Cambridge Companion to English Renaissance Drama.* Cambridge: Cambridge UP, 1990.

Bronner, Stephen Eric, and Douglas MacKay, eds. *Critical Theory and Society: A Reader.* New York: Routledge, 1989.

Brooks, Lou. Telephone interview. 10 May 1999.

Budick, Emily Miller. "Absence, Loss, and the Space of History in Toni Morrison's *Beloved.*" *Arizona Quarterly* 48.2 (1992): 117–38.

Burgess, Anthony. *A Dead Man in Deptford.* London: Hutchinson, 1993.

———. *Nothing Like the Sun.* London: William Heinemann, 1964.

Burgin, Victor. *The End of Art Theory: Criticism and Postmodernity.* Atlantic Highlands, N.J.: Humanities Press International, 1986.

Burnham, Clint. *The Jamesonian Unconscious: The Aesthetics of Marxist Theory.* Durham: Duke UP, 1995.

Burton, Philip. *You, My Brother: A Novel Based on the Lives of Edmund and William Shakespeare.* New York: Random, 1973.

Bush, Ronald. "Monstrosity and Representation in the Postcolonial Diaspora: '*The Satanic Verses,*' '*Ulysses,*' and '*Frankenstein.*'" *Borders, Exiles, Diaspora.* Ed. Elazar Barkan and Marie-Denise Shelton. Stanford: Stanford UP, 1998. 234–56.

Butler-Evans, Elliott. *Race, Gender, and Desire: Narrative Strategies in the Fiction of Toni Cade Bambara, Toni Morrison, and Alice Walker.* Philadelphia: Temple UP, 1989.

Cain, William E. "Making Meaningful Worlds: Self and History in *Libra.*" *Michigan Quarterly Review* 29 (1990): 275–87.

Chapman, Robin. *Christoferus, or Tom Kyd's Revenge.* London: Sinclair-Stevenson, 1993.

Chevrier, Yves. "*Blade Runner;* or, The Sociology of Anticipation." Tr. Will Straw. *Science-Fiction Studies* 11 (1984): 50–60.

Chidester, David, and Edward T. Linenthal, eds. *American Sacred Space.* Bloomington: Indiana UP, 1995.

Christian, Barbara. "Fixing Methodologies: *Beloved.*" *Cultural Critique* 24 (1993): 5–15.

Ciucci, Giorgio. "The City in Agrarian Ideology and Frank Lloyd Wright: Origins and Development of Broadacres." *The American City: From the Civil War to the New Deal.* By Ciucci et al. Cambridge: MIT P, 1979. 243–388.

Civello, Paul. "Undoing the Naturalistic Novel: Don DeLillo's *Libra.*" *Arizona Quarterly* 48.2 (1992): 33–56.

Creed, Barbara. "From Here to Modernity: Feminism and Postmodernism." *Screen* 28.2 (1987): 47–67.

Crew, Spenser R., and James E. Sims. "Locating Authenticity: Fragments of a Dialogue." Karp and Lavine 159–75.

Davis, Mike. "*Chinatown,* Part Two? The 'Internationalization' of Downtown Los Angeles." *New Left Review* 164 (1987): 65–87.

———. "Urban Renaissance and the Spirit of Postmodernism." *New Left Review* 151 (1985): 106–13.

DeCurtis, Anthony. "Matters of Fact and Fiction." *Rolling Stone* 17 Nov. 1988: 114+. Rpt. as "'An Outsider in This Society': An Interview with Don DeLillo." Lentricchia, *Introducing* 43–66.

DeLillo, Don. "American Blood: A Journey through the Labyrinth of Dallas and JFK." *Rolling Stone* 8 Dec. 1983: 21+.

———. *Americana.* New York: Penguin, 1971.

———. *Libra.* New York: Viking, 1988.

———. *Players.* New York: Penguin, 1977.

———. *The Names.* 1982. New York: Vintage-Random, 1983.

———. *White Noise.* 1985. New York: Penguin, 1986.

Derrida, Jacques. *Of Grammatology.* 1967. Trans. Gayatri Chakravorty Spivak. Baltimore: John Hopkins UP, 1976.

———. *Positions.* Chicago: U of Chicago P, 1981.

———. *Writing and Difference.* 1967. Trans. Alan Bass. Chicago: U of Chicago P, 1978.

Deutelbaum, Marshall. "Visual Memory/Visual Design: The Remembered Sign in *Blade Runner.*" *Literature/Film Quarterly* 17 (1989): 66–72.

Dick, Philip K. *Blade Runner (Do Androids Dream of Electric Sheep?).* 1968. New York: Del Ray-Ballantine, 1982.

Duncan, Carol. "Art Museums and the Ritual of Citizenship." Karp and Lavine 88–103.

During, Simon. "Postmodernism or Post-colonialism Today." *Textual Practice* 1.1 (1987): 32–47.

Duvall, John N. "From Valparaiso to Jerusalem: DeLillo and the Moment of Canonization." *Modern Fiction Studies* 45 (1999): 559–68.

Eysteinsson, Astradur. *The Concept of Modernism.* Ithaca: Cornell UP, 1990.

Finney, Patricia. *Firedrake's Eye.* New York: St. Martin's, 1992.

Fisher, William. "Of Living Machines and Living-Machines: *Blade Runner* and the Terminal Genre." *New Literary History* 20 (1988): 187–98.

Fishman, Robert. *Urban Utopias of the Twentieth Century: Ebenezer Howard, Frank Lloyd Wright, Le Corbusier.* Cambridge: MIT P, 1982.

Foucault, Michel. *The Archaeology of Knowledge and the Discourse on Language.* 1969. Trans. A. M. Sheridan-Smith. New York: Pantheon, 1972.

Frank, Joseph. *The Widening Gyre.* Bloomington: Indiana UP, 1963.

Fraser, Nancy, and Linda J. Nicholson. "Social Criticism without Philosophy: An Encounter between Feminism and Postmodernism." *Feminism/ Postmodernism.* Ed. Linda J. Nicholson. New York: Routledge, 1990. 19–38.

Freed, James Ingo. "The Holocaust Memorial Museum." *Partisan Review* 61 (1994): 448–56.

Freud, Sigmund. "The Future Prospects of Psycho-Analytic Therapy." S.E. 11: 139–51.

———. "Group Psychology and the Analysis of the Ego." S.E. 18: 65–143.

———. *The Interpretation of Dreams.* S.E. 4 & 5.

———. *The Standard Edition of the Complete Psychological Works of Sigmund Freud.* Trans. and Ed. James Strachey. London: Hogarth and the Institute of Psycho-Analysis, 1966.

———. "The Uncanny." S.E. 17: 217–56.

Friedberg, Anne. "*Les Flâneurs du Mal(l):* Cinema and the Postmodern Condition." *PMLA* 106 (1991): 419–31.

Frow, John. "Tourism and the Semiotics of Nostalgia." *October* 57 (1991): 123–51.

Fukuyama, Francis. *The End of History and the Last Man.* New York: Free, 1992.

Gates, Henry Louis, Jr. "The Blackness of Blackness: A Critique of the

Sign and the Signifying Monkey." *Critical Inquiry* 9 (1983): 685–723.

Gay, Peter. *Freud: A Life for Our Time.* New York: Norton, 1988.

Goldstein, Philip. *The Politics of Literary Theory: An Introduction to Marxist Criticism.* Tallahassee: Florida State UP, 1990.

Goodheart, Eugene. "Some Speculations on Don DeLillo and the Cinematic Real." Lentricchia 117–30.

Gourevitch, Philip. "Behold Now Behemoth: The Holocaust Memorial Museum, One More American Theme Park." *Harper's* July 1993: 55–62.

Grant, Robert. "Absence into Presence: The Thematic of Memory and 'Missing' Subjects in Toni Morrison's *Sula.*" *Critical Essays on Toni Morrison.* Ed. Nellie Y. McKay. Boston: Hall, 1988. 90–103.

Green, Jeremy. "Disaster Footage: Spectacles of Violence in DeLillo's Fiction." *Modern Fiction Studies* 45 (1999): 571–99.

Greenblatt, Stephen. "Resonance and Wonder." Karp and Lavine 42–56.

Grimes, William. "Toni Morrison is '93 Winner of Nobel Prize in Literature." *The New York Times* 8 Oct. 1993: A1+.

Gurian, Elaine Heumann. "Noodling Around with Exhibition Opportunities." Karp and Lavine 176–90.

Gutman, Israel. "Oneg Shabbat." *Encyclopedia of the Holocaust.* Ed. Israel Gutman. 4 vols. New York: Macmillan, 1990.

Halevy, Julian. "Disneyland and Las Vegas." *The Nation* 7 Jun. 1958: 510–13.

Hall, Stuart. "The Local and the Global: Globalization and Ethnicity." *Dangerous Liaisons: Gender, Nation, and Postcolonial Perspectives.* Ed. Anne McClintock, Aamir Mufti, and Ella Shohat. Minneapolis: U of Minnesota P, 1997. 173–87.

Haraway, Donna. *Simians, Cyborgs, and Women: The Reinvention of Nature.* New York: Routledge, 1991.

Harvey, David. *The Condition of Postmodernity: An Inquiry into the Origins of Cultural Change.* Oxford: Blackwell, 1989.

Haynes, Alan. *Invisible Power: The Elizabethan Secret Services, 1570–1603.* Phoenix Mill, UK; Wolfeboro Falls, N.H.: Alan Sutton, 1992.

Hearings Before the President's Commission on the Assassination of President Kennedy. Washington, D.C.: United States Government Printing Office, 1964. 26 vols.

Henderson, Mae, G. "Toni Morrison's *Beloved:* Re-Membering the Body as Historical Text." *Comparative American Identities:*

Race Sex, and Nationality in the Modern Text. Ed. Hortense J. Spillers. New York: Routledge, 1991. 62–86.

Hilfer, Anthony. "Critical Indeterminacies in Toni Morrison's Fiction: An Introduction." *Texas Studies in Literature and Language* 33.1 (1991): 91–95.

Hofstadter, Richard. *The Paranoid Style in American Politics and Other Essays.* New York: Knopf, 1966.

hooks, bell. *Yearning: Race, Gender, and Cultural Politics.* Boston: South End, 1990.

Horkheimer, Max. Foreword to Studies in Prejudice. Adorno et al. v–viii.

Hutcheon, Linda. *Irony's Edge: The Theory and Politics of Irony.* London: Routledge, 1995.

———. *"Orientalism* as Postimperial Witnessing." *Cultural and Postcolonial Studies: Essays in Honor of Edward Said.* Ed. Hussein Kadhim. Forthcoming.

———. *A Poetics of Postmodernism: History, Theory, Fiction.* New York: Routledge, 1988.

———. *The Politics of Postmodernism.* New York: Routledge, 1989.

———. *A Theory of Parody: The Teachings of Twentieth-Century Art Forms.* London: Methuen, 1985.

Huyssen, Andreas. *After the Great Divide: Modernism, Mass Culture, Postmodernism.* Bloomington: Indiana UP, 1986.

———. *Twilight Memories: Marking Time in a Culture of Amnesia.* New York: Routledge, 1995.

Jameson, Fredric. "Afterword—Marxism and Postmodernism." Kellner 369–87.

———. "Architecture and the Critique of Ideology." 1985. *The Syntax of History.* Vol. 2 of *The Ideologies of Theory: Essays 1971–1986.* Theory and the History of Literature 49. Minneapolis: U of Minnesota P, 1988. 35–60.

———. "Cognitive Mapping." *Marxism and the Interpretation of Culture.* Ed. Cary Nelson and Lawrence Grossberg. Urbana: U of Illinois P, 1988. 347–57.

———. *The Geopolitical Aesthetic: Cinema and Space in the World System.* Bloomington: Indiana UP, 1992.

———. *The Ideologies of Theory: Essays 1971–1986. Vol. 1: Situations of Theory.* Minneapolis: U of Minnesota P, 1988.

———. *Marxism and Form.* Princeton: Princeton UP, 1971.

———. *The Political Unconscious: Narrative as a Socially Symbolic Act.* Ithaca: Cornell UP, 1981.

———. "Postmodernism and Consumer Society." *The Anti-Aesthetic: Essays on Postmodern Culture.* Ed. Hal Foster. Port Townsend: Bay P, 1983. 111–25.

———. "Postmodernism, or, The Cultural Logic of Late Capitalism." *New Left Review.* 146 (1984): 53–92.

———. *Postmodernism, or, The Cultural Logic of Late Capitalism.* Durham: Duke UP, 1991.

———. *The Seeds of Time.* New York: Columbia UP, 1994.

———. *Signatures of the Visible.* New York: Routledge, 1990.

———. "*Ulysses* in History." *Modern Critical Views: James Joyce.* Ed. Harold Bloom. New York: Chelsea House, 1986. 173–88.

Jencks, Charles. *What Is Post-Modernism?* New York: St. Martin's, 1986.

Johnson, Carol Siri. "The Limbs of Osiris: Reed's *Mumbo Jumbo* and Hollywood's *The Mummy.*" *MELUS* 17 (1991–1992): 105–15.

Johnson, Ken. "Art and Memory." *Art in America* Nov. 1993: 90–99.

Johnston, John. "Generic Difficulties in the Novels of Don DeLillo." *Critique* 30 (1989): 261–75.

———. "Superlinear Fiction or Historical Diagram?: Don DeLillo's *Libra.*" *Modern Fiction Studies* 40 (1994): 319–42.

Kadir, Djelal. "Postmodernism/Postcolonialism: What Are We After?" *World Literature Today* 69.1 (1995): 17–21.

Karp, Ivan, and Steven D. Lavine, eds. *Exhibiting Cultures: The Poetics and Politics of Museum Display.* Washington: Smithsonian Institution P, 1991.

Kellner, Douglas. *Postmodernism: Jameson: Critique.* Washington: Maisonneure, 1989.

Kronick, Joseph. "*Libra* and the Assassination of JFK: A Textbook Operation." *Arizona Quarterly* 50.1 (1994): 113–32.

Kucich, John. "Postmodern Politics: Don DeLillo and the Plight of the White Male Writer." *Michigan Quarterly Review* 27 (1988): 328–41.

Lacan, Jacques. "The mirror stage as formative of the function of the I." *Écrits: A Selection.* Trans. Alan Sheridan. New York: Norton, 1977. 1–7.

Laub, Dori, M.D. "An Event without a Witness: Truth, Testimony and Survival." *Testimony: Crises of Witnessing in Literature, Psychoanalysis, and History.* Coauthored by Shoshana Felman and Dori Laub. New York: Routledge, 1992. 75–92.

LeClair, Tom. "An Interview with Don DeLillo." *Anything Can Happen: Interviews with Contemporary American Novelists.* Ed.

Tom LeClair and Larry McCaffery. Urbana: U of Illinois P, 1983. 79–90.

Lentricchia, Frank, ed. *Introducing Don DeLillo*. Durham: Duke UP, 1991.

———. "*Libra* as Postmodern Critique." Lentricchia 193–215.

Levy, Andrew. "Telling *Beloved*." *Texas Studies in Literature and Language* 33.1 (1991): 114–23.

Linenthal, Edward T. *Preserving Memory: The Struggle to Create America's Holocaust Museum*. New York: Viking Penguin, 1995.

Lowenthal, David. *The Past Is a Foreign Country*. Cambridge: Cambridge UP, 1985.

Lyotard, Jean-François. *The Postmodern Condition: A Report on Knowledge*. 1979. Trans. Geoff Benningtion and Brian Massumi. Theory and History of Literature 10. Minneapolis: U of Minneapolis P, 1984.

Mailer, Norman. *The Executioner's Song*. 1979. New York: Warner, 1980.

———. "Superman Comes to the Supermarket." 1960. *The Presidential Papers*. 1963. New York: Berkley Medallion, 1970. 25–61.

The Making of Luxor. Dir. Scott Morris. Scott Morris Productions, Inc., 1994.

Marcuse, Herbert. "The Obsolescence of the Freudian Concept of Man." Bronner and MacKay 233–46.

Martin, Reginald. *Ishmael Reed & The New Black Aesthetic Critic*. New York: St. Martin's, 1988.

Mason, Theodore O., Jr. "Performance, History, and Myth: The Problem of Ishmael Reed's *Mumbo Jumbo*." *Modern Fiction Studies* 34 (1988): 97–109.

McCoy, Esther. "The Bradbury Building." *Arts & Architecture* (Apr. 1953): 20+.

McDowell, Deborah E. "Recycling: Race, Gender, and the Practice of Theory." *Studies in Historical Change*. Ed. Ralph Cohen. Charlottesville: UP of Virginia, 1992. 246–63.

McHale, Brian. "Postmodernism, or The Anxiety of Master Narratives." *Diacritics* 22.1 (1992): 17–33.

———. *Postmodernist Fiction*. London: Methuen, 1987.

McKay, Nellie. "An Interview with Toni Morrison." *Contemporary Literature* 24.4 (1983): 413–29.

McNamara, Kevin. "*Blade Runner*'s Post-Individual Worldspace." *Contemporary Literature* 38 (1997): 422–46.

———. *Urban Verbs: Arts and Discourses of American Cities.* Stanford: Stanford UP, 1996.

Mercer, Kobena. "'1968': Periodizing Politics and Identity." *Cultural Studies.* Ed. Lawrence Grossberg, Cary Nelson, and Paula Treichler. New York: Routledge, 1992. 424–38.

Michaels, Walter Benn. "'You who never was there': Slavery and the New Historicism, Deconstruction and the Holocaust." *Narrative* 4 (1996): 1–16.

Mobley, Marilyn Sanders. "A Different Remembering: Memory, History and Meaning in Toni Morrison's *Beloved.*" *Modern Critical Views: Toni Morrison.* Ed. Harold Bloom. New York: Chelsea House, 1990. 189–99.

Molesworth, Charles. "Don DeLillo's Perfect Starry Night." Lentricchia 143–56.

Montrose, Louis. *The Purpose of Playing: Shakespeare and the Cultural Politics of the Elizabethan Theatre.* Chicago: U of Chicago P, 1996.

Morrison, Rachela. "*Casablanca* Meets *Star Wars:* The Blakean Dialectics of *Blade Runner.*" *Literature/Film Quarterly* 19 (1980): 2–10.

Morrison, Toni. "Behind the Making of *The Black Book.*" *Black World* Feb. (1974): 86–90.

———. *Beloved.* New York: Plume, 1987.

———. "A Conversation, Gloria Naylor and Toni Morrison." *Southern Review* 21.3 (1985): 567-93.

———. "Living Memory." *City Limits.* 31 Mar.–7 Apr. (1988): 10–11.

———. "The Site of Memory." *Inventing the Truth: The Art and Craft of Memoir.* Ed. William Zinsser. Boston: Houghton Mifflin, 1987. 103–24.

Mott, Christopher M. "*Libra* and the Subject of History." *Critique* 35 (1994): 131–45.

Nazareth, Peter. "Heading Them Off at the Pass: The Fiction of Ishmael Reed." *Review of Contemporary Fiction* 4 (1984): 208–26.

Nietzsche, Friedrich. *Untimely Mediations.* Cambridge: Cambridge UP, 1983.

Nicholl, Charles. *The Reckoning: The Murder of Christopher Marlowe.* London: Jonathan Cape, 1992.

"Nobel Prize in Literature a 'Knockout' for Morrison, First Black Award Recipient." *Jet* 25 Oct. (1993): 34–35.

Nora, Pierre. "Between Memory and History: *Les Lieux de Mémoire.*" *Representations* 26 (1989): 7–25.

Norden, Edward. "Yes and No to the Holocaust Museums." *Commentary* Aug. 1993: 23–32.

Nye, Robert. *Mrs. Shakespeare: The Complete Works.* London: Sinclair-Stevenson, 1993.

O'Brien, John, ed. *Interviews with Black Writers.* New York: Liveright, 1973.

O'Donnell, Patrick. "National Trauma and the Cultural Imaginary: Narrating Paranoia in DeLillo's *Libra* and Stone's *JFK*." Paper delivered at "Narrative: An International Conference." Albany, New York. 2 Apr. 1993.

Ogburn, Charlton. *The Mysterious William Shakespeare: The Myth and the Reality.* New York: Dodd, 1984.

Oswald, Robert L. *Lee: A Portrait of Lee Harvey Oswald by His Brother.* With Myrick and Barbara Land. New York: Coward-McCann, 1967.

Owens, Craig. "The Discourse of Others: Feminists and Postmodernism." *The Anti-Aesthetic: Essays on Postmodern Culture.* Ed. Hal Foster. Port Townsend: Bay P, 1983. 57–82.

Park, Robert E. "The City as Social Laboratory." 1929. *On Social Control and Collective Behavior.* Ed. Ralph H. Turner. Chicago: U of Chicago P, 1967. 3–18.

Patraka, Vivian M. "Spectacles of Suffering: Performing Presence, Absence, and Historical Memory at U.S. Holocaust Museums." *Performance and Cultural Politics.* Ed. Elin Diamond. New York: Routledge, 1996. 89–107.

Pearlman, Bob. "Parataxis and Narrative: The New Sentence in Theory and Practice." *American Literature* 65 (1993): 313–24.

Pinsker, Sanford. "America's Conspiratorial Imagination." *The Virginia Quarterly Review: A National Journal of Literature and Discussion* 68 (1992): 605–25.

Rainwater, Catherine. "Worthy Messengers: Narrative Voices in Toni Morrison's Novels." *Texas Studies in Literature and Language* 33.1 (1991): 96–113.

Reed, Ishmael. *Mumbo Jumbo.* New York: Atheneum, 1988.

Rigney, Barbara Hill. *The Voices of Toni Morrison.* Columbus: Ohio State UP, 1991.

Rooke, Leon. *Shakespeare's Dog.* Toronto: Stoddard, 1981.

Rose, Margaret A. *The Post-Modern and the Post-Industrial.* Cambridge: Cambridge UP, 1991.

Rowe, Colin, and Fred Koetter. *Collage City.* Cambridge: MIT P, 1978.

Rubeli, Paul. *Theming—The Casino Marketing Strategy of the 90s.* Brooklyn: Conference Copy, Inc., 1991. Sound cassette.

Said, Edward W. *Culture and Imperialism.* New York: Knopf, 1993.
———. *Orientalism.* 1978. New York: Vintage, 1979.
———. "Representing the Colonized: Anthropology's Interlocutors." *Critical Inquiry* 15 (1989): 205–25.
———. *The World, the Text, and the Critic.* Cambridge, Mass: Harvard UP, 1983.
Sammartino, Peter. *The Man Who Was William Shakespeare.* New York: Cornwall, 1990.
Savoy, Eric. "You Can't Go Homo Again: Queer Theory and the Foreclosure of Gay Studies." *English Studies in Canada* (1995): 129–52.
Shakespeare in Love. Dir. John Madden. Universal, 1998.
Shirvani, Hamid. "Postmoderism: Decentering, Simulacrum, and Parody." *American Quarterly* 46 (1994): 290–97.
Silberman, Neil Asher. "The Battle Disney Should Have Won." *Lingua Franca* Nov.-Dec. 1994: 24–28.
Silliman, Ron. "What Do Cyborgs Want? (Paris, Suburb of the Twentieth Century)." *Jean Baudrillard: The Disappearance of Art and Politics.* Ed. William Stearns and William Chaloupka. New York: St. Martin's, 1992. 27–38.
Soja, Edward. *Postmodern Geographies: The Reassertion of Space in Critical Social Theory.* London: Verso, 1989.
Sontag, Susan. *Under the Sign of Saturn.* New York: Farrar, 1980.
Sorrentino, Gilbert. *Mulligan Stew.* New York: Evergreen-Grove, 1979.
Stafford, Jean. *A Mother in History.* New York: Farrar, 1966.
Stephanson, Anders. "Regarding Postmodernism: A Conversation with Fredric Jameson." Kellner 43–74.
Tafuri, Manfredo. *Architecture and Utopia.* Tr. Barbara Luigia La Penta. Cambridge: MIT P, 1980.
———. "*Machine et Mémoire:* The City in the Work of Le Corbusier." *Le Corbusier.* Ed. H. Allen Brooks. Princeton: Princeton Architectural Press, 1987. 203–18.
Taylor, Mark C. *Hiding.* Chicago: U of Chicago P, 1997.
Thomas, Glen. "History, Biography, and Narrative in Don DeLillo's *Libra.*" *Twentieth-Century Literature* 43 (1997): 107–24.
Trilling, Lionel. *Freud and the Crisis of Our Culture.* Boston: Beacon, 1955.
Tweedale, Ralph L. *Wasn't Shakespeare Someone Else?* N.P.: Shakespeare Oxford Society, 1966.
Venturi, Robert, Denise Scott Brown, and Steven Izenour. 1977.

Learning from Las Vegas: The Forgotten Symbolism of Architectural Form. Cambridge: MIT P, 1994.

Walker, Joseph S. "Criminality, the Real, and the Story of America: The Case of Don DeLillo." *Centennial Review* 43 (1999): 433–66.

Weixlmann, Joe. "African American Deconstruction of The Novel in the Work of Ishmael Reed and Clarence Major." *MELUS* 17 (1991–1992): 57–79.

West, Cornel. "Ethics and Action in Fredric Jameson's Marxist Hermenutics." *Postmodernism and Politics.* Ed. Jonathan Arac. Minneapolis: U of Minnesota P, 1986. 123–44.

Whalen, Richard F. *Shakespeare—Who Was He?* Westport: Praeger, 1994.

White, Hayden. *The Content of the Form: Narrative Discourse and Historical Representation*. Baltimore: Johns Hopkins UP, 1987.

———. *Tropics of Discourse: Essays in Cultural Criticism*. Baltimore: Johns Hopkins UP, 1978.

Willman, Skip. "Art after Dealey Plaza: DeLillo's *Libra.*" *Modern Fiction Studies* 45 (1999): 621–40.

———. "Traversing the Fantasies of the JFK Assassination: Conspiracy and Contingency in Don DeLillo's *Libra.*" *Contemporary Literature* 39 (1998): 405–33.

Young, James E. "The Art of Memory: Holocaust Memorials in History." *The Art of Memory: Holocaust Memorials in History.* Ed. James E. Young. New York: Prestel, 1994. 19–38.

———. *The Texture of Memory: Holocaust Memorials and Meaning.* New Haven: Yale UP, 1993.

Young, Robert. *White Mythologies: Writing History and the West.* London: Routledge, 1990.

Contributors

Paul Budra is Associate Professor of English at Simon Fraser University. He is author of *A Mirror for Magistrates and the de casibus Tradition* (Toronto, 2000) and has co-edited *Part Two: Reflections on the Sequel* (Toronto, 1999).

Thomas Carmichael is Associate Professor of English at the University of Western Ontario. He is co-editor of *Constructive Criticism: The Human Sciences in the Age of Theory* (Toronto, 1996) and *Postmodern Times : A Critical Guide to the Contemporary* (Northern Illinois, 1999). His essays have appeared in *Contemporary Literature, boundary 2,* and *Mosaic.*

Kimberly Chabot Davis received her Ph.D. in English from the University of Virginia. She is a Mellon Postdoctoral Fellow in the English Department at Cornell University. She is working on a book manuscript, "Moving Subjects: Sentimental Postmodernism and the Politics of Identification." Her work has appeared in *Twentieth-Century Literature.*

John N. Duvall is Associate Professor of English at Purdue University and Editor of *Modern Fiction Studies.* He is author of *Faulkner's Marginal Couple: Invisible, Outlaw, and Unspeakable Communities* (Texas, 1990) and *The Identifying Fictions of Toni Morrison: Modernist Authenticity and Postmodern Blackness* (Palgrave, 2000).

W. Lawrence Hogue, Professor of English at the University of Houston, is the author of *Discourse of the Other: The Production of the Afro-American Text* (Duke, 1986) and *Race, Modernity, Postmodernity: A Look at the History and Literatures of People of Color Since the 1960s* (SUNY, 1996). He is currently completing a study titled "Beyond Racial Victimization/Otherization: Celebrating African American (Male) Differences."

Linda Hutcheon is Professor of English and Comparative Literature at the University of Toronto. Of her many books, this collection responds primarily to her work on postmodernism in *The Poetics of Postmodernism: History, Theory, Fiction* (Routledge, 1988) and *The Politics of Postmodernism* (Routledge, 1989).

Kevin McNamara, Assistant Professor of Literature at the University of Houston–Clear Lake, is author of *Urban Verbs: Arts and*

Discourses of American Cities (Stanford, 1996). He is presently at work on a study of Los Angeles in the American imagination of utopia and dystopia, portions of which have appeared in *Contemporary Literature* and *Arizona Quarterly.*

Stacey Olster is Associate Professor of English at SUNY–Stony Brook. She has written *Reminiscence and Re-Creation in Contemporary American Fiction* (Cambridge, 1989) and is currently completing a book manuscript, "The Trash Phenomenon," on contemporary American authors who chart American history with respect to the artifacts of American popular culture.

Nancy J. Peterson is Associate Professor of English at Purdue University. She has edited *Toni Morrison: Critical and Theoretical Approaches* (Johns Hopkins, 1997) and authored the recent study *Against Amnesia: Contemporary Women Writers and the Crises of Historical Memory* (Pennsylvania, 2001).

Shelton Waldrep is Assistant Professor of English at the University of Southern Maine. In addition to co-authoring *Inside the Mouse: Work and Play at Disney World* (Duke, 1995), he edited *The Seventies: The Age of Glitter in Popular Culture* (Routledge, 2000).

Michael Zeitlin is Associate Professor of English at the University of British Columbia and has published essays on modern and postmodern fiction in such journals as *Contemporary Literature, Mosaic,* and *College Literature.*

Index